LEE'S LAST STAND
SAILOR'S CREEK, VIRGINIA, 1865

By
Derek Smith

WHITE MANE BOOKS
SHIPPENSBURG, PENNSYLVANIA

This White Mane Books publication
was printed by
Beidel Printing House, Inc.
63 West Burd Street
Shippensburg, PA 17257-0708 USA

The acid-free paper used in this book meets the guidelines for permanence and durability of the Committee on Production Guidelines for Book Longevity of the Council on Library Resources.

For a complete list of available publications
please write
White Mane Books
Division of White Mane Publishing Company, Inc.
P.O. Box 708
Shippensburg, PA 17257-0708 USA

Library of Congress Cataloging-in-Publication Data

Smith, Derek, 1956 Nov. 3-
    Lee's last stand : Sailor's Creek, Virginia, 1865 / by Derek Smith.
        p. cm.
    Includes bibliographical references and index.
    ISBN 1-57249-251-1 (alk. paper)
        1. Sailor's Creek, Battle of, Va., 1865. 2. Lee, Robert E. (Robert Edward),
    1807-1870--Military leadership. I. Title.

E477.67 .S65 2002
973.7'38--dc21

2002027232

CONTENTS

ILLUSTRATIONS AND MAPS

PREFACE

Amid the predawn of April 6, 1865, Captain Franklin Harwood of the U.S. Army military engineers climbed into the saddle and rode down a narrow country road outside Jetersville, Virginia. Somewhere in front of him lay the Confederate Army of Northern Virginia, a wounded panther limping to escape—yet perhaps brought to bay in or near the hamlet of Amelia Court House. Robert E. Lee was on the run, but still could be a potent and dangerous aggressor if trapped. And the Union brass apparently believed they had the Rebel Leonidas and his army hemmed in at Amelia less than 10 miles away.

Harwood trotted past knots of soldiers of the Army of the Potomac's celebrated VI Corps. Through the half-light, he heard the crisply shouted commands of officers, yawns and bits of a thousand conversations from the infantrymen. In the fields and valleys around him, two other Union corps and most of the army's cavalry, a juggernaut of almost one hundred thousand men, were stirring. Cries of regiments cheering in unison echoed around distant campfires, and couriers calling out for directions to various officers or brigades swerved their horses among the men, kicking up dirt clods and wholesale commotion. The Yankee titan was awake. From the lowliest drummer boy to General Ulysses "Sam" Grant himself, all were ready to put an end to this infernal war.

Kill all the Secesh, some said.

Just get me home and back to my dear mother, others proclaimed.

I am tired of fighting, I only want to see my sweetheart, many confessed.

We'll lick the Rebels sure!—was the consensus.

Harwood was on temporary assignment with the VI Corps. His task was to find roads that would put the VI Corps in position to cut off the Southerners' flight or destroy Lee's remaining divisions in a pitched battle. For the engineer and thousands of other soldiers on both sides, the momentous events, naked emotions and indelible memories of this coming day would paint a mind's-eye portrait they would forever remember.

No book such as this study of the battle of Sailor's Creek is created without the influence, positive thought, and energy of many people. Much gratitude is due Walter Wright, whose ancestor William S. Basinger was among the Confederate heroes of Sailor's Creek and who provided copies of Basinger's personal letters. Special thanks also to Henry Kennedy whose exhaustive history of the Savannah Volunteer Guards helped me fill in some gaps in the narrative. A grand bow also goes to the staffs of the Georgia Historical Society, the Chatham-Effingham Regional Library (both in Savannah, Georgia), and the Erie County Public Library in Buffalo, New York, for their able and kind assistance in my research. There is no truer friend than Dale K. Hooks whose computer wizardry aided me immensely in completing this book. Fellow writer Marlyce Kling offered encouragement, friendship, and a sense of perspective.

Cynthia Benderson has been my gentle inspiration through most of this project. I love you, Czarina.

As always, special thanks go to my parents, Gordon and Willene Smith, who fostered my love of history.

Yet the masters of this work are the soldiers—those who marched and went about their bloody business on April 6, 1865. Most lived through it and some described it. Others died and were described. All compose the panorama of that terrible day.

The Spelling Bee Battle

Did the blue and gray clash at Sailor's, Saylor's, Sailer's, or Sayler's Creek? Anyone who has read about this specific engagement or the Appomattox campaign in general knows that no other Civil War battle *or* location is more commonly spelled so differently.

With some uniformity, the officers on both sides whose combat accounts are included in *The War of the Rebellion: Official Records of the War of the Union and Confederate Armies* refer to "Sailor's" Creek. Past that, however, historians and writers, as well as soldiers giving firsthand accounts, have utilized free license in spelling the name.

Who is right?

Chris M. Calkins, a Civil War author and well-recognized authority on the battles from Petersburg to Appomattox, has done the most extensive research into this name game. The only mariners who fought there on April 6, 1865, were the Confederate sailors and marines of Commodore John R. Tucker's naval battalion. But the creek, located more than one hundred miles from the Virginia coast, had its own identity long before these saltwater Rebs arrived.

In his book, *The Appomattox Campaign*, Calkins describes the conclusion of his search to solve the spelling, based on the premise that the stream was named for a person who lived in the region of Prince Edward, Amelia, and Nottoway Counties where the creek flows. Calkins found that a Marten Saylor was associated with a 1795 plan to extend and clear the Appomattox River for flatboats to transport cargos of tobacco. Between this time and 1809, Saylor and George King were partners in a Prince Edward County tannery, the records showed.

A man identified as J. D. Sayler opposed the change of a court date in 1842, but Calkins uncovered nothing to determine exactly where either "Sailor" lived or if they had any influence on the creek's name. Peter Jefferson and Joshua Fry distributed *A Map of the most inhabited part of Virginia, all of the province of Maryland, part of Pennsylvania, New Jersey and North Carolina*, a 1751 chart showing Sailor's Creek emptying into the Appomattox.

The U.S. Army completed the 1867 *Michler Survey Map* depicting Big and Little Sailor's Creeks. But the 1879 *Jacob's Official Map of Prince Edward County* called the creek Sayler's, although no homesteader or store proprietor was displayed on the document. In 1960, however, the U.S. Board of Geographic Names decided what name would be used on Virginia maps. They decided on Sayler's Creek. Yet for anyone trying to find the site, Sailor's Creek Battlefield State Park is Calkins' description in 1990's *The Civil War Battlefield Guide*, published by the Houghton Mifflin Company.

Sayler's Creek Battlefield Historical State Park is described in a 1985 Virginia Division of Tourism brochure about battlefields, but the state later changed the name of the park *and* the battle to Sailor's. The stream name remained the same, however. Thus, visitors to the battle-ground of Sailor's Creek will see Big and Little Sayler's Creeks winding through the countryside.

For simplicity's sake, all references to the battle *and* the stream in this book will be Sailor's Creek. I believe the Saylers, Saylors, and Sailers, as well as the sailors, would have wanted it that way.

INTRODUCTION

A few more Sailor's Creeks and it will be all over—ended—just as
I have expected it would end from the first.

—Confederate General Robert E. Lee,
quoted by a special courier from
Confederate President Jefferson Davis, April 8, 1865,
in Strode, *Jefferson Davis—Tragic Hero*

The complete isolation of Ewell from Longstreet in his front and
Gordon in his rear led to the battle of Sailor's Creek, one of the
severest conflicts of the war, for the enemy fought with desperation to escape capture, and we, bent on his destruction, were no
less eager and determined.

—Union Major General Philip H. Sheridan
in his memoirs finished less than three
months before his death in August 1888,
in Sheridan, *Civil War Memoirs*

Weuns have found the last ditch.

—Rebel teamster's scrawled chalk
message on an abandoned
wagon near Sailor's Creek—April 6, 1865,
in Rodick, *Appomattox: The Last Campaign*

The battle that exploded along Little Sailor's Creek and its pasto-
ral Virginia countryside on April 6, 1865, was the last major engagement fought between the Confederate Army of Northern Virginia and
the U.S. Army of the Potomac during the Civil War. More importantly,
it proved to be the coup de grâce to General Robert E. Lee's Rebel
army, setting it on a virtual funeral procession to Appomattox Court
House where Lee surrendered three days later.

Few histories of the Civil War deal with Sailor's Creek in any detail. Most regard it as an unimportant clash that occurred when Lee's defeat was already inevitable. What is most overlooked is the fact that Lee lost one-half to one-third of his legendary army in this engagement. Never before had he suffered such devastating casualties in proportion to his number of troops.

While Confederate blunders contributed to Lee's defeat, the events at Sailor's Creek were just as largely shaped by the hunters: Lieutenant General Ulysses S. Grant, general in chief of the United States armies; Major General Philip H. Sheridan, leader of the Union Cavalry Corps; and Major General George Gordon Meade, commander of the Army of the Potomac. This Federal triumvirate hounded and bled Lee without respite until the starving Rebels marched to defeat almost four years to the day when Southern batteries sent shells arcing over the Charleston, South Carolina, harbor toward Fort Sumter to inaugurate the conflict.

War ambitions had turned dramatically against the Southerners to reach this point in the spring of 1865. By the first week of April, Lee's Army of Northern Virginia had been engaged in trench warfare, guarding the Confederate capital at Richmond and its supply base at Petersburg for more than nine months. Grant had many more men in this deadly chess match, and he was willing to swap them body for body with Lee while the Rebels were pinned in their defenses.

Most of the major supply routes feeding Richmond, either by land or by the Appomattox River, connected at Petersburg, 23 miles distant. From there the Richmond & Petersburg Railroad was the life-or-death pipeline joining the cities. If Petersburg could be taken, Grant knew that only the Richmond & Danville Railroad, running west from Richmond, stood between his army and virtually choking off the Rebel Carthage from the outside world. The Confederate defenders had about 59,000 men to oppose Grant's more than one hundred thousand troops. These Rebels were spread paper-thin in a trench system of some 50 miles running from northeast of Richmond to south of Petersburg.

The last act of the Union's final, epic drive to victory opened on April 1, 1865, when Federal forces smashed through the Confederate line and captured the critical crossroads at Five Forks, southwest of

Petersburg. Grant had launched his spring offensive three days earlier, piling legions of infantry against Lee's right flank. The break in the Rebel defenses at Five Forks, coupled with a titanic follow-up assault by Grant the next day, effectively snapped the spinal cord of Lee's Richmond-Petersburg defenses.

Now the Southerners either had to hunker in their earthworks and eventually be gobbled up by Grant's boys coming at them from all sides or they had to escape to fight another day.

To Lee, there *was* no choice. The army had to march out of this hellhole if there was any chance for the Confederacy's survival.

After nearly 10 months in the siege lines and with almost no rations for his men or pack animals, Lee abandoned his trenches on the night of Sunday, April 2, sending his tattered troops streaming off on routes to the west. These roads converged at Appomattox Court House a week later, but not before the Confederates suffered one of their greatest reversals of the war at Sailor's Creek.

Lee's loss of some eight thousand troops at Sailor's Creek, the inability to feed his soldiers, mistakes by his junior generals, and the raw aggressiveness of overwhelmingly superior Union armies were slashing wounds from which the South could never recover.

The piecemeal Rebel army of General Joseph E. Johnston fought on for two weeks after Lee's capitulation, and scattered Confederate forces beyond the Mississippi River endured even longer. But the wistful dream of an independent Southern nation died in the tears, stacking of muskets, and burning of blood-spattered battle flags at Appomattox on Palm Sunday, April 9, 1865.

This is the saga of that violently brutal spring day at Sailor's Creek, which set a course for the mass grave burial of the Confederacy—and the preservation of the Union.

CHAPTER 1
"WE ARE AFTER LEE, AND WE ARE GOING TO HAVE HIM."

The ragged Rebel veterans of Major General Joseph B. Kershaw's division clambered out of their trenches on the Petersburg-Richmond line before daylight on the morning of April 3, 1865, and marched into Richmond. The once-defiant capital of the Confederacy was a hell of chaos, civilians and soldiers scurrying about, explosions and gunshots ripping the air, and the dust and smoke of a dying nation fogging the streets. Kershaw met with Lieutenant General Richard S. Ewell, commander of the Richmond Defense Corps, and detached two battalions to control mobs sacking some sections of the city.

The past 72 hours had been a nightmarish sequence of bloody battles for the struggling Confederacy along the miles of trenches and forts protecting Richmond. The first of the catastrophes erupted late on the afternoon of Saturday, April 1, at Five Forks, a crossroads held by Confederates guarding the South Side Railroad. A combined Union force of about 22,000 infantry and cavalry under Major General Philip H. Sheridan had swept down on this vital road junction, surprising Confederate Major General George E. Pickett and his command of less than 11,000 troops. Pickett's defenders were overpowered and routed, leaving the door open for Union forces to spear forward and cut the rail line, although the Rebels managed to hold on through the night. If the South Side was severed, however, Lee's army would be shut off in their defenses and most likely starved into surrender.

General Grant did not waste any time in exploiting Sheridan's Five Forks victory. On the morning of April 2, he ordered an all-or-nothing breakout by four Union corps, the II, IX, and VI, from the Army of the Potomac, and the XXIV of the Army of the James, to smother the Richmond-Petersburg defenses. A II Corps division, led by Brigadier General Nelson A. Miles, battled its way to Sutherland Station on the South Side Railroad and captured the depot.

Just as crucial as Miles gaining the railroad was the success of Union Major General Horatio G. Wright's VI Corps, which knifed through this breach, spreading the gap and threatening to break up Lee's army on either side of their thrust.

Confederate General Robert E. Lee
Library of Congress

At his headquarters outside Petersburg, Lee began receiving the grim reports from the front and realized that he could not stave off the enemy much longer. He sent a telegraph dispatch to Confederate Secretary of War John C. Breckinridge stating the precarious position of the Rebel army: "I see no prospect of doing more than holding my position here till night. I am not certain that I can do that...I advise that all preparations be made for leaving Richmond tonight. I will advise you later, according to circumstances."[1]

Confederate President Jefferson Davis was attending worship services at Saint Paul's Episcopal Church when a courier arrived with another dispatch from Lee. Davis had received Lee's first message a few minutes earlier while walking to church, but did not seem to comprehend its seriousness. Lee was more insistent in his second message, however, writing that Richmond and Petersburg should be abandoned that night. The general's latest words must have convinced the chief executive of the colossal danger. Other worshippers recalled how he paled while reading the note, then grimly strode out of the sanctuary.

The Confederate setbacks of the day were compounded by the loss of Lieutenant General Ambrose Powell Hill, commander of Lee's Third Corps. Hill, one of Lee's most reliable combat captains, had been shot dead from the saddle while attempting to capture a pair of blue infantrymen. The news of Hill's death brought tears to Lee's eyes, but the immediacy of the Rebels' plight left no time for grieving. Hill's death also prompted Lee to consolidate the Third Corps with that of Lieutenant General James Longstreet's First Corps.

The Army of Northern Virginia had to move or be trapped in the siege lines and potentially be destroyed. After almost 10 months in the mud and dirt of the Petersburg trenches, the premier army of the Confederacy was about to march again, but under very different circumstances from its other campaigns because of its physical condition. Lee's soldiers, horses, and pack animals were emaciated due to battle fatigue and a lack of rations. Many of the troops were barefooted and wore little more than shreds. Boys and old men filled gaps in the ranks of divisions and brigades that had almost ceased to exist due to wartime attrition. Any loyal Southerner of almost any age who could pull a trigger or lanyard was welcomed, so desperate was the shortage of soldiers. The Confederate artillery was in just as bad shape as the foot soldiers, consisting of about two hundred guns pulled by scrawny, starving mules and horses.

As Lee studied his options that Sunday, the survival of what remained of his army was of greater importance to the Confederacy than holding Richmond or Petersburg. With his divisions scattered by the Union hammer strike, Lee made plans for the evacuation of his defensive network. The withdrawal would begin just after nightfall.

Lee already had decided to move west and regroup his army at Amelia Court House, about 40 miles from Petersburg. The town was about the same distance to the southwest of Richmond and Lee ordered Ewell's defense forces to rendezvous there as well. Lee had explained his intent to reassemble at Amelia in his second Sunday telegram to Jefferson Davis.

From Amelia, the army would march to Burke's Station, or Burkeville, where the Richmond & Danville intersected the South Side

Railroad. Here, Lee intended to turn southwest and, following the railroad line, move to Danville. Every mile would bring him closer to the Confederate army of General Joseph E. Johnston, the only other Rebel force of any strength still putting up a fight. Johnston's 20,000 were doing all they could to slow Major General William T. Sherman's 60,000 Union veterans in their rampage through North Carolina. The Southerners hoped that if Lee could join Johnston their combined army could conceivably defeat Sherman...then they would turn to deal with Grant's blue hordes.

The Rebel units in the Petersburg area would have to cross the Appomattox River and march west to reach Amelia Court House. Lee's evacuation orders specified that the Confederate guns that could be moved should be across the river by 3 a.m. on April 3. Even as he put together the specifics of the withdrawal, Lee had other issues with which to deal. None of them were good.

Jefferson Davis drew Lee's seldom-seen ire with his replies to the general's morning telegrams. Davis questioned the immediacy of abandoning Richmond, writing that to leave that night would "involve the loss of many valuables, both for the want of time to pack and of transportation."[2] Lee read one of these dispatches and angrily tore it to bits. "I am sure I gave him sufficient notice," he said, adding more calmly that it was "absolutely necessary" to withdraw that night.[3] Lee also had received telegrams from Lieutenant General Richard Taylor in Alabama indicating that Mobile was about to fall into enemy hands.

Lee rode across a makeshift bridge over the Appomattox during the night and reined in at a road fork. In the quiet darkness he watched the butternut columns file by, the only sound coming from the boom of Union artillery in the distance and the occasional creak or jangle of one of his wagons or their teams. No one wanted to alert the Yanks that Petersburg had "gone up," so the soldiers and their officers proceeded in silence.

Little more than two months earlier, the 58-year-old Lee had been appointed general in chief of the Confederate States armies. *Was it as much a grandiose promotion or an opportunity for some in the Richmond government to wash their crimsoned hands of the secession holocaust?* If he had thoughts such as these, Lee never voiced them.

About 12,500 infantry were with Lee when Petersburg was evacuated. This total grew to approximately 28,000 to 30,000 troops from the entire Confederate defensive system around Richmond and Petersburg. Of course, many of these were not combat veterans but were convalescents. Like the rest of the army, units of the Richmond defense force contained old men and boys. Also among these Confederates was a force of Southern sailors and marines now serving as infantry. They would play a key role at Sailor's Creek three days later. And unknown to most in the Rebel exodus was the presence of black troops wearing gray. All were on the march west. Lee's retreat would be encumbered by a train of more than one thousand heavily laden wagons that often stretched to 30 miles in length. The bony teams that pulled this train were in the same poor condition as the artillery animals.[4]

Few, if any, numbers favored the Confederates. The Union forces arrayed around Richmond-Petersburg vastly outnumbered Lee's command. Grant had a total of some one hundred twenty thousand troops in the Army of the Potomac and the Army of the James to draw on against Lee. These forces were spread from Richmond to the Virginia peninsula, but they could be called to the chase with the stroke of Grant's pen if needed. For the most part, these Federals were battle-toughened, well-supplied soldiers energized by the belief that their longtime foe was wounded and about to be brought to a death fight. Grant had stacked his superiority, through manpower, weaponry, spirit and, least savory, a terrible body count of boys in blue, to finally be in a position to defeat Lee. Now he was preparing to reap the rewards. The Rebs had stolen a few hours' march on the Yanks with their evacuation, but this advantage couldn't last unless they maintained a rapid pace and outlegged the bluebellies despite empty stomachs and dwindling hopes. When the Federals ascertained the direction of their withdrawal, they would come after the Confederates with Judgement Day's wrath.

Lee's troops had to march some 55 miles to reach Burke's Station from Petersburg. Grant had infantry at Sutherland Station, where the South Side Railroad had been cut, that could reach Burke's Station by a route of about 36 miles. And when Lee expected to turn southwest to link with Johnston, his path would put him squarely in the line of Grant's pursuing columns south of the Appomattox River. The chase had not yet started, but it already was a question of endurance and hours.

The first Federal squads inched into the murky streets of Petersburg shortly after 4 a.m. on April 3. A few Reb skirmishers, wounded, and stragglers were captured, but Lee's army had made its escape. Grant, who had expected the Confederates' evacuation, and Meade conferred between 5 a.m. and 6 a.m. Monday outside Petersburg and Meade was instructed to begin an immediate pursuit of Lee.

Union General Ulysses S. Grant
Library of Congress

Corduroying muddy sections of roads with discarded Confederate muskets from Five Forks, the Union II, V and VI Corps, along with the Federal cavalry, were on the move within a few hours.

Richmond also had fallen, the formal surrender at 8:15 a.m. being no more than a sideshow to Federal infantry and cavalry tromping through the smoky, somber avenues before light. "We heard today that Richmond has been evacuated and is in flames," wrote Lieutenant Colonel Elisha Hunt Rhodes of Rhode Island. "Well, let it burn, we do not want it. We are after Lee, and we are going to have him."[5]

Other than a scattering of black civilians who cheered the blue soldiers, Petersburg was a scene of complete desertion when Grant and his staff rode into the abandoned Rebel stronghold about 9 a.m. on April 3. Grant quietly reined in at a fine brick house on one of the town's main street and established temporary headquarters there.

Less than a month shy of his 43rd birthday, Grant already had achieved the pinnacle of American military greatness where only George Washington had stood before. His coordination of colossal Federal offensives over the past year since being named general in chief had stoked Union hopes for all-out victory and had the Confederacy reeling in retreat across the board. Now, as he savored captured Petersburg, Grant was anxious to ride west and join the lead infantry columns, but politics, as well as courtesy, interceded. On Sunday, the general had invited President Abraham Lincoln to join him at the front and Lincoln had accepted, saying that he would be there on Monday.

As Meade girded his corps to pursue Lee, Grant and his staff lounged on the piazza, waiting for the arrival of the president. Lincoln arrived from the vast Federal supply depot at City Point, Virginia, where he had been monitoring virtually every phase of the Union operations. Now, he strode through the front yard gate, followed by his younger son, Tad, as the generals snapped to attention.

Colonel Horace Porter of Grant's staff wrote of a delighted Lincoln:

> He seized General Grant's hand as the general stepped forward to greet him, and stood shaking it for some time and pouring out his thanks and congratulations with all the fervor of a heart that seemed overflowing with its fullness of joy. I doubt whether Mr. Lincoln ever experienced a happier moment in his life.[6]

Lincoln and Grant both believed that the demise of Lee's army and that of Joseph Johnston would not be long in coming, and the president spoke of mercy and magnanimity guiding his efforts to reunite the country. To the west the armies raced to continue the war with the fervency of four years of bloodshed.

CHAPTER 2
"Unremitting Fatigue, Hunger, Trouble, and Disaster"

Deep hunger tore at their bellies as the mud of the roads clung to the legs of the Confederate soldiers on the march. Unlike the forgiveness preached by Lincoln scant miles away in Petersburg, there were few, if any, thoughts of mercy or good will among the fragmented portions of Lee's army on the night march of April 2–3. Realizing the preciousness of every hour, Lee was urgent in pressing his men to move in all haste. The troops were dirty, sullen, and without food.

While the lead Union platoons edged into Richmond and Petersburg, daybreak that Monday found the rangy Army of Northern Virginia back in the countryside where it was most dangerous. The retreat had times when the air of triumph flushed the Southerners like a long-ago breath from Chancellorsville or Fredericksburg. "Maybe in a few days the enemy might find us assailing him unaware, falling upon him flank and rear as we were used to when (Stonewall) Jackson led us," one Reb observed.[1]

Even though there were no signs of a Union pursuit on Monday, the hard pace chiseled at the Confederates. Some of the weaker men already were dropping on the roadsides as the number of stragglers grew. Exhausted teams stumbled and fell, unable to pull the heavy wagons and guns any further. Yet the gray columns plodded on, seemingly drawn by the sun that was sinking behind the western hills.

The approximately six thousand Confederates who had survived or eluded capture at Five Forks had been badly scattered in the rout.

8

Many had been fighting as detached units since Saturday, trying to make their way back to Lee's main army or rejoin their shattered commands. Others, principally the corps of Lieutenant General Richard H. Anderson, simply had been isolated from Lee when the Union breakthrough occurred.

Anderson's troops left their lines shortly after twilight on the disastrous April 1 and linked with the Confederate cavalry corps of Major General Fitzhugh Lee about 2 a.m. on Sunday. Lee, 29, was a nephew of the army commander.

With the cavalry as his rearguard, Anderson began his movement, collecting shreds of Rebel brigades and divisions as he marched. Pickett and remainders of the Five Forks defenders joined Anderson on Monday in the area of Bevill's Bridge. [Although attached to Longstreet's Corps, what remained of Pickett's Division would fight under Anderson at Sailor's Creek.] Anderson was unable to collect all of the troops disorganized by the Federal attacks on the Petersburg lines. Many of these bands of Rebels fought on alone, eventually becoming casualties or escaping.

By Monday night, Lee still had reason to be optimistic. The troops in his column were some 20 miles west of Petersburg and still had not been accosted by the enemy. He also was in contact with Anderson and other units from the Petersburg defenses about the rendezvous at Amelia Court House. Longstreet, at the head of the column, had sent units to recross to the south side of the Appomattox at Goode's Bridge. He posted a force there to guard the crossing of Lee's other troops.

Rebel sharpshooter Berry Benson had these memories of the hardships:

> From Goode's Bridge on, our march was one of unremitting fatigue, hunger, trouble, and disaster. I do not remember that we had rations issued at any time, but must shift for ourselves as best we could. The march was kept up day and night. We rested at odd and uncertain intervals, sleeping as we lay down with gun in hand, bundled up with whatever baggage we carried, which was rarely more than blanket, haversack, canteen, and cartridge box. As we marched along in column, many short halts occurred, caused by

some obstacle in front. At 1st I would stand waiting, as did nearly all, expecting any moment to go on. But soon, along with many others, I fell into the practice of lying down whenever there was a halt, and so got many a good little rest, for in our exhausted state it took but a moment to drop off to sleep.[2]

Lee was concerned by the lack of contact and information about Ewell's troops and their status. A messenger with orders for Ewell rode to find him Sunday night but was unable to locate the general or his force. Lee dispatched another courier to Ewell on Monday morning with instructions to cross the Appomattox wherever possible and proceed to Amelia Court House.

At the time, Lee had no way of knowing that Ewell's men were engaged in street-to-street fighting in the heart of Richmond. The absurdity was that their foe was not wearing Yankee blue.

Ewell had received orders on Sunday morning to bring his troops into the capital as part of the evacuation and to destroy supplies that could not be removed. His command consisted of the divisions of Major Generals Kershaw and George Washington Custis Lee, eldest son of Robert E. Lee. Ewell also held authority over the various cadet and convalescent units scraped together as part of the Richmond defense force. Ewell reported that his troop strength was about six thousand at the time of Richmond's abandonment.

Lee's division of three brigades was composed mostly of heavy artillerymen, Virginians and Georgians, who were in serious need of animals to pull their guns. They seized a few horses, but not nearly enough for their needs. Brigadier General Seth M. Barton and Colonel Stapleton Crutchfield headed two of Lee's brigades. The third consisted of bottom-of-the-barrel reservists and local Richmond defense troops led by Lieutenant Colonel Thomas J. Spencer.

Crutchfield, a 29-year-old Virginian, had been the chief of artillery for General Thomas J. "Stonewall" Jackson until he was wounded and lost a leg at Chancellorsville. He was among many disabled Confederates recalled to duty in the waning months of the war. Crutchfield had graduated from Virginia Military Institute in 1855 and had taught math, philosophy, and tactics at the Lexington school. He also had served briefly as V.M.I. commandant in 1861.

By far, Ewell's best men were of Kershaw's Division. The reputation of these Georgians and Mississippians had been forged at Gettysburg, Chickamauga, Spotsylvania, the Wilderness, and on dozens of other fields.

Troops were detailed to guard Union prisoners being transferred from Libby Prison and Castle Thunder, and Ewell soon found himself with only a handful of reliable soldiers in the city.

The government was of little help in this crisis. A train carrying President Davis, most of the Confederate cabinet, and other politicians had huffed out of Richmond heading toward Danville late on Sunday night. The day's awful tumults had convinced Davis that if the Confederacy was to survive, he had to relocate the capital, at least temporarily, and wait for Lee to regroup.

As if there wasn't trouble enough, looting began after dark and intensified into the night and early morning hours of Monday. Mobs roamed the streets and several buildings were set afire. Ewell used a force of convalescent soldiers, his staff, and couriers to try to restore order, but failed.

Kershaw's Division, which had been assigned to Ewell from Longstreet's Corps amid the confusion of Saturday, could not have arrived soon enough. Ewell quickly ordered Kershaw to hurry forward soldiers to suppress the pillage. Kershaw complied and his troops quickly regained control of the capital, at least stopping any large-scale looting.

By sunrise Monday, the mob had dispersed, but Richmond was on a deathwatch, with flames and dirty columns of smoke soiling the sky. Much of the city was ablaze. Exploding shells from arsenals rocked the ground as fiery debris from stocked warehouses filled the air. The earthquake blasts of Confederate gunboats that the Rebels were destroying in the James River had echoed through the night.

Amid this mayhem, Ewell evacuated Richmond. Trying to make their escape south, Kershaw's regiments found Mayo's Bridge over the James River on fire. Some boatmen helped to quell the flames, and the

Rebels double-quicked over the smoldering span while it remained sturdy. Kershaw was followed by elements of Brigadier General Martin W. Gary's cavalry. Custis Lee's Division had to cross the James at another point and joined with Ewell and Kershaw near the village of Manchester. The 10th Virginia Battalion of Heavy Artillery was among Crutchfield's cannoneers in the retreat, leaving the explosions of dying Richmond behind them.

These men typified the retreating Rebels. "Our cartridge boxes were filled, but haversacks were very light, as we were living from hand to mouth," related Captain Thomas B. Blake, who led the 10th's Company E, soldiers from Henrico County. "It had been a hard winter."[3]

The train carrying Jefferson Davis and the Confederate cabinet reached Danville about 3 p.m. on April 3. The 140-mile trip had been terribly slow with delays due to other trains also in flight from Richmond and Petersburg. Danville became the temporary capital of the Confederacy, and Davis tried in vain to find out what was happening with Lee's army.

As he settled in to the mansion of Major W. T. Sutherlin on Main Street, Davis hoped Lee was marching toward him as a first step in uniting with Joe Johnston. If Lee and Johnston could join forces and turn on the enemy, the Confederacy would have its best chance of survival—at least temporarily.

CHAPTER 3

"IN FULL VIEW OF THE DISASTROUS END"

Heading to Amelia Court House, Robert E. Lee crossed to the south side of the Appomattox River at Goode's Bridge about 7:30 a.m. on April 4, with the sound of battle to his front. This was unsettling for Lee to hear since Amelia was less than nine miles away and the Confederates had experienced little opposition up to this point. He learned that Longstreet's Corps, in the lead, had run in to enemy cavalry, and skirmishing was in progress, thus slowing the army's march.

Lee knew that his troops direly needed food and had made arrangements to feed them at Amelia. Through the commissary general, Lee had collected some three hundred fifty thousand reserve rations from Richmond. From this cache, Lee had ordered provisions for the expected fifty-six thousand or so Confederates descending on Amelia Court House. The rations were to be sent by train. Other supplies were to come down by rail as the army headed south parallel to the Richmond & Danville Railroad.

Lee's anticipation of the rations for his men quickly turned to dread at Amelia. Some train boxcars were on a siding but they contained only munitions. The provisions had not been sent! The arrangements for the ration train had been lost in the war's whirlwind, whether in paperwork at Lee's headquarters or in bureaucratic confusion.

Almost mockingly, Amelia and the train cars brimmed with military stores, as if the Confederacy was urging her troops forward with lead and powder rather than bread. The Southerners found almost 100 full caissons, 200 boxes of artillery rounds, and 164 cases of harnesses for artillery horses. A Rebel officer described Lee at the time: "No one who looked upon him then, as he stood there in full view of the disastrous end, can ever forget the intense agony written upon his features."[1] "No face wore a heavier shadow than that of General Lee," wrote Lee biographer John Esten Cooke. "The failure of the supply of rations completely paralyzed him. An anxious and haggard expression came to his face."[2]

Lee had no choice but to order a halt. His army had to have sustenance and the only way to obtain it quickly was to send out wagons to scour the countryside for victuals of any kind. Lee realized that such a move would allow the enemy to regain the precious time he had stolen on the night of the Petersburg evacuation. There also was the very real threat that the Federals would cut the railroad ahead of him and he would lose his grip with Danville where more than a million and a half rations were stored.[3]

Lee issued orders to have two hundred thousand of the Danville provisions sent by rail to meet his advance. Still, Danville was about five days' march from Amelia and, even if these rations could reach him, it would take some time, so Lee appealed to the local populace in writing:

> To the Citizens of Amelia County, Virginia.
>
> The Army of Northern Virginia arrived here today, expecting to find plenty of provisions, which had been ordered to be placed here by the railroad several days since, but to my surprise and regret I find not a pound of subsistence for man or horse. I must therefore appeal to your generosity and charity to supply as far as each one is able the wants of the brave soldiers who battled for your liberty for four years. We require meat, beef, cattle, sheep, hogs, flour, meal, corn and provender in any quantity that can be spared. The quartermaster of the army will visit you and make arrangements to pay for what he receives or give the proper vouchers or certificates. I feel assured that all will give to the extent of their means.[4]

In conjunction with this appeal, Confederate forage wagons spread out from Amelia.

As his exhausted men settled in for some much-needed rest in and around the village, Lee used the time to streamline his army. Any excess animals were harnessed with other teams to help pull the wagons and guns. The artillery and wagon trains also were trimmed, cannon and wagons deemed nonessential were culled from the column. The excess fieldpieces were moved by rail to Danville while the extra wagons would head west on a route that would put Lee's army between them and Union forces to the south. If the railroad could not be used, the artillery was to follow the wagon train.

Lee's quartermaster, Colonel James L. Corley, was responsible for the wagons while Brigadier General William N. Pendleton, chief of the Confederate artillery, would see to the cannon.[5] Mind-numbing explosions rocked the little town throughout the day as the Confederates destroyed munitions they could not carry with them.

Riding through the streets, Lee was cheered as always by his troops, despite their dire condition. "I saw General Lee and Longstreet," wrote William Owen of the New Orleans Washington Artillery after a morning glimpse of the commanders. "As usual they both looked confident."[6]

Captain J. D. Cummings of the Washington Artillery also penned a description of Lee that day:

> Here I saw General Lee for the last time...I had never seen him look so grand and martial and handsome on horseback. He was the finest specimen of a man I ever looked at, then apparently about 60 years of age, deep brown eyes, clear skin, a well-shaped Roman nose, abundant gray hair, silky beard and mustache, well and neatly trimmed, wearing a gray coat and soft hat, his uniform buttoned up and fitting to perfection. He was a picture worth seeing...General Lee and staff rode up and rested a few minutes under the slight shade of the new leaves...presently the party moved on...and when they disappeared it seemed as if a great light had gone out.[7]

In the afternoon, Union cavalry was spotted south of the railroad and west of Amelia, in the direction of Burke's Station. Longstreet threw out a battle line, but the blue troopers did not appear interested in a

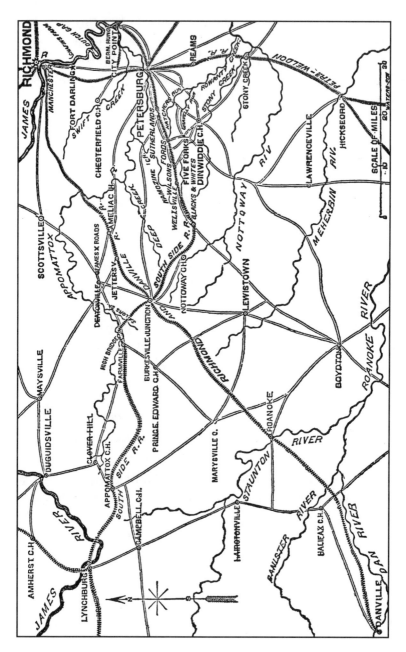

Petersburg to Appomattox

The Blue and the Gray

pitched firefight. They merely wanted to determine the location of Lee's army and pester it until Meade's infantry could reach the field. Hearing the commotion, Robert Lee rode toward the action to see what was happening. He soon met the 14th Virginia Cavalry about to launch a counter-charge against Union horsemen in their front. But the Federals suddenly retreated, except for one blue trooper who cantered toward Lee as if on a Grim Reaper mission. Rebel cavalrymen leveled carbines and revolvers at the rider, before Lee called out, "Don't shoot!" The Yank rode into the Southern lines

**Union Major General
George G. Meade**

U.S. Army Military History Institute

where a Johnny grabbed his bridle and brought him to a halt. As Lee suspected, the Northerner had been wounded and was unable to control his horse.[8]

The enemy withdrew in the early evening, allowing Longstreet to recall his units.

The bluecoats involved in this skirmish were elements of the Union Cavalry Corps under General Sheridan. Smelling blood, Sheridan's hard-riding troopers had been pushing west since Monday morning, pitiless in their effort to run down Lee's army. The cavalry squadrons were followed rapidly by the Union V Corps of Brigadier General Charles Griffin. He had been in corps command literally only a matter of hours, replacing Major General Gouverneur K. Warren, who had not deployed his divisions quickly enough, at least in the opinions of Grant and Sheridan, in the fighting at Five Forks.

There was brisk combat along Deep Creek, at Mannboro, Namozine Church, and Sweathouse Creek in the opening hours of the chase. For the most part, however, the Union anaconda was barely slowed by pesky

Rebel cavalry, stopping briefly to swallow prisoners, abandoned guns and wagons marking Lee's retreat.

Brigadier General Wesley Merritt, with Sheridan's First and Third Divisions, tailed the Confederates on the Namozine Road, the main route west toward Amelia Court House.

These divisions, the First under Brigadier General Thomas C. Devin and the Third led by Brigadier General George Armstrong Custer, were elements of the U.S. Army of the Shenandoah which had most recently sharpened their sabers in combat from Winchester to Cedar Creek. Major General George Crook's Second Cavalry Division, Army of the Potomac, completed Sheridan's mounted squadrons.

Grant and Meade were committing about 76,000 men to their pursuit of Lee. In addition to the cavalry and Griffin's Corps, the II Corps, commanded by Major General Andrew A. Humphreys, followed by the VI Corps of Major General Horatio G. Wright, also were marching west on the Namozine Road. To the south moved the columns of Major General Edward O. C. Ord's Army of the James heading west on the Cox Road, which roughly paralleled the South Side Railroad. Two divisions of Major General John G. Parke's IX Corps were bringing up the rear after ensuring that conquered Petersburg was securely in Union hands. Crook, followed by the V Corps, was ordered by Sheridan to try to block Lee's advance along the Danville Railroad at Jetersville, which was some eight miles southwest of Amelia Court House and 10 miles northeast of Burke's Station.[9]

On Tuesday morning, while Lee's columns were descending on Amelia Court House, Crook was sent to strike the Richmond & Danville between Burke's Station and Jetersville. He was then to move to the northeast to Jetersville.

After Sheridan's scouts reported gray infantry concentrating at Amelia, the V Corps also was put on the march to Jetersville. Unwilling to wait for Crook's Division to reach its destination, Sheridan then set off toward Jetersville with his two-hundred-man escort of the 1st U.S. Cavalry.

Sheridan reached the village about 5 p.m. and learned without doubt that Lee's army was at Amelia. The escort troopers were deployed facing northeast along the railroad. Sheridan was determined to hold until reinforced by Crook and the V Corps. In a flurry, he sent off a message to Meade asking that the II and VI Corps join him as rapidly as possible at Jetersville and other dispatches for the rest of his cavalry to come up.

Riding through the night toward Jetersville late Tuesday, the Union cavalry divisions were tired and hungry. Many swayed in their saddles, sound asleep as the horses followed the mount ahead of them. Federal pioneer troops, eager to unload boxes of ammunition, handed them fistfuls of Spencer rounds along the lanes. Some of the cavalrymen balked at taking more rounds since they usually only carried no more than 75. But orders were for each trooper to have 125, indicating that something big was in the works.

Sheridan's men also intercepted a dispatch from Lee's commissary general to the Rebel quartermasters at Danville and Lynchburg ordering three hundred thousand rations from each depot to be sent to meet the Confederates at Burke's Station. Sheridan figured to try to obtain these provisions for his own soldiers who had far outdistanced their supply lines. He sent out two pairs of scouts, each with a copy of Lee's original dispatch, to find the telegraph line and make doubly sure the message clicked over the wire to the Rebels. Meade complied with Sheridan's request for reinforcements and the II and VI Corps were soon on the march. It would be sometime Wednesday before they would be within distance to help Sheridan, however.

Settling in to Jetersville, one of Sheridan's bluejackets described it as "A small village on the railroad of scarcely a dozen buildings, a store or two. Blacksmith shop, Post Office, and small Railroad Depot where were found a few cars...The little place wore an air of comfort and respectability."[10] Another Yankee was less kind, calling the town "an insignificant station on the railroad, comprising a half-dozen buildings all told, with nothing to boast of but an old Revolutionary Church, built in some remote period in the history of the state."[11]

"Still following the demoralized Army," wrote a Union infantry officer in the VI Corps, doggedly pressing its march. "The road is filled with broken wagons and the things thrown away in the flight of the Rebels. I do not know just where we are but do not care, for Grant is at the head and we shall come out all right."[12]

The V Corps arrived in the late afternoon Tuesday and began to entrench "with a view to holding Jetersville until the main army could come up," Sheridan reported.[13]

"As the enemy was within striking distance no fires were lighted, and the corps was kept in readiness for battle," recalled another bluecoat.[14] "This place is on the Danville Railroad, and about ten miles west of Amelia Court House, where Lee is said to be tonight, with his main force," Colonel Charles S. Wainwright, commander of the V Corps artillery, confided in his journal. "So we have got ahead of him, and cut him off from his direct route to join Johnston..."[15]

Sheridan knew he had the chance of a lifetime if he could clamp down on the Confederate army which so many times had set Union forces of greater might in full retreat. He also realized that Lee likely could crush him if the Rebels made a quick and concentrated attack on his outnumbered infantry and cavalry.

At Amelia Court House, Robert Lee knew that the enemy was nearby as he impatiently waited for his supply wagons to return and for some contact from General Ewell. What he did not know, as Tuesday evening settled over the Virginia hills, was that a Union infantry corps and a good portion of Sheridan's cavalry, were already blocking his most direct route to Danville. Major General Henry Heth arrived with the remnants of the late Hill's Third Corps in the afternoon, and Anderson's Corps was marshaling nearby, both forces having fought off Union cavalry attacks on Tuesday. The Second Corps of Major General John B. Gordon went into camp for the night about five miles east of the village.[16]

After dark on Tuesday, Lee finally received word from Ewell, who had been held up by the swollen waters of the Appomattox. Ewell wrote that his engineers were planking the railroad bridge at Mattoax so that his troops could cross there. The division of Major General William Mahone, which had been guarding Goode's Bridge, also was headed toward Amelia.

At Danville, Jefferson Davis spent a drizzly Tuesday hoping for some word as to Lee's fate, but he received none. Davis and his cabinet members busied themselves in trying to reestablish some semblance of a government. The president also issued a proclamation "to the People of the Confederate States of America," opening with news of Richmond's fall. Davis quickly added, however, "We have now entered upon a new phase of the struggle. Relieved from the necessity of guarding particular points, our army will be free to move from point to point, to strike the enemy in detail far from his base. Let us but will it, and we are free."[17]

Attempting to contact Lee, Davis ordered a train sent east from Danville. Aboard was volunteer courier Lieutenant John S. Wise, son of Brigadier General Henry A. Wise, a former governor of Virginia who commanded one of Lee's brigades. Davis also sent out telegram inquiries trying to obtain news about Lee's army. The only response he received from the telegraphers was indeed ominous. There was no word from Lee, but other stations along the lines were regularly going dead.

Unbeknown to Davis at the time, the Yankees were closing down all of his links to his shrinking domain.

Ewell's men and Fitz Lee's cavalry did not reach Amelia Court House until the early morning of Wednesday, April 5. Dawn heralded a rainy day, adding to the dreariness blanketing the Confederate bivouacs in and around the village.

"It was a forced march; we halted only to rest on our arms," recounted artillery Captain Thomas Blake of Crutchfield's Brigade. "To add to other discomforts, a cold rain set in, drenching us to the skin. Footsore, well-nigh starved, and almost exhausted, we continued the retreat."[18]

Custis Lee's Division was joined at Amelia by the Naval Battalion under Commodore John Randolph Tucker and a detachment of Richmond civilians and militia commanded by Major Frank Smith. Tucker's Brigade of three hundred sailors and two hundred marines had been manning batteries at Drewry's Bluff outside Richmond. With virtually no navy left, these Confederates were now fighting afoot.

The gray leathernecks suffered a blow this day when their commander, Major George H. Territt, was captured near the town.[19] Territt had led the marines from their evacuation of their base at Camp Beall on the James River. They would now be commanded by Tucker and marine captains John D. Simms, George Holmes, and Thomas S. Wilson.[20] At least one Confederate was not impressed with Tucker's men. "I remember the Naval Battalion particularly," wrote Lieutenant Colonel William W. Blackford, a Virginia cavalryman and military engineer. "The sailors did well enough on the march, but there were the fat old captains and commodores, who had never marched anywhere but on a quarter-deck before in their lives, limping along, puffing and blowing and cursing everything black and blue."[21] Other amused Rebels called the navy men the "Aye Ayes" due to their shouted answers to orders.

Blackford was even more critical of Smith's Richmond contingent, which he described as:

> a perfect army of bureau clerks, quartermasters, commissaries, and ordnance officers, all dressed in fine clothes and uniforms, with white faces, scared half to death, fellows who for the most part had been in their bomb-proof offices ever since the war began and who did not relish the prospect of smelling powder, nor of having to rough it a bit like ordinary mortals in the field.[22]

Still, the diverse blend of Custis Lee's ranks stirred one Confederate officer to write:

> Infantry, cavalry, light and heavy artillery and sailors, we had thus in our small division all the elements of a complete army and navy, and with the Richmond Locals and Defences some material for civil government besides.[23]

An assortment of Rebeldom's luminaries and others completed the procession from Richmond. Blackford saw them as "citizens in broadcloth, politicians, members of Congress, prominent citizens, almost all on foot, but sometimes there were wagons and carriages loaded with them. Some ladies too might be seen occasionally and generally they were calmer than the men."[24]

Lee had reassembled his broken army in the field despite battle disaster, bad communications, forces separated by many miles and an aggressive, powerful enemy. But any cheer brought by the arrival of Ewell and Mahone was offset by the return of the forage wagons Wednesday morning. Eager soldiers hopefully watched the first of them rattle into the streets, their longings quickly turning to gloom. The wagons were nearly empty, the teamsters finding little food or crops in a farmland already stripped. Lee's appeal for food from Amelia's citizens also met with little response.

There was no doubt that Lee's dead-tired and filthy soldiers were starving. They had been ordered out of their Richmond-Petersburg trenches with little notice or, in most cases, no time for the Rebels' scant commissaries to fill their haversacks. Riding along his column, Ewell reported seeing some men eating "raw fresh meat as they marched in ranks." A small ox wandered close to the road at one point, was instantly butchered and eaten on the spot by a group of men. Other soldiers chewed on spring buds snapped from tree branches.[25]

"The Quartermasters said there were plenty of rations for the army at Amelia C.H.," recounted a Virginia cavalryman who rode into the village on Tuesday night, "only to meet the bitterest disappointment. And now it really did seem that famine would accomplish what all of Grant's bayonets could not effect and compel the veteran army of Lee to surrender; but that alternative impressed the men as worse than starvation."[26]

Gun crews of the Jeff Davis Artillery reached Amelia Court House on Wednesday and were among a few lucky Rebels to be issued their first provisions since leaving the Petersburg trenches. "These rations consisted of three small ears of corn, and this was the last rations I received from the Confederate Government," Georgian John Francis Methvin wrote after the war.[27]

The artillery battalion of Colonel Wilfred E. Cutshaw had been forced to leave its guns behind in the trenches. Reaching Amelia, the cannoneers were assigned to Brigadier General James A. Walker's Division in Gordon's Corps and about two hundred twenty-five men were issued muskets. "Not a cartridge-box, cap box, belt, or any other convenience ornamented the persons of these new-born infantrymen," reflected Rebel Carlton McCarthy. "They stored their ammunition in their pockets along with their corn, salt, pipes, and tobacco."[28]

Cutshaw's men fell in to be fed shortly afterward and McCarthy remembered the depressing scene:

> When application was made for rations, it was found that the last morsel belonging to the division had been issued to the command, and the battalion was again thrown on its own resources, to wit: corn on the cob intended for the horses. Two ears were issued to each man. It was parched in the coals, mixed with salt, stored in the pockets, and eaten on the road.[29]

"We had nothing to eat; hunger became an ally of the enemy," recalled Major Henry Kyd Douglas, a brigade commander in Walker's Division. "Once I took some corn from my horse, beat it between stones and tried to swallow it. The little army was willing to march and fight, but starvation made stragglers of them; commands were reduced to skeletons, as their men had been some time before."[30]

John Methvin of Gordon's Corps had shucked one ear of his corn ration and was parching it in half of an old canteen over a small fire when his older brother, Thomas, marched by in another unit. With an officer's permission, Thomas stopped briefly to pour some meal into his grateful brother's haversack before hustling back into ranks. "I did not have time to cook any of the meal he gave me, but finished parching my corn, put it into my haversack to cool, and lit out," John Methvin recounted. "A few minutes after I left there I got into a scrape with the Yankees, but came out alright."[31]

CHAPTER 4

SHERIDAN—BRIMSTONE AND BLOOD

At Jetersville, Sheridan had been in the saddle since early morning Wednesday trying to determine the Rebels' next move. Through the night of April 4–5 he had waited for Lee to attack, but there was nothing. Now, before first light, he was riding along his lines, wondering why the Confederates did not surface.

The 34-year-old Sheridan had emerged as one of the conflict's foremost commanders, waging offensive, lightning war well suited to the brimstone and blood combat fought by Grant and Sherman. Chivalry be damned; seek and destroy the enemy, was the coda of "Little Phil" Sheridan. He and Sherman shared a similar definition of war in which the enemy was not only a rival soldier but the civilian populace as well.

By spring 1865, hundreds of homefront Southerners in Georgia and in the Shenandoah Valley could painfully attest to the scorched-earth righteousness of both of these loathsome Yankees. Sheridan theorized that "the loss of property weighs heavy with the most of mankind; heavier often, than the sacrifices made on the field of battle."[1] At 5'4", Sheridan did not have the stature of an imposing war chief. Lincoln, after his first meeting with Sheridan, described him as a "brown, chunky, little chap, with a long body, short legs, not enough neck to hang him, and such long arms that if his ankles itch he can scratch them without stooping."[2]

His Minié bullet-shaped head was crowned by a short burst of black hair. The dark eyes, however, defined the shark. An aide and confidant,

John Schuyler Crosby, told how
"one could tell from his eyes in a
moment whether he was serious,
sad, or humorous, without noticing
another feature of his face."[3] Raised
by Irish immigrant parents who
settled in Somerset, Ohio, Sheridan
in different records claimed both
that village and Albany, New York,
as his birthplace.

Sheridan received his early
education in Somerset's one-room
schoolhouse and, as a youngster,
worked in a general store. The
teenager read of battles and daring exploits of the Mexican War
and daydreamed of being a soldier.

**Union Major General
Philip H. Sheridan**

U.S. Army Military History Institute

When he learned that the 1848 appointee to West Point from his district
had failed the entrance exam, Sheridan quickly applied for the vacancy,
and Congressman Thomas Ritchie granted it.[4]

Sheridan and his temper quickly landed him in trouble at the Academy. He did not take to the traditional hazing, clashed with cadets from
the South, and did poorly in his studies.

Sheridan served eight years on the frontier, being posted in Texas,
California, and Oregon with the 1st and later the 4th U.S. Infantry. After the war opened, Sheridan was ordered back East and served on the
staffs of Generals Samuel Curtis and Henry W. Halleck.

In May 1862, the captain was promoted to colonel of the 2nd
Michigan Cavalry and saw his first serious battle at Booneville, Mississippi, on July 1. Outnumbered as much as six to one, Sheridan's
827 troopers fought off a Confederate division. The Yankees were
armed with 12-shot Colt revolving rifles, which added immensely to
their firepower, but the victory was significant nonetheless to the Union
brass. In September 1862, Sheridan was appointed brigadier general
of volunteers to rank from the date of his Booneville triumph. He

fought tenaciously at Perryville and Stones River and earned his major generalship in March 1863.

Sheridan's comet dimmed at Chickamauga in September 1863 when his division crumbled with most of the U.S. Army of the Cumberland in this ringing Union defeat. The victorious Rebels of General Braxton Bragg besieged these Yankees in Chattanooga until Grant and Sherman orchestrated a breakout attempt on November 24–25, 1863. On the second day, Sheridan's Division attacked and captured Confederate positions at the base of Missionary Ridge, a mountaintop Rebel bastion.[5] Weathering a murderous fire from the enemy above, Sheridan's men charged up the slopes without orders. Their bantam general, astride his sable warhorse Rienzi, galloped ahead of his troops and the seemingly invincible gray lines were overrun. Sheridan continued his pursuit for miles, snapping up hundreds of prisoners. "Sheridan showed his genius in that battle...," Grant recalled. Sheridan's relentness nature, much like his own, also had to impress Grant.[6]

When Grant headed to Washington in March 1864 to assume his general-in-chief duties, Sheridan was given command of the Army of the Potomac's cavalry. Friction between General Meade and Sheridan was shortly forthcoming. Sheridan wanted to craft his squadrons into hawkish fighters who would go head-to-head with Confederate Major General J. E. B. Stuart's vaunted horsemen who, for the most part, had dominated the Union cavalry for three years. Meade was more old school, insisting that the cavalry's role remained that of picket duty, escort, and scouting. Grant sided with Sheridan and the burgeoning Yankee mounties, ten thousand strong, went after Stuart.

Sheridan's squadrons overwhelmed the outnumbered and depleted Confederate cavalry at Yellow Tavern, Virginia, on May 11, 1864, mortally wounding Stuart in the process and rampaged to the outskirts of Richmond. Cavalry dominance had now swung to the Union. After Rebel Lieutenant General Jubal Early's abortive raid up Virginia's Shenandoah Valley against Washington in July, Sheridan was put in command of the Middle Military Division, which essentially was the U.S. Army of the Shenandoah. Sheridan had orders to close off this open back door to the capital. He also was to destroy any and everything he deemed usable by the enemy in the valley, which was known as the "breadbasket of the Confederacy." Sheridan's forces whipped Early's undermanned army at Winchester on September 19, 1864, and, more decisively, at Fisher's Hill three days later.

With the Rebs apparently beaten, Sheridan's soldiers sent the Shenandoah up in flames. Crops, mills, farms and all else the Yankees believed could contribute to the Southern war effort were torched. By the third week of October 1864, Sheridan's army of 32,000 had encamped along Cedar Creek between Strasburg and Middletown intent on rest and recuperation from the hard campaign. But the resurgent and unpredictable Early, reinforced by Joseph Kershaw's Division from Lee, was preparing a very unpleasant surprise for these Yanks.

Sheridan, unaware of any threat, left on Sunday, October 16, for a conference in Washington, leaving Major General Horatio G. Wright of the Union VI Corps in overall command. Sheridan was near Winchester, en route back to his army, on Wednesday, October 19, when he received mind-jumbling news: Early had launched a surprise predawn attack at Cedar Creek and part of his army was fleeing!

An American legend was born over the next few hours.

Mounting Rienzi, Sheridan clattered down the Valley Pike, heading to the battlefield some 14 miles away. Stragglers told him of the disaster ahead and Sheridan shouted for the soldiers to rally and help drive the Rebs back. Hundreds did just that and by afternoon, Sheridan had regained control of his forces and was preparing a counterattack against Early. This massive blow fell about 4 p.m., and the outnumbered Confederates were unable to withstand it. Their retreat disintegrated in rout and Early had lost control of the Shenandoah forever.

The Union victory was immortalized in the poem *Sheridan's Ride*, by T. Buchanan Read, and Sheridan became a virtual Paul Revere for the North. Rienzi garnered celebrity as well.

The electric triumph at Cedar Creek unquestionably aided Republican President Lincoln's 1864 reelection a few weeks later against the popular General George McClellan, the "peace at any price" Democrat.

On Grant's orders, Sheridan continued his scorching of the Valley through the last weeks of 1864 and early into 1865. The fiery destruction was so complete that "Little Phil" bragged that "a crow would be compelled to carry his own rations" in flying over the Shenandoah.[7] Sheridan rejoined Grant in March 1865, intent on being in on the final kill as Grant opened his spring campaign destined to be the last of the war in Virginia. Sheridan coordinated the infantry and cavalry force that seized Five Forks on April 1, leaving Lee with little choice but to evacuate Richmond and Petersburg. Four days later, Sheridan had been the lead warhound snapping after the Rebels. As he rode among his bluejackets and peered down the Amelia Road, which was now blocked to Lee's army, it appeared his obstinate persistence was about to pay off.

Tension and anticipation mounted among the dug-in Federals in Jetersville through the morning of April 5. "In the same position, and Lee said to be still at Amelia, yet no fight," wrote artillery Colonel Wainwright.[8] That morning, hours before the II and VI Corps reached his line, Sheridan ordered Crook to send the cavalry brigade of Brigadier General Henry E. Davies on a patrol north about seven miles toward Painesville, or Paines Cross Roads. If the Rebs were not going to attack him, Sheridan figured to see if there was any enemy movement outside his left flank.

Unfortunately for the Confederates, Davies' command rode into Painesville in the early afternoon, discovered that a portion of Lee's wagon train had passed through there a short time earlier and was only about four miles ahead of them. The target proved to be the baggage train of Custis Lee's Division that had left Richmond with Ewell and taken a different route from the infantry in trying to reach Amelia Court House. It consisted of about two hundred Confederate vehicles, including ammunition, rations and headquarters wagons, ambulances and caissons.

An estimated four hundred soldiers, about half of whom were blacks recently recruited in Richmond, guarded the column. These men were apparently a part of a "Negro brigade" assembled after the Virginia legislature, in mid-March, decided to allow blacks to join state units. The Confederate Congress had narrowly rejected a similar proposal a few weeks earlier. Robert Lee favored recruiting black Confederates, writing to Ewell on March 30: "If we do not get these men, they will soon be in arms against us, and perhaps relieving white Federal soldiers."[9] Ewell had privately supported the enlistment of black soldiers as early as 1861 and Lee had given him the task of organizing what would become two companies.[10]

So with some of these unlikely Rebels on vigilance, the train had proceeded unmolested and had crossed the Appomattox River at Clementown on Tuesday night. Resuming its trek in the morning, the caravan was within four miles of Amelia when Davies closed in. Excitedly, the Union horsemen went after the train, the 1st Pennsylvania galloping along the road and the rest of the brigade following cautiously at a trot. Hell, there was no sense riding into a Reb ambush.

Davies' cavalry caught up with the enemy wagons as the Rebels frantically tried to ready a cannon to fire on his command. Before the gun could be primed, the Union detachment plunged through a swamp and quickly overpowered the guards and teamsters. Davies' yipping troopers madly rode along and amid the now-stalled train, firing at wagoneers or gray cavalrymen in the startled escort. Many of the Rebels in the column were heavy artillerymen who were unarmed.

The Yanks were "dashing up and down the road, now shooting the drivers, now charging the guards, now unceremoniously overhauling the contents of a heavily laden wagon, or attempting to drive off mules, drivers, wagons, and all," one of the marauders recounted.[11]

A Confederate not involved in the action happened upon a point where he could see the attack. He described the fate of the ebony Rebels in the escort:

> I saw a wagon train guarded by Confederate negro soldiers...When within about one hundred yards of and in the rear of the wagon train, I observed some Union cavalry a short distance away on elevated ground forming to charge and the negro soldiers forming to meet the attack, which was met successfully...The cavalry charged again, and the negro soldiers surrendered.[12]

The overall issue was decided in minutes. The Federals captured some six hundred forty prisoners, half of whom were black soldiers or teamsters. Also taken were eleven flags and about four hundred horses and mules. Davies soon decided that the weaker draft animals could not move fast enough to pull the wagons triumphantly into Jetersville and the decision was made to torch the captured train.

"The escort was dispersed and the dingy vehicles consigned to the flames," a bluejacket observed.[13] Most critical, some twenty thousand rations that would have been manna for the ravenous gray soldiers at Amelia were fired by the Federals.

With the smoke of the column licking skyward, the Northerners jubilantly gathered their war prizes and rode toward Sheridan's lines. Nearing Flat Creek, Davies' troopers surprised a small force of Confederate artillery from the command of Lieutenant Colonel John C. Haskell's Battalion that was on the march. These Southerners, led by Captain James N. Lamkin, were quickly snapped up, adding to the bluecoats' spoils. Davies' plunder here included eight to 10 heavy mortars that had been in the Rebel defenses around Richmond and five British-made Whitworth rifled guns.

Still, the Yankees would not be allowed to hold a victory parade. Confederate cavalry, led by Brigadier General Martin W. Gary's Brigade camped three miles distant, descended on the Union force. Gary's men rode through the sacked and blazing wagon train to find and attack Davies.

Lieutenant Edward M. Boykin of the 7th South Carolina Cavalry described the action:

> We soon reached the point they had [first] attacked and set fire to the wagons—the canvas covers taking fire very easily. Their plan of operation seemed to be to strike at the train, which was several miles long, at a given point, fire as many wagons as they could, then making a circuit and striking it again, leaving an intermediate point untouched...The burning caissons, as we rode by, were anything but pleasant neighbors, and were exploding right and left, but I do not recollect any of our men being hit. We could hear the enemy ahead of us, as we pressed our tired horses through the burning wagons and the scattered plunder which filled the road, giving our own wagon rats and skulkers a fine harvest of plunder. Many of the wagons were untouched, but [later were] plundered by our own cowardly skulkers, that I suppose belong to all armies.[14]

At a bend in the road, the South Carolinians were ambushed and five troopers plummeted from their saddles. The Yanks couldn't exploit their surprise, however, and a brief saber fight ended with several Federals taken prisoner and the Johnnies still on the attack. Gary's command repeatedly stove in Davies' rearguard as the Rebel cavalry continued to mass. The fighting churned desperately before the arrival of blue cavalry brigades under Colonel Charles H. Smith and Colonel J. Irvin Gregg sent by Crook to reinforce Davies.

With this support, Davies battled his way into Jetersville, the Southern troopers hitting him to within a mile of the village before turning back due to the strong infantry presence there. Incredibly, casualties were light and both sides claimed a measure of victory.

Wrote a Virginia trooper:

> This affair did more to revive the drooping spirits of the Cavalry Corps than anything else could, but it is doubtful if they would have fought so fiercely if they had not been so hungry, and the first demand, on taking a prisoner, was "hand me your haversack, quick, or I'll blow your brains out."[15]

Davies' reconnaissance had been fruitful. Sheridan was now convinced that Lee would try to escape when he was free of his wagon trains.

General Meade, meanwhile, had left his headquarters at Deep Creek that morning, heading to find Sheridan. He met with the cavalryman at Jetersville about midafternoon and reassumed command of the V Corps, which had operated under Sheridan's orders at Five Forks. Bad blood had flowed between Meade and Sheridan for some time. Both generals were known for their tempers, their seethings a sizzling powder keg. During the Wilderness campaign they had engaged in an explosive argument with Meade accusing Sheridan of blundering in troop deployment. An aide recalled that Sheridan was "equally as fiery... His language throughout was highly spiced and conspicuously italicized with expletives."[16]

The road to Sailor's Creek would do nothing to heal these wounds.

CHAPTER 5
"OUR ARMY IS RUINED, I FEAR."

With little or nothing to feed the troops from the forage parties, Lee put the army in motion toward Danville about 1 p.m. on April 5. Perhaps if they followed the railroad west they would eventually meet the supply train. The excess baggage and artillery column had creaked out of camp with a cavalry escort about two hours earlier. With the army moving again, Lee was aware of the attack on Custis Lee's wagons but still did not realize the magnitude of the enemy buildup at Jetersville.

The cavalry division of Major General William H. F. "Rooney" Lee, the second son of the army commander, was sent down the railroad, nosing toward Jetersville. These troopers had stayed with the main army while the rest of Fitz Lee's cavalry was, even then, engaged against Davies. Behind this cavalry screen came the head of Longstreet's Corps followed by the infantry of Generals Pickett and Mahone. Next came the rest of Anderson's Corps. Ewell, with his divisions of Kershaw and Custis Lee, were among the last Confederates to leave the village, getting a few hours of invaluable rest after their forced march. John Gordon's men followed.

Kershaw, 44, was from Camden, South Carolina, and had been an attorney, state legislator, and delegate to the Secession Convention in 1860. A citizen soldier, who had an exemplary record throughout the conflict, Kershaw's first military experience had been as a lieutenant in the Palmetto Regiment militia in the Mexican War. As colonel of the 2nd South Carolina, he was with state forces that bombarded Fort Sumter

in April 1861 and fought at First
Bull Run. Promoted to brigadier
general in February 1862, Kershaw
was an integral commander in the
Confederate First Corps in almost
all of the Army of Northern Virginia's campaigns. When the corps
was sent west in September 1863,
Kershaw went with Longstreet and
was in the heaviest of the struggle
at Chickamauga. Appointed major
general in May 1864, Kershaw assumed division command and saw
action at the Wilderness, on detached duty in the Shenandoah
Valley under Jubal Early and at
Petersburg.

**Confederate Major General
Joseph B. Kershaw**

Author's Collection

The 32-year-old Custis Lee
was seeing his first actual combat duty of the war. Lee graduated at the
head of the West Point class of 1854, topping other future Confederate
generals who included J. E. B. Stuart, John Pegram, and Stephen Dill
Lee, no relation.[1] Lee mirrored his father's early military career, serving as an engineer in various parts of the country. He resigned his U.S.
Army lieutenantcy in May 1861 and shortly became a captain of engineers for the Confederates. Custis was employed in the construction of
Richmond's earliest defenses and in August 1861 was appointed colonel to serve on the staff of President Davis. While he could never
begin to approach his father's battlefield acclaim, Custis performed
admirably as a military liaison for Davis and sometimes even was
consulted by "Marse Robert" himself.[2] Lee was promoted brigadier
general to rank from June 1863 and attained major general in February 1865. In the war's last weeks, Custis had organized the local defense brigade in Richmond, ultimately under Ewell's Department of
Richmond command.

Gordon's men brought up the rearguard and had some time to relax while the rest of the troops snaked out of the village. Sudden but volcanic blasts from the train depot startled the weary men. The engineers were destroying as much of the excess munitions and other stores as possible to keep it from the enemy. Mountains of ammunition, including almost one hundred loaded caissons, had been stacked near the hamlet's southern end and were being detonated.

Confederate Major General George Washington Custis Lee

Author's Collection

"Towards evening...the men were lying around, chatting and eating raw bacon...when suddenly the earth shook with a tremendous explosion," recounted Carlton McCarthy. "Whole regiments broke and fled...till it was known that the ammunition had been purposely fired and no enemy was threatening the line. Then what laughter and hilarity prevailed for a while among these famishing men!"[3]

The soldiers' amusement was brief, however, as they returned to the starkness of their plight and Gordon's men soon rejoined the procession.

Spring rains from earlier in the week added to the Rebels' woes on the march. Wagons sunk to their axles in the muck, and weakened horses and mules collapsed in the road as the Confederates marched past them, barely taking notice. The Rebel infantry was well on its way Wednesday afternoon until cavalry pickets galloped back to the main column. The news was alarming to say the least: Union cavalry, with infantry in close support, were dug in before Jetersville, blocking the army's path. And the Federals were steadily being reinforced.

Robert Lee rode to the front and inspected the Union positions and the lay of the land through field glasses. Trotting along his front,

Lee appeared more than ready to fight. "I never saw General Lee seem so anxious to bring on a battle in my life as he seemed this afternoon," remembered Brigadier General E. P. Alexander, Longstreet's artillery chief.[4]

In deciding his course the commander conferred with son, Rooney, and later with Longstreet. With no concise maps and having not been in the region before, Lee also called in area farmers to help describe the countryside around them, but they were of little assistance. What Lee saw were Sheridan's cavalry and the Union V Corps doggedly holding their positions while the lead brigades of Humphreys' Corps were arriving in the village. The first units of Wright's VI Corps also were hard on the march and would be in Jetersville about 6 p.m.

By now the sun was sinking low and Lee had second thoughts about attacking, based on the dwindling daylight and the reported size of the enemy. He decided that the Union forces were making a general advance toward Burke's Station and that the enemy to his front was too strong for him to gamble on a breakout.

The blue roadblock obviously was another setback for the Confederates. "This deprived us of the use of the railroad," Lee later reported, "and rendered it impracticable to procure from Danville the supplies ordered to meet us at points of our march."[5]

Not wanting his men brought to bay to perhaps face a major battle at dusk or the next dawn, Lee altered his plans. The troops would continue on through the rest of the day and make a night march, skirting north of the Union left flank and moving west to Farmville, about 23 miles away on the South Side Railroad. In addition to the earlier dispatch that had been captured by Sheridan, Lee also issued orders for rations to be sent from Lynchburg to Farmville. From there he could then turn southwest again toward Danville. Lee briefly considered a suggestion by Mahone to mass his army and strike the enemy flank at Jetersville, but decided otherwise. As always, frantic speed was of the essence.

Longstreet's divisions retreated along the road away from Jetersville and then turned north toward Amelia Springs as Lee's new orders were spread through the army late in the afternoon. An infantry officer wrote that he felt this was "the most cruel marching order" issued to Lee's men during the war.[6]

Again, the Southerners stumbled to their feet, shouldered muskets and slogged along the road. Although many realized they were in a death race, time's reality was lost in this infinite nightmare. "From this time forth the army was little more than a mob," wrote Captain William Brunson who commanded what was left of a unit of sharpshooters in McGowan's Brigade. "We fought day and night without much system, surrounded by Yankee cavalry. The Sharpshooters were ordered from one flank to another, and from front to rear."[7]

"The country through which we were passing had been swept bare," the Virginia Captain Thomas Blake recounted. "There was nothing we could find to eat except the few grains of corn left on the ground where horses had fed. These we gathered up wherever we could find any and ate them raw."[8]

Unaware that Lee's army was on the march, Sheridan sent a 3 p.m. dispatch to Grant, informing him of the success of Davies' raid. In closing, he wrote: "I feel confident of capturing the Army of Northern Virginia if we exert ourselves. I see no escape for Lee..."[9] The message also contained this line: "I wish you were here yourself," implying to Grant that Meade and Sheridan were not seeing eye-to-eye on the conduct of the operations. Grant well knew of the differences between his highly charged generals. With the dispatch, Sheridan sent Grant a letter, written by a Confederate officer to his mother that had been captured earlier that day:

> Dear Mamma:
> Our army is ruined, I fear. We are all safe as yet. Shyron left us sick. John Taylor is well—saw him yesterday. We are in line of battle this morning. General Robert Lee is in the field near us. My trust is still in the justice of our cause, and that of God. General Hill is killed. I saw Murray a few minutes since. Bernard, Terry said, was taken prisoner, but may yet get out. I send this by a negro passing up the railroad to Mecklenburg. Love to all.
> Your devoted son,
> Wm. B. Taylor, Colonel.[10]

The dispatch was carried by a veteran scout named Campbell, who wore a Confederate uniform in making his way to Grant. At the time, Grant was with Ord's Corps marching along the line of the South Side Railroad near Nottoway Court House. When Campbell approached, some of the Federals opened fire on him, but the shooting was quickly stopped when Grant's staff recognized the scout. Campbell had the correspondence folded into tin foil and encased in a wad of chewing tobacco he had in his mouth. The somewhat soggy message of Sheridan's success was soon shared with the blue infantry on the move along the railroad.

"This news was given to the passing troops and lusty cheers went up from every throat," wrote Lieutenant Colonel Horace Porter of Grant's staff. "They had marched about fifteen miles already that day, and now struck out as if they were good for fifteen more, and swore they were going to beat the record of the cavalry."[11]

At Jetersville, the incoming infantry of Humphreys and Wright found the V Corps entrenched and expecting to be attacked. The Federals dug in to lines along a four-mile front and rested while they waited for the Rebs. "We had unexpectedly intercepted him [the enemy] with three infantry corps supporting our cavalry," a Federal surgeon wrote.[12]

"Was ever a mortal permitted to endure such tortures as I have suffered today?" moaned a Maine soldier in the II Corps. "Quite early in the day my heels were galled to the bone. The blood dried into the stockings and boots, and when I removed them, the flesh was actually torn from my heel. I thought I had known suffering from this cause before, but all previous experiences have been simply skirmishes compared with the agony of the moment."[13]

"Still plodding along following up Lee," a VI Corps officer scrawled in his diary. "Every step we see proof of the demoralized condition of Lee's troops. We shall catch him if we keep on, and when we do the war will end. He has often followed us, and we him, but this is the last time. At night we joined Sheridan's Cavalry at Jetersville."[14]

Sheridan, never disposed to give much, if any, credit to his enemy, later recognized that Lee missed an excellent opportunity to punch out of the Federals' trap if he had attacked Jetersville before the Union troops had had time to erect defenses and be reinforced.

"It seems to me that this was the only chance the Army of Northern Virginia had to save itself, which might have been done had General Lee promptly attacked and driven back the comparatively small force opposed to him and pursued his march to Burkeville Junction," he recounted.[15] In agreement with Sheridan was artillery Colonel Wainwright who wrote on Wednesday: "It seems to me queer for Lee must have known that there was only one corps of infantry here, until quite late in the afternoon. I cannot understand it; for it was a grand chance for him, if he has any large force with him. Now we are much too strong for him to break through and shall probably attack him tomorrow if he remains overnight."[16]

Hungry and foot-sore soldiers of the VI and II Corps hunkered into camps around Jetersville, waiting for their supply trains to come up. Some of these Federals set out into the countryside to find their supper, leaving their friendly bivouac fires and tromping out into the darkness. A fortunate few happened upon a squirrel, chicken, or rabbit to add to the stew pot. For the most part, however, these foraging Yanks instead found a foreign land beset by deserters and stragglers from Lee's army, many of whom were crazed by starvation and battle fatigue. These were often brutal meetings.

"A few of our men went to check the poultry interests of this section," Private John W. Haley of the 17th Maine wrote in his April 5 journal entry. "They were beset by guerrillas who served them as they had served the hens; cut their throats and plucked their clothing. This game of stripping the dead is a favorite sport with Rebels. If they do it from necessity then I can only say that when a so-called government gets *that* poor it is quite time to go out of business."[17]

Jefferson Davis spent another frustrating day in Danville with still no reports of Lee's whereabouts. His courier, John Wise, had hopefully evaded capture and was en route to find the army, but Davis had no word as to his progress either. The proclamation he had written on Tuesday was printed in the *Danville Register* and also dispatched by telegraph.[18]

Grant by Wednesday night reasoned that Lee and his army were trying to reach Danville. He had established his headquarters at Wilson's Station on the South Side Railroad when he wrote General Sherman that evening:

> Sheridan, who was up with him [Lee] last night, reports all that is left, horse, foot, and dragoons, at 20,000, much demoralized. We hope to reduce this number one-half. I shall push on to Burkeville, and if a stand is made at Danville, will in a very few days go there. If you can possibly do so, push on from where you are, and let us see if we cannot finish the job with Lee's and Johnston's armies. Whether it will be better for you to strike for Greensborough [Greensboro, N.C.] or nearer to Danville, you will be better able to judge when you receive this. Rebel armies now are the only strategic points to strike at.[19]

Grant's intention was clear. If Bobby Lee and Joe Johnston were hell-bent on combining their forces, then so be it. Such a move would mean that he and Sherman might snare the whole lot at one time! Excited by the success reported in Sheridan's afternoon communiqué, Grant decided to ride the 20 or so miles to Jetersville that night to join Meade and Sheridan, and plot how best to deal with Lee. He also had to be curious about how his top generals were getting along, based on the tone of Sheridan's note.

Leaving his jaded pony, Jeff Davis, and mounting his bay, Cincinnati, Grant set out with a 14-man escort and some of his staff guided by Campbell, Sheridan's scout. Moonlight was their only way to navigate through the wilderness, and there was a threat of bumping into Rebel cavalry, but there were no encounters.

Entering Sheridan's picket lines about 10 p.m., Grant was recognized by a number of blue cavalrymen who hailed him from the orange glow of their campfires.

"Why, there's the old man!" some called. "Boys, this means business!" "Great Scott! The old man's out here himself. The Rebs are going to get busted to-morrow for certain!" "Uncle Sam's joined the cavalry sure enough. You can bet there'll be lively times here in the morning!"[20]

Grant reached Sheridan's camp and enjoyed a supper of coffee and cold chicken with his cavalry chief. By candlelight in a log cabin, Sheridan, who had been asleep when Grant arrived, showed his commander what was happening in the Jetersville sector. New York *Herald* reporter Sylvanus Cadwallader, whom Grant had befriended earlier in the war, described the scene:

> Sheridan...ended by declaring this to be the final battle ground. Meade's troops must be forced to certain positions during the night, and then not a man of Lee's army could escape. He was enthusiastic, positive, and not a little profane in expressing his opinions.[21]

After Sheridan briefed Grant on his situation, Grant sent a message to General Ord to watch the roads running south from Burke's Station and Farmville.

The events of the next few hours are obscured by various accounts. Some narratives state that Grant and Sheridan rode to Meade's headquarters, which had been set up in a house about a half-mile away that also was being used by the cavalry as a hospital. The generals' accounts of the midnight war conference are conflicting, the facts lost in time. Even the question of whether they actually met or whether Grant simply sent a note to Meade is still debated. Grant did dispatch a message to Meade stating:

> I would go over to see you this evening, but I have ridden a long distance today. Your orders directing an attack tomorrow will hold in the absence of others, but it is my impression that Lee will retreat during the night, and, if so, we will pursue with vigor.[22]

Sheridan had a much different view of what occurred:

> Grant stated that the orders Meade had already issued would permit Lee's escape, and therefore must be changed, for it was not the aim only to follow the enemy, but to get ahead of him, remarking... that he had no doubt Lee was moving right then.[23]

The apparently stormy decision process of the Union high command at Jetersville that night will likely never be known, but the outcome was this: The Federal forces would launch a large-scale strike against Lee at Amelia Court House on Thursday morning. Yet even as Grant, Meade, and Sheridan communicated in whatever capacity, Lee's army was on the march to escape them.

CHAPTER 6

"LEE WILL LEAVE AMELIA TONIGHT..."

"Night was day. Day was night," a Confederate recalled of the overnight march of April 5–6. "There was no stated time to sleep, eat, or rest, and the events of [Wednesday] morning became strangely intermingled with the events of the evening. Breakfast, dinner, and supper were merged into 'something to eat,' whenever and wherever it could be found."[1]

All around the Rebels were images of an army marching to hell's gate. Burning wagons and abandoned equipment of every sort, along with the contorted carcasses of soldiers, horses, and mules, were strewn along the road. The retreat was punctuated by exploding ammunition. "I did not see how the men could be held together much longer without food, or where the scantiest supply could be obtained or where they could get enough if scattered in such a country," wrote a major in Custis Lee's Division.[2]

The Confederate order of march was this: The combined First and Third Corps of Longstreet continued to lead the army, followed by Anderson and Ewell's Richmond Defense Corps. The main wagon train followed Ewell with Gordon's Second Corps serving as the rearguard. The division of Major General Bryan Grimes of Gordon's command was in stationary battle line for much of Wednesday, confronting the enemy until after dark when they scrambled to rejoin the main body. Grimes recalled that his men "were very much impeded on the march by the wagon train and its most miserable mismanagement, which, as I apprehended, would cause us some disaster."[3]

The new route through the hilly Virginia countryside snaked across Flat Creek, through the resort at Amelia Springs and the crossroads at Deatonville. It then reached bottomlands sliced by Little Sailor's Creek and, further west, by Big Sailor's Creek, both small tributaries of the Appomattox River. These streams intersected at Double Bridges, a pair of small farm lane spans to the north of Lee's intended course. Also to the north was the Appomattox, which the army could cross only at Farmville or three miles to the northeast, at High Bridge, the South Side Railroad's expansive trestle which had a wagon bridge over the river beneath it.

This rural region was connected by a primitive web of dirt roads and country lanes, often funneling through swampy backwaters and creeks. Both sides were hampered by inadequate maps of this portion of the state.

Lee's decision to make an end run around Sheridan resulted in immediate stumbling blocks for his army. "The change of route threw the troops over the roads pursued by the artillery and wagon trains west of the railroad, which impeded our advance and embarrassed our movements," he later wrote.[4] In other words, the night march was painfully slow due to the mass of wagons and weary soldiers piled against each other on the narrow roads. The Rebel sharpshooter Berry Benson related:

> Every hour brought news of the capture or burning of portions of our wagon trains, while wagons, broken down horses, pieces of artillery, stragglers, and all kinds of munitions of war were being abandoned to fall into the hands of our pursuers. A fusillade off at a distance would tell of a descent upon a wagon train by their cavalry. Then a column of smoke rising above the tree tops would tell of its capture and destruction.[5]

The carnage of Davies' strike on the wagon train added to the delays. For some six hours, much of the main army's baggage and artillery vehicles were motionless due to the wreckage cluttering the rural lanes. This lack of movement also disrupted the infantry's march. "Night came and found us toiling on at a snail's pace," wrote Captain McHenry

Howard of Custis Lee's staff. "Nothing is so fatiguing and demoralizing to soldiers as an irregular step and uncertain halts."[6]

"The movement of the division was regulated to suit the movements of the wagon trains, which should have been destroyed on the spot, and the column allowed to make its best time as, owing to the delay they occasioned, the Army lost the time it had gained on the enemy in the start and was overtaken...," recalled one of Gordon's veterans.[7] "We hurried on, with the enemy harassing us on all sides, weary and footsore, with nothing to eat but a little corn," related a Rebel in Ewell's ranks. "Still we marched on, fighting, starving, dying."[8]

Firing erupted in the black woods between 9 and 10 p.m. as Yankee patrols probed the gray columns. A bead of skirmishers marching parallel to the road could not stop the Federals' penetration and the Confederates suffered casualties. The white spit of carbines and muskets was too much for the green Richmond militia. "Most of the men became panic-stricken, broke and sought cover behind trees or fences, while not a few skulked disgracefully to the rear," Howard wrote. "They began to discharge their pieces at random, in many instances shooting their own comrades."[9]

Among the killed, whether by friendly fire or that of the enemy, was Major Frank Smith of Norfolk who was mortally injured only hours after joining Lee's Division. Other wounded were taken to a nearby farmhouse and left behind. "The whole division was disheartened by this unhappy occurrence and for some time marched on, discussing it in subdued but eager tones, presently relapsing into a gloomy silence," recalled Howard.[10] These clashes were a minor hindrance to the Rebels, but they further slowed the army's progress.

R. S. Rock, a teenager on Crutchfield's staff, had settled down in a field of broom sedge with 11 other exhausted comrades, including his black servant, Ben. "The night was chilly, and we lay on the broom straw with no covering, but slept as if on beds of down," Rock remembered.[11]

Sniping lasted through the night and tragedy again played her trump card. A horse tied to a fence broke loose and galloped along one of the columns, dragging a fence rail behind it. The sudden uproar again roused the jumpy Confederates, who immediately thought they were under attack. Muskets flared and other Rebels on the march returned fire. Several Southerners were killed or wounded before order was restored. Panic zigzagged through the ranks at least twice more during the night, ending in shooting and more bloodshed.[12]

Not expecting the sudden change in direction, Confederate engineers had not bolstered a small bridge across Flat Creek. During the night, the little span collapsed under the weight of the artillery and wagon teams. The butternut infantry had little problem fording the stream, but the baggage and guns were held up for several more hours until the engineers came up and repaired the bridge. The setbacks to the wagons and artillery continued to hold up the rest of the army.

Ever the stalwart commander, Lee still held the purest devotion among most of his troops, yet there was a noticeable change in the general's countenance. While Lee remained stoic and cool under fire, "His carriage was no longer erect, as his soldiers had been used to see it," a Rebel remembered. "The troubles of those last days had already plowed great furrows in his forehead. His eyes were red as if with weeping; his cheeks sunken and haggard; his face colorless."[13]

About 3 a.m., a courier from Gordon reached Lee, who was supervising the bridge repair work at Flat Creek. Gordon's rearguard had captured two men dressed in Confederate uniform and believed to be Yankee spies. Several documents were found on them and the Georgian thought that at least one order, discovered in the boot of one of the men, was important enough to interrupt Lee.

Among the papers taken from the prisoners, Gordon's men found a note from U. S. Grant to General Ord. The letter was dated "Jetersville, April 5, 1865—10–10 p.m." In the dispatch, Grant ordered Ord to move at 8 a.m. the next day and guard the roads between Burke's Station and Farmville.

In closing it read:

> I am strongly of the opinion that Lee will leave Amelia tonight to go south. He will be pursued at 6 a.m. from here if he leaves. Otherwise, an advance will be made upon him where he is.

The note bore the signature of "U. S. Grant, lieut-genl."[14]

Lee reasoned that the dispatch was not a Yankee trick. Grant was at Jetersville, probably meaning that most of the Union army was with him or nearby. If this were true, the message also meant that at least some of Ord's troops had arrived from their positions east of Richmond, having marched farther than any of the other Federal forces.

Lee wrote detailed instructions for the aide to return to Gordon. The orders included wagon and infantry routes and directed Gordon to burn all bridges behind him, adding that the head of the army would try to obtain rations at Rice's Station or Farmville.

Lee wrote to Gordon:

> I hope the rear will get out of harm's way and I rely greatly upon
> your exertions and good judgment for its safety. I know that men
> and animals are much exhausted, but it is necessary to tax their
> strength...You must of course, keep everything ahead of you...[15]

The gray fox had eluded the hunters at least one more time with his flank march while sparing his beleaguered troops another battle. Yet Lee knew, as well as the most ardent Rebel in the scarecrow divisions following him, that the hourglass sand was almost gone.

CHAPTER 7

"WE WERE PELTING AFTER OLD LEE..."

A spring drizzle dampened the silent men of Longstreet's and Anderson's Corps as they trudged past Amelia Springs in the predawn hours of Thursday, April 6.

Longstreet's vanguard, the division of Major General Charles W. Field, was leading the army's thrust toward Farmville about 19 miles away.

"My column marched before daylight on the 6th," Longstreet penned in his memoir. "The design from the night we left Petersburg was that its service should be to head off and prevent the enemy's infantry columns passing us and standing across our march."[1]

"No note was taken of day or night," a Confederate artillery officer wrote, "one long, confused, dreadful day. There seemed to be no front, no rear, for firing might be heard ahead and behind, and on both sides at once. There were no headquarters except where the ambulance happened to be."[2]

Sergeant David E. Johnston of the 7th Virginia Infantry remembered:

> If all our marchings, sufferings, hardships, privations and sacrifices for all the preceding years of the war were summed up, shaken together and pressed down, they would not equal those we were now undergoing on this tramp.[3]

A few miles to the southwest of the Rebels, Captain Frank Harwood of the Union army engineers was trying to locate roads for Wright's VI Corps to reach Lee at Amelia Court House and also to find routes to cut off any chance of the enemy's escape. Despite Grant's belief that Lee had evacuated the village, there had been no confirmation that the main Rebel army had left Amelia. Davies' discovery of the Confederate wagon train apparently was not enough evidence for Grant and Meade, despite the fact that the enemy column had been on the move beyond the Union left flank. Other than Ord, Grant was aiming almost everything at Amelia.

On the roads behind Harwood, the VI Corps already was on the march, and the blue regiments of the II and V Corps, along with Sheridan's cavalry, also were on the hunt by about 6 a.m. Based on Grant's instructions, Meade had ordered the army to action at daylight. The three infantry corps were to move along the South Side Railroad toward Amelia Court House and attack the Confederate army. There was no detailed battle plan other than to engage and overrun the Johnnies wherever they were found.

"The day opened dark, with a misty rain...," a Federal surgeon wrote. "The pursuit of General Lee's army was resumed with great activity."[4]

As his VI Corps infantry moved across country, General Horatio Wright could not know that he would be one of the Union's stars in the suspenseful drama unfolding this day. A native of Clinton, Massachusetts, Wright, 45, graduated second in the West Point class of 1841 and joined the Corps of Engineers. His duties before the war were with this department, including 10 years in Florida assisting with the construction of Forts Jefferson and Taylor in the Dry Tortugas. His first major war mission was a failed attempt to destroy the Norfolk Navy Yard facilities before Union forces abandoned them in April 1861. Wright was captured there by Virginia troops but soon released. After combat at First Bull Run, Wright was named a brigadier general of volunteers in September 1861, and participated in the expedition that took Port Royal, South Carolina. He led a division in the Federals' defeat at Secessionville, South Carolina, and, after a stint in Ohio, returned east in May 1863. Political wrangling resulted in Wright's promotion to major general being held up and, at one time, revoked before he was reappointed and confirmed in May 1864. During this time, he led a VI Corps division at Gettysburg, at Rappahannock Bridge, and in the Mine Run campaign. When Major General John Sedgwick was killed at Spotsylvania, Wright assumed command of the VI Corps.[5]

His troops were the mainstay of Washington's defenses when Lieutenant General Jubal Early's Rebel army assailed the capital in July 1864. That fall the VI Corps had joined Sheridan in the Shenandoah campaign. In the absence of Sheridan, who was away for a conference in Washington, Wright commanded the U.S. Army of the Shenandoah on October 19, 1864, when Early's Confederates made the daring surprise attack at Cedar Creek.

**Union Major General
Horatio Gates Wright**

U.S. Army Military History Institute

The Federals had a sizable manpower advantage, but Wright was unable to regroup his force from the assault's initial shock. With victory within Early's grasp, Sheridan made his famous and rallying ride to the battlefield to turn the tide for a Union triumph. And Wright missed a stellar opportunity for a national hero's grandeur. Sheridan wore the victor's mantle instead.

George Meade himself was on the warpath by 6 a.m. following his seemingly endless corps columns toward Amelia. "We were pelting after Old Lee as hard as the poor doughboys' legs can go," one of Meade's staff officers recalled.[6] Union couriers from Humphreys' Corps, however, brought in information about 9 a.m. that altered the direction of the pursuers.

Lee had disappeared from Amelia! Infantry in the divisions of Brigadier Generals Nelson A. Miles and Gershom Mott had spotted the Confederate rear echelon, heading westward along the opposite ridge of Flat Creek. Even then, Humphreys was preparing to engage the enemy.

The VI Corps had marched about three miles toward Amelia when Wright received word that Lee's army had left the town during the night and was attempting to pass around the Union left toward Farmville. The blue ranks immediately were halted while the high command changed its plan of attack.

Meade now set the course of the II and V Corps from a north-easterly to a more northwesterly direction with the II Corps moving toward Deatonville. This three-pronged sweep resulted in the VI Corps now being on the left, taking the road Sheridan's cavalry had ridden out that morning, the II Corps in the middle, and the V Corps serving as the right spear point. With some luck, hardtack, sweat, and shoe leather, these bluecoats figured to trap Bobby Lee's army before the sun went down!

The Union cavalry had orders to move on the extreme left of the Federal infantry, and Sheridan used the opportunity to take a tactical swipe at Meade. After the war, Sheridan wrote that he was convinced that Lee would evacuate Amelia Court House on the night of April 5, long before Meade's infantry reached the hamlet. Because of this Sheridan wrote that he "did not permit the cavalry to participate in Meade's useless advance, but shifted it out toward the left to the road running from Deatonsville [*sic*] to Rice's station."[7] Sheridan actually would be moving along a series of farm lanes and across country, riding parallel and to the south of Lee in an effort to catch the enemy.

As his troopers rode out that morning, Colonel Charles H. Smith related: "To-day will see something big in the crushing of the rebellion."[8]

A Maine cavalryman remembered:

> The men awoke in fine spirits. Never before during their three years or more of service had there been any prospect of the end. All the hard marching and fighting of three summer campaigns, and the long hours on picket and in dull winter quarters, had been with no such encouragement as they now had...Richmond was captured...the goal for which they had marched and fought, and for which so many brave boys had died, was reached—the backbone of the

rebellion...had now been broken... and was beyond healing...It was exciting to even think of the situation that spring morning.[9]

General George Crook's Division led the mounted blue squadrons out on the road leading to Deatonville and beyond to Rice's Station and Farmville. George Custer's Third Division rode behind Crook, followed by General Devin's First Division.

Among Crook's riders were troopers of the 1st New Jersey Cavalry in Davies' Brigade who were anxious for revenge. Their commander, Colonel Hugh H. Janeway, had been killed, shot through the head while leading a charge in the cavalry combat near Jetersville the day before. "This cast a gloom over the whole regiment," wrote Janeway's successor, Major Walter R. Robbins. "His superior we never knew; a brave skillful officer, a courteous gentleman, a true, earnest patriot, qualities which have endeared him to every officer and man of the regiment."[10]

CHAPTER 8

"ALL THE PLAGUES OF EGYPT'S KING"

The gaunt Army of Northern Virginia had stumbled through the night and early morning, bloodied, tired and ravenous, but not yet beaten. The delays suffered, however, had cost it the golden hours gained by Lee's night march around Jetersville.

The bulk of Fitz Lee's cavalry had gone into camp at Amelia Springs after their running fight with Sheridan's troopers on Wednesday afternoon. The exhausted horsemen were serenaded during the night by Union bands playing songs from the Federal lines not far in the distance.

Longstreet's Corps passed the cavalry bivouac early Thursday and Robert Lee arrived at Fitz Lee's camp near the village's hotel before sunrise. Lee ordered Fitz to put his cavalry on the road behind Longstreet at first light. The gray troopers of Rooney Lee's Division were with Gordon's Corps to assist the rearguard. Rooney, 27, was born at Arlington, Virginia, in May 1837. Harvard-educated, he was a noted college oarsman who was commissioned into the U.S. Army in 1857. After two years in the service, he resigned to become a gentleman planter, but followed his father into the Confederate military. Rooney fought with Stuart's cavalry for most of the war, becoming a brigadier general in September 1862. Seriously wounded and captured at Brandy Station in June 1863, he was not exchanged until March 1864 and was soon promoted to major general, the youngest of that rank in the Confederate armies.[1]

Behind Longstreet were his corps wagons. Then came Anderson and Ewell who continued ahead of the rest of the main baggage train

followed by Gordon. The army was
moving on the Jamestown Road toward the crossroads of Deatonville
en route to Farmville. At daybreak,
Fitz Lee started the major portion
of his squadrons, under Major General Thomas L. Rosser, who found
a place in the column behind
Anderson's infantry.

One of Rosser's men remembered how civilians the horsemen
passed looked on in woe, knowing
that the Yankees were not far behind: "For they dreaded what was
to come...more than if all the
plagues of Egypt's King had been
turned loose in their land and were
approaching the plantations..."[2]
Based on orders from Robert Lee,

**Confederate Major General
Fitzhugh Lee**

Author's Collection

Fitz remained behind "to explain in person to the first infantry officer
who came on the situation of things and to urge the importance of his
keeping sharp watch upon his left flank, as it was feared by the commanding general [that] the enemy might tap the marching column coming down from the Amelia Springs and Jetersville road."[3] The night
strikes against the Southerners' left reinforced the Lees' fears that a
concentrated assault might come from that vicinity. They also kept the
Confederates falling into battle line to repel any sustained attacks.

"Do you remember the night march before Sailor's Creek?" Rebel
Major Campbell Brown, Ewell's stepson, wrote to Colonel Charles
Venable after the war. "I saw men apparently fast asleep in ranks, standing up, & walking enough to move on a few yards at a time as the
wagons & troops in front gave us a little space. During the whole night
our command could not have made three or four miles."[4]

Ewell's men reached Amelia Springs by 8 a.m. Thursday, having
covered only seven miles from Amelia Court House. And the army's

largest wagon train, along with Gordon's Corps, still was behind them. "The march, though not a long one, was exceedingly tiresome," recalled one of Gordon's men, "as the main roads being crowded, the column moved by plantation roads, which were in wretched condition and crowded with troops and trains."[5]

Colonel Edmund Pendleton of the 15th Louisiana "Tigers" in Gordon's rearguard paused to scribble a note to his wife on the back of an envelope this morning:

> The whole army of Gen'l Lee is now within ten miles of Farmville. After a severe battle at Petersburg...in which our lines were broken & our communications cut, we have been compelled to fall back to a more defensible line. I am sorry to think that this implies the abandonment of the greater part of Va. & it is not unlikely you & my dear children will be left in the Enemy's hands, tho' I hope not. I shall use my utmost exertions to come to see you. Our Army is not whipped...indeed it is strong & ready to fight to-day...I write this hasty note on the march & will endeavor to write you more fully in two or three days. Love to all.[6]

The tortoise pace of the overnight march would prove to be the undoing of many of these Confederates a few hours later. Hundreds of Rebels staggered or limped forward as if in a trance, savoring any morsel of food they might find along the road. Captain Howard of Custis Lee's Division parched a handful of corn in a borrowed frying pan during a stop just before dawn. He had settled in for a quick nap "when the drum beat assembly and we took the road once more. By this time the command was fearfully reduced in numbers, and men were falling out continually. They were allowed to shoot from their places in the ranks pigs, chickens, or whatever of the sort came in their way, commanding officers looking on without rebuke."[7]

The Rebel orderly R. S. Rock and his companions were asleep and left behind by their brigade as the army marched through the night. "We awoke early, and could hear the combined booming of guns in the distance," he recalled. Rock set out alone to rejoin his company and soon fell in with a number of other stragglers. "All the money I had, $50, I gave to a man for a piece of honey, which was full of dust and dirt," he remembered. Continuing on, Rock encountered a sickly soldier "who soon grew delirious with fever." Rock helped him to a nearby farmhouse where a woman took them in and gave Rock a piece of bread, the only food he had had for four days other than some corn. Leaving the ill man in her care, Rock returned to the fighting:

> After leaving the house I heard cannonading a few miles away, and hurrying on I caught up with my command at Sailor's Creek, where Gen. Lee had concentrated the ragged, starving soldiers to fight the last battle of [the] war.[8]

The night hours also brought more desertions and increased straggling as companies and regiments simply dissolved, soldiers melting into the woods to fight no more. Robert Lee was at Amelia Springs when Commissary General Isaac St. John arrived to see him. St. John had left Richmond shortly before Federal troops entered the capital. He explained that he had vainly been trying to bring rations to Lee's men by wagon train, since the Danville Railroad had been cut. He also told Lee that some eighty thousand rations were waiting for the army at Farmville. Sheridan's deception of sending the telegrams to capture this food had not persuaded the Rebels to keep from sending it from Lynchburg and, ultimately, to Farmville based on Union movements. St. John headed to Farmville to ready the rations for distribution to Lee's troops.

Adding to his problems, Lee received word that Ord's Corps was pushing toward the railroad at Rice's Station. Longstreet was quickly ordered to intercept it. Leaving Amelia Springs, Lee rode forward to the vicinity of Rice's Station to await the arrival of Longstreet's Corps and deal with the threat ahead of him. Lee biographer Douglas Southall Freeman wrote that as the general trotted along, beside, and among his ragamuffin soldiers, "There was something akin to despair in the eyes that were turned on him and there was delirium in the loyal cheers that greeted him."[9]

"Gen. Robert E. Lee rode by," recalled artillery Captain Blake in Custis Lee's Division. "In a moment every man was on his feet cheering. None of us knew where we were going; we only knew we were following 'Marse Robert.' Faith in him never wavered."[10] With Lee headed a few miles to the front, Ewell was left as the ranking officer over the column behind Longstreet. In his study of Lee's field generals, Freeman described this potential dilemma:

> Ewell had no instructions to exercise command beyond that of the troops he had brought from Richmond. Whatever he did in any sudden emergency would have to be based on his seniority, which he was always hesitant to assert. His was as dolorous a part as any officer had in that tragic retreat.[11]

The 48-year-old Ewell was among the most droll and enigmatic officers in the Rebel hierarchy. A profane, hot-tempered professional soldier, Ewell had been amid Lee's top generals only to plummet from that pinnacle due to severe battle wounds, other physical and mental ills, and lackluster combat performance. John Gordon, who had served with Ewell since First Bull Run, described him thusly:

> He was a compound of anomalies, the oddest, most eccentric ge-nius in the Confederate army...No man had a better heart or a worse manner of showing it. He was in truth as tender and sympathetic as a woman, but, even under slight provocation, he became exter-nally as rough as a polar bear, and the needles with which he pricked sensibilities were more numerous and keener than porcupines' quills.[12]

Rebel officer John Cheves Haskell wrote that Ewell was "a queer character, very eccentric, but upright, brave and devoted. He had no very high talent but did all that a brave man of moderate capacity could."[13] To the front-line Johnnies, Ewell was Old Dick, Fightin' Dick, or Old Bald Head, the latter based on Ewell's hairless dome. His blue popeyes, large-beaked nose, and fidgety movements made him almost birdlike to some observers. Born in Georgetown outside Washington in February 1817, Ewell was an 1840 West Point graduate who spent some 20 years on army duty in the Southwest. He was commended for gallantry in the Mexican War, and resigned his commission to side with the Confed-eracy in May 1861. Commissioned a brigadier general in the Confeder-ate Provisional Army a month later, Ewell fought well at First Bull

Run, and was promoted to major general in January 1862. He distinguished himself in the Shenandoah Valley campaign that year and the
Seven Days' battles before falling with a musket wound to his left leg at
Groveton on August 28, 1862. The leg was amputated above the knee
the next day. Ewell spent some nine months in complicated recupera-
tion and was contemplating his return to the army in May 1863 when
Lee and Stonewall Jackson earned their stunning victory at
Chancellorsville. Jackson, however, was accidentally shot and mortally
wounded by his own troops, dying on May 10. This huge blow prompted
Lee to reorganize his army. Longstreet retained command of the First
Corps while Lee recommended that Ewell take over Jackson's Second
Corps and A. P. Hill would lead the newly formed Third Corps.

Writing to Jefferson Davis about his command choices, Lee described Ewell as "an honest, brave soldier, who has always done his duty
well." He added, "I do not know where to get better men than those I have
named."[14] The command structure was approved, and Ewell and Hill were
promoted to lieutenant general on May 23, 1863. Three days later, Ewell
married his first cousin and longtime love, Lizinska Campbell Brown.
Within the week he had rejoined Lee's army with a wooden leg and
crutches, strapped into the saddle when riding on his own.

But Ewell's terrible wound apparently bled away some of the bold-
ness he exhibited earlier in the war. To some, the general appeared pale
and feeble. The "Widow Brown," as Ewell's new wife was often called
in the ranks, was domineering and blamed by some Rebels for the apparent softening of the general. "From the military point of view the
addition of the wife did not compensate for the loss of the leg," wrote
one Confederate. "We were of the opinion that Ewell was not the same
soldier he had been when he was a whole man—and a single one."[15]

Nevertheless, Lee plunged into his invasion of Pennsylvania in
mid-June 1863 with Ewell's Corps as the spearhead. But Ewell's hesi-
tancy in attacking Cemetery Hill at Gettysburg on July 1 and his subse-
quent failures to achieve any major gains in this battle doomed him.
Feverish illness and problems with his leg forced Ewell to take sick
leave in early November 1863, but he was back in command by Grant's
1864 spring offensive. Ewell fought his corps at the Wilderness and

Spotsylvania, suffering a fall in the latter battle when his horse was killed under him. Shaken by his tumble, Ewell bungled the retreat of his corps, losing almost five hundred troops who were left behind.

As the armies tramped toward Cold Harbor, Ewell again fell ill, and relinquished his corps command to Jubal Early on May 26. But fearing that Lee would use his sickness to replace him, Ewell almost immediately began requesting a return to service. Lee refused, however, stating in so many words that Ewell needed time to regain his health and that it also might be dangerous to the army to change

Confederate Lieutenant General Richard S. Ewell

Author's Collection

commanders when the fighting was almost continuous. Personal pleas to Davis and Lee were fruitless, even to the point of Ewell being allowed to return to division command.[16]

His decision cloaked in the issue of Ewell's health, Lee clearly had lost confidence in Ewell, dating to his lack of aggressiveness at Gettysburg. Ewell fought competently at the Wilderness, but Gordon complained to Lee that Ewell had missed a great opportunity to make a crushing flank attack on May 6. Ewell's poor performance at Spotsylvania was the final straw that apparently convinced Lee that he was no longer fit for corps command. Not wanting to embarrass Ewell any more than necessary, Lee recommended that he be placed in charge of the Richmond defenses, a post that Ewell assumed on June 15, 1864.[17]

To Ewell's thinking, his desk-bound duties would effectively take him out of harm's way. The only adversaries he likely was to encounter would be those paper-shuffling pompous Richmond bureaucrats. Little did Fightin' Dick know that he was fated for a starring role in the war's final act.

CHAPTER 9

"IT IS NOW A RACE FOR LIFE AND DEATH."

Union infantry of General Humphreys' II Corps had been the first to sight the tail of Lee's army on Thursday morning. Marching in three columns, these Yankees had only been on the roads about two hours when their point units encountered gray cavalry. The butternut troopers in their front were part of the cavalry screen for the rear of Gordon's Corps. Humphreys sent an 8 a.m. dispatch to Meade stating that he had made contact with the enemy about two miles from Jetersville.

With a showdown suddenly looming, the morning already had been tumultuous for Humphreys and his Second Division commander, Brigadier General William Hays. Humphreys had ridden to Hays' headquarters about 6:30 a.m. to see how the division's advance was progressing. Instead he found Hays and his staff asleep.[1] Infuriated, Humphreys located Brigadier General Thomas A. Smyth, whose Third Brigade was supposed to lead the division's march, and determined that none of the troops were moving. On the spot, Humphreys relieved Hays and gave Smyth the division command temporarily before assigning it to Brigadier General Francis C. Barlow. The disgraced Hays was immediately posted to the Army of the Potomac's Artillery Reserve.[2]

Humphreys, 54, was a Philadelphian whose grandfather had drawn up the plans for *Old Ironsides* and her five sister frigates. His father also was a naval contractor, but Humphreys had decided on an army career. An 1831 graduate of West Point, he spent almost 30 years as a military and civil engineer. Humphreys became an aide to General George B. McClellan in 1861 and made brigadier general of volunteers in April 1862. After a stint as chief topographical engineer for the Army of the Potomac, he was assigned to lead a new V Corps division, which he commanded in the Maryland campaign, at Fredericksburg and Chancellorsville. Transferred to a II Corps division, Humphreys' actions at Gettysburg earned him promotion to major general of volunteers and a brevet brigadier's post in the regular army. Humphreys granted Meade's request to serve as his chief of staff, a position he held until November 1864. At that time, Major General Winfield S. Hancock had to leave the service due to a serious wound

Union Major General Andrew A. Humphreys

U.S. Army Military History Institute

suffered at Gettysburg and Humphreys succeeded him in command of the II Corps.[3] Having taken care of his minor crisis with Hays, Humphreys hastened toward the front with his First Division under General Miles.

Some 45 minutes after spotting the Reb cavalry, his soldiers beheld their main prey near Amelia Springs. Humphreys dashed off another message to Meade saying that he had sighted enemy wagons and a large body of infantry some three miles to the west of his left column. The Confederates were moving to the west, southwest. Humphreys added that he would order Brigadier General Gershom Mott to send a brigade from Mott's Third Division to probe the Rebels.

In an 8:45 a.m. order to Mott, Humphreys wrote:

> From the head of the First Division we see a long column of infantry about two miles and a half distant in a northwest direction, moving apparently west or a little south of it. It may be that they intend an attack on your flank or rear. I have halted the column. Send out a force to feel from your center.[4]

Mott hustled forward his First Brigade, commanded by Brigadier General Philippe Regis de Trobriand, which soon hit the Confederate rearguard. Hearing the firing along the skirmish line, Mott rode ahead to determine the situation. He and de Trobriand were assessing developments about 9 a.m. when Mott was wounded in the leg. He had to be taken from the field and turned over command of the Third Division to de Trobriand. In turn, Colonel Russell B. Shepherd of the 1st Maine Heavy Artillery was to lead de Trobriand's Brigade.

At 9:40 a.m., Humphreys sent a dispatch to Meade, stating that he had ordered Mott's Division (actually de Trobriand's by now) out the Amelia Springs Road in the direction of Deatonville, about three miles away. Miles' Division, about half a mile north of de Trobriand, was ordered in the same direction, as was Barlow, even further to the north, both marching across country toward the Confederate column.

De Trobriand, however, was in the immediate presence of the enemy and almost immediately decided not to wait for Miles, much less Barlow, to come to his aid. "Knowing that part of the enemy's train was within our reach if we advanced promptly, I did not deem it necessary to wait for the First Division," he would later report.[5]

Born near Tours, France, the son of a French army general and baron, de Trobriand, 48, was likely the most international infantry officer in Meade's army. A globehopper who was a poet, lawyer and bon vivant, as well as a soldier, de Trobriand married a New York heiress, became an American citizen, and recruited the Lafayette Guard militia for the war effort. The unit would become the 55th New York Infantry with de Trobriand as colonel. The rakish Frenchman was in combat in the Peninsula campaign and at Fredericksburg, Chancellorsville, and at Gettysburg where he led a III Corps brigade in the Peach Orchard fighting.[6]

On this morning de Trobriand formed his division in battle line and pressed forward without Miles or Barlow as support. "The elan of the men was remarkable from the start and augured well for the success of the day," he related.[7] Gordon's Southerners recoiled before this Union sweep. They hastily threw up breastworks near the Truly Vaughan farm, but were quickly overpowered after a weak resistance. Humphreys would later use the farmhouse as a hospital.

The speed of the relentless bluecoats allowed the Confederates little time to offer any semblance of a stand. Through orders, Humphreys and Mott each impressed upon de Trobriand the importance of pressing the enemy without loss of time, and the Frenchman was focused on doing just that.

Humphreys wrote that there was "constant combat...through a country where forests with dense undergrowth and swamps alternated with cultivated fields..."[8] He added, "The lines of battle followed closely on the skirmish line with a rapidity and nearness of connection that I believe to be unexampled, and which I confess astonished me. Nothing could have been finer than the spirit of the officers and men."[9]

After the war, Grant paid tribute to the Rebels who fought in these sharp flare-ups: "There was as much gallantry displayed by some of the Confederates in these engagements as was displayed at any time during the War."[10]

Federal troops who had switched direction to chase Lee's army found themselves on the same roads taken by the fleeing Confederates. The scenes they encountered inspired jubilation but, at the same time, were sobering. Exhausted Johnnies, including veterans of many a fight, had dropped in their tracks or curled into fence corners, farm buildings, or by the roadsides. Dead Rebels and the wrecks of caissons, wagons of every sort and artillery, along with bone-bare mules and horses that had fallen in their traces or died from starvation and exertion, offered a trail of Confederate tears. Muskets with bayonets fixed were plunged barrel down in woods and fields. Canteens, haversacks, clothing, and accoutrements of all description had been tossed aside on the route.

"Weuns have found the last ditch," a despondent Reb had scrawled in chalk on the side of one of the wagons left behind.[11] Amid the discarded vehicles were carriages and farm carts, loaded with furniture and other possessions, packed by area residents who vainly had tried to escape the Union advance. Indeed, in some cases, the Yanks actually were slowed by civilian traffic clogging the roads.

Rummaging through some of the enemy wagons, the Federals found many still contained much if not all of their loads. "Cooking utensils, frying pans, stewpans, kettles were plentiful," wrote de Trobriand. "When a ship threatens to founder, they throw the freight into the sea. Lee's army refused to lighten itself in this way and was engulfed with its cargo."[12]

Confederate Berry Benson remembered the Southern retreat:

Not much of what was captured, however, was of service to the enemy for we were too poor to own food, clothing, blankets or anything but powder and lead—and not enough of that. The horses were mere skeletons, and fell all along the road, dying out of sheer exhaustion and starvation, and the men were in not much better condition. Straggling became the rule rather than the exception. From sheer weakness and lack of sustenance, many a brave man lagged behind his command who had never lagged before.[13]

"Marched all day and nearly all night," New Orleans artillerist William Owen etched in his diary. "When the batteries halt to rest, the men throw themselves upon the ground and immediately go to sleep. When the order is given to move forward, the horses often move on without their drivers, so hard is it to arouse the men. Tired and hungry we push on. It is now a race for life and death. We seldom receive orders now. The enemy has the shortest line to Danville and Burkeville and is heading us off."[14]

Georgia infantryman W. L. Timberlake recalled:

The road from Amelia Springs, by which the weary, sleep-longing, hungry, yet dauntless Confederate army moved toward Rice's Station and Farmville, is a narrow, winding, and lonely one that never before that fatal day had seen a battle flag, heard the clattering march of cavalry, or felt the heavy tread and jar of thundering guns, nor had it ever dreamed of the sound it was to hear before the sun went down; the shriek of disemboweled horses, the piercing cries of the wounded, and the faint, intermittent—speech of the dying.[15]

"The horrors of the march from Five Forks to Amelia Court House and thence to Sailor's Creek beggars all description," George Pickett wrote to his wife, Sally, a few days later. "For forty-eight hours the man or officer who had a handful of parched corn in his pocket was most fortunate."[16]

A Rebel in Gordon's corps had a similar recollection:

That the night was spent in the most trying manner may best be learned from the fact that when the morning dawned the column was only six or seven miles from the starting point of the evening before.[17]

In their haste to catch Lee's army, the Yankees all but ignored the gray dead they found on the march. They did, however, concentrate on rounding up Reb stragglers who had wandered from their lines in quest of food or those who simply did not have the stamina, willpower, or desire to fight any longer. The II Corps Federals ripping at Gordon backpedaled at one point when the Southerners planted several artillery pieces, supported by cavalry, and commenced a very accurate fire on the blue infantry. De Trobriand's onslaught through some woods, as well as that of Miles' Division skirmishers who were now on the scene, was broken up due to this shelling. De Trobriand dealt with this by bringing up a section of the 11th New York Artillery and putting it in a prime position to batter the enemy. A few well-placed rounds from the New Yorkers sent the gray horsemen and gunners fleeing for cover. Weaving out of the trees de Trobriand's skirmishers scuttled forward and occupied some piecemeal defenses with the Rebels retreating to a stronger position on a hilltop outside Deatonville.

A Maine infantryman wrote in his journal:

For a mile or two we moved rapidly, the enemy making but slight resistance until they came to their line of works at Deatonville, undoubtedly thrown up to detain us till their trains can be pushed out of our reach.[18]

Near the crossroad some of Gordon's beleaguered soldiers stopped to hastily eat a pitiful meal. "But before the simplest articles of food could be prepared, the order to march was given," a Virginian recounted.[19] Humphreys had reached de Trobriand by now, stressing the importance of taking enemy guns whenever possible. "This was accomplished afterward, but not before we had felt again the accuracy of their fire," de Trobriand remembered.[20]

The Union battle line, composed of six regiments, moved forward to the defenses seized by their skirmishers and de Trobriand ordered an uphill charge against the stronger position:

> At the command forward the whole line sprang over the works and rushed through the open ground under a heavy fire of musketry and artillery, each regiment anxious to be the first to reach the enemy's entrenchments and to plant there its flying colors.[21]

Maine, New York, and Pennsylvania troops "emulated each other in their ardor of this attack," de Trobriand wrote, and crashed over the Confederate outpost, taking some four hundred prisoners and several battle flags.[22] The Federal surge did not abate until all of the Rebels had been flushed out of Deatonville, [which was little more than a house and a few outbuildings], and into the countryside beyond. Miles' Division joined de Trobriand about this time and the drive was resumed. These generals were confident that their flanks were safe due to the presence of the VI Corps on the left and Barlow, as well as the V Corps, to the right. This advantage allowed them to be more aggressive in their frontal attacks. The Rebel rearguard, meanwhile, had taken up yet another defensive position on a hill west of the crossroad and Gordon ascended the crest. From the hilltop he could see formations of blue cavalry on the flank of the Confederate procession, which was winding its way behind him to the west.

The dashing 33-year-old Gordon was among Lee's closest companions as well as one of his most reliable and daring lieutenants in the last year of the war. "He's so purty, it'd put fight in a whupped chicken just to look at him," a Rebel remarked of Gordon's soldierly bearing.[23] A fellow officer described the Georgian as "a picture of the sculptor."[24] Gordon had been one of Jubal Early's spear points in the Rebels' surprise attack at Cedar Creek the previous October, and Lee had entrusted him to lead the almost suicidal attack on Fort Steadman at Petersburg on March 25. Born in Upson County, Georgia, in February 1832, Gordon attended the University of Georgia. He did not graduate but studied

**Confederate Major General
John B. Gordon**

Author's Collection

to become a lawyer. Gordon was developing coal mines in northwestern Georgia when the war flamed. Despite no military experience, he was elected captain of the "Racoon Roughs," a militia unit of mountaineers. He was appointed major in the 6th Alabama Infantry and sent to join Confederate forces in Virginia. Gordon fought superbly at First Bull Run and in the ensuing battles waged by the Army of Northern Virginia except when he was recuperating from wounds. His severest injury occurred at Antietam where he led the 6th Alabama as its colonel. Shot in the head, he collapsed unconscious and likely would have drowned in his own blood but for a hole in his hat. He was promoted to brigadier general in November 1862.[25]

Gordon compiled a stellar record as a brigade leader from Chancellorsville to Gettysburg, and was given a division command in May 1864, just before Spotsylvania, where he was a stalwart in stemming the Federal onslaught against the Confederates' Mule Shoe salient. He was appointed major general to rank from May 14, 1864. Ordered to the Shenandoah Valley with Jubal Early on June 12, 1864, Gordon again displayed sound abilities and initiative although Early's Confederate Army of the Valley was overmatched and outmanned by the enemy. Defeats at Fisher's Hill and Cedar Creek, among lesser battles, painfully convinced Lee that the Shenandoah was lost. He began pulling back units from Early to strengthen his main army. By mid-December 1864, Gordon was ordered to rejoin Lee's army as commander of the Second Corps, which had been decimated in the Shenandoah fighting.

When Gordon rode out of Petersburg on the road to Appomattox a few months later, he left behind his wife, Fanny Haralson Gordon, who had just given birth to their third son.

———————

Even as Gordon was digging in above Deatonville, other elements of Lee's legions were crossing Little Sailor's Creek, whether by fording or on wooden fence rails. The Confederate impetus now was on the Rice's Station Road after passing an intersection where the Jamestown Road forked to the north just over a mile from the creek. This junction was known as Hott's or Holt's Corner by local residents, its name derived from a farmer named John Holt who had settled in the area.[26] From Holt's Corner the Jamestown Road led across Big and Little Sailor's Creeks near their confluence with the Appomattox River, eventually heading into Rice's Station about five miles to the west. Both branches of the creek snaked through a valley some six hundred to eight hundred yards wide. A series of gulches, called The Devil's Tavern, interlaced the valley, which was overgrown with willow, pine, and dogwood.

The Rice's Station Road edged along the southern end of the valley past the James Moses Hillsman family farm, which Pickett was using as a temporary hospital for his division. The farm was some four hundred yards east of the point where Little Sailor's Creek bisected the narrow road. Moses Overton built the four-room main house in the 1700s. Among his descendants was the family of James Hillsman, at home when the war came to their doorstep. Hillsman, a captain of sharpshooters in the 44th Virginia Infantry, had been captured at Spotsylvania the previous May and remained in a Federal prison camp. But his wife, Lucy Blanton Hillsman, and mother, Martha Overton Hillsman, along with two children and eight servants, found refuge in the basement when the guns opened.

Everywhere the Yankees continued to find stark images of the Southerners' death march, including carriages and wagons abandoned by panicky Richmond or Petersburg civilians that brimmed with furniture, paintings, elaborate clothing, and household goods and wares. "We have now driven them till they are crowded onto their main trains, loaded with furniture, plate, libraries, costly wardrobes—almost everything that

Hillsman House

Photo by Author

can be moved," wrote Private John Haley of the 17th Maine. "The wealthy of Richmond and Petersburg are fleeing, they know not whither."[27]

At some points the blue infantry were able to scoop up Rebel wagons that had fallen behind or strayed from the column. A few of these Yanks were killed or wounded by Confederate drivers or their escorts, defiant in not giving up their vehicles. Haley wrote:

> The guards would jump from their wagons and hide behind some defensive point and pepper us. To think these fools risked their lives and fought like fiends for goods in which they had not one cent of interest; everything in those wagons belonged to the aristocracy. Our men made a lively search for small articles, and in many cases were well repaid.[28]

De Trobriand reported that he was preparing to assault Gordon's hilltop line when a VI Corps brigade, that he did not or could not identify, along with a force of Union cavalry, temporarily blocked his advance. When the way was clear, the bluecoats stormed up the slope and

overran the Confederates. The 40th New York, which had seen a great
deal of action throughout the morning, captured a cannon in the attack.
By now, the fighting had torn through the Virginia woods, hills and
fields for several miles with Union skirmishers repeatedly having to be
relieved to replenish their ammunition.

"The skirmishers were almost constantly engaged with the
rearguard of the enemy," wrote General Miles, "but the great length of
the line enabled us to expel them from all their positions by overlapping
their flank...Whenever it appeared probable that the enemy might check
us, the skirmish line was reinforced by a regiment."[29]

Federal artillery also was playing on the Confederates at every
opportunity. When the Rebel wagon train presented targets, the II Corps
gunners, riding forward with the advance line, unlimbered and opened
fire. Batteries of the 1st New Hampshire, the 10th Massachusetts, and
the 4th U.S. Artillery were among these flying squadrons. By late
morning Humphreys was at Amelia Springs. A civilian informed him
that Lee himself had left there about daybreak and that a Confederate
officer had told the man that the Rebel army would be some six to
seven hours in passing. According to the civilian, the officer also said
that another gray column was moving on the Painesville Road. "He
[the civilian] thinks there is considerable of their force in rear of the
column I have broken into," Humphreys wrote in an 11:10 a.m. message to Meade.[30]

Sheridan sent this dispatch to Grant shortly after noon:

> My information is that the enemy are moving to our left with their
> trains and whole army. The train and army were moving all last
> night and are very short of provisions and very tired indeed. I think
> that now is the time to attack them with all your infantry. They are
> reported to have begged provisions from the people of the country
> all along the road as they passed. I am working around farther to
> our left.[31]

De Trobriand's First Brigade under Colonel Shepherd had been in
the II Corps lead all day, and was replaced on the point by the Second
Brigade of Brigadier General Byron R. Pierce. If Shepherd's battle account is accurate, de Trobriand had every reason to be very proud of his

brigade. Shepherd reported a haul of 1,390 enlisted men and 17 commissioned officers captured along with five artillery pieces, 28 wagons, and three battle flags.[32] With his right connected with Miles, Pierce resumed the advance, "Charging every position the enemy took with success."[33]

None among the Confederates knew the grimness of the fighting and the battle delirium any more than Gordon's men. In a postwar account, Gordon described the nightmare.

> Fighting all day, marching all night, with exhaustion and hunger claiming their victims at every mile of the march with charges of infantry in the rear and of cavalry on the flanks, it seems the war god had turned loose all his furies to revel in havoc. On and on, hour after hour, from hilltop to hilltop, the lines were alternately forming, fighting and retreating, making one almost continuous shifting battle. Here, in one direction, a battery of artillery became involved; there, in another, a blocked ammunition train required rescue. And thus came short but sharp little battles which made up sideshows of the main performance...On that doleful retreat...it was impossible for us to bury our dead or carry with us the disabled wounded. There was no longer any room in the crowded ambulances which had escaped capture...We could do nothing for the unfortunate sufferers who were too severely wounded to march except leave them on the roadside with canteens of water.[34]

"I am about three miles beyond Deatonville and pushing the enemy," Humphreys wrote to Grant early in the afternoon. "The road is literally lined with their tents, baggage, and cooking utensils. We have taken one gun. I am pushing on."[35]

"We soon had the Rebs in close quarters again with their large train in sight," the Maine private Haley related. "Now there was wild screaming and clawing to get out of the way of the confounded Yankees. Our column dashed forward to secure the spoils, but every rock and tree, every fence and hillock seemed alive and offered resistance. Wagon after wagon was overturned, its contents confiscated and scattered to the winds."[36]

Anderson's Corps reached Holt's Corner about 10:45 a.m. at approximately the same time George Crook's Federal cavalry was closing on Little Sailor's Creek on a collision course with these Confederates. Behind Crook, but not yet within striking distance, were the cavalry divisions of Custer and Devin. Like the rest of the army, the blue squadrons had altered their direction earlier and were galloping over fields and gullies and through woods to intercept Lee, whose troops were becoming more and more strung out on the road. "The country was broken, intersected with ravines and ditches," Devin later reported.[37]

Nearing the creek, Crook's point troopers reined in to behold an awesome sight. There, spread before them, was Lee's main wagon train, snaking slowly along a country road as far as they could see. The Rebel procession was moving parallel to Crook and was accompanied by heavy masses of infantry and cavalry. Seeing Crook's horsemen in the distance and expecting an attack, Anderson posted skirmishers and ordered the divisions of Pickett and Major General Bushrod R. Johnson to dig in facing south to protect the Rice's Station Road in the vicinity of Holt's Corner. The baggage and artillery trains in this part of the line were halted so that they could be better defended. "We reached Sailor's Creek...weary, starving, despairing," Pickett later wrote to Sally.[38]

At this point occurred one of the monumental mistakes made by the Rebel brass during the Confederate exodus. When he stopped his march, Anderson failed to notify General William Mahone who was in column in front of him. Uninformed of Anderson's halt, Mahone continued moving westward toward Rice's Station, where Lee was waiting, as yet unaware of any serious trouble to the rear. Lee's general orders for the army behind Longstreet were for it "to close upon it [Longstreet's corps] as fast as the progress of the trains would permit or as they could be directed on roads farther west."[39] But the swiftness of Longstreet's basically unimpaired march, plus the agonizingly slow movement of the wagons, were factors that spelled coming disaster.

Preparing to attack the Rebels, George Crook himself was little more than two weeks out of a Confederate prison, having been exchanged on March 20 after a most embarrassing incident in late February. The

36-year-old Ohioan was an 1852 West Point graduate who served in northern California and Washington prior to secession hostilities. As colonel of the 36th Ohio Infantry, Crook saw action in western Virginia and was appointed brigadier general in August 1862. He fought at South Mountain and Antietam, and led a cavalry division in the U.S. Army of the Cumberland in the Chickamauga campaign. Reassigned to western Virginia, Crook defeated a lesser Rebel force at Cloyd's Mountain in May 1864. Placed over one of Sheridan's three corps in the Shenandoah, Crook was promoted to major general of volunteers in October 1864.

In one of the war's more daring missions, Rebel raiders captured Crook at his headquarters in Cumberland, Maryland, on the night of February 21, 1865. The general was staying at the Revere House, a hotel operated by a man named Daily, whose daughter, Mary, was engaged to Crook. The innkeeper's son, however, was in a band of Confederate partisan rangers led by Captain Jesse McNeill. In the night, about 60 of these Rebels slipped through some ten thousand Union troops stationed about the town and awakened the surprised Crook. Also captured was Union Brigadier General Benjamin F. Kelley, who also was courting a Cumberland lass whom he would later marry.[40]

Crook plowed into Anderson's battle line about 11 a.m. with Colonel Charles Smith's Brigade leading the way. They quickly found the Reb wagons strongly guarded by both infantry and cavalry. Smith's riders inflicted and suffered some casualties, but made little headway in trying to break into the Southerners' column.[41] The most important result of Crook's aggressiveness, however, was that the gap between Mahone's Division and Anderson's stalled infantry grew to a width of about two miles by early afternoon. On the road behind Anderson, Ewell's troops were taking a brief rest when the clatter of gunfire off to their southwest alerted them to Crook's assault. To the rear, the ever-present sputter of musketry told Ewell that Gordon also was being pressed.

After warding off Crook's thrusts, Anderson resumed his march on the Rice's Station Road and Ewell followed, but not before another huge blunder was made. The confusion and catastrophe of the day have

not yet yielded who made the decision, but the section of the wagon
train between Ewell and Gordon
was ordered to proceed past Ewell
and Anderson's commands. This
apparently was done so that Gordon would not have the vehicles
in front of him if he needed aid
from those two corps. In the end,
however, this continued delay allowed Union cavalry to race ahead
of Anderson, which was critical to
both armies. Ewell allowed a number of the wagons to move ahead
of him and, for whatever reason,
left the remainder between his rear
and Gordon's lead units. Ewell
then marched ahead to close with

**Union Major General
George Crook**

Gil Barrett Collection
U.S. Army Military History Institute

Anderson, whose men remained at a standstill due to the train's pas-
sage.[42] The portion of the wagon column Ewell and Anderson permitted to pass them creaked ahead into the exposed road between Mahone
and Anderson.

If he intended to close with Gordon, why did Ewell leave some
wagons between him and the rearguard before continuing his march?
That question is among the enigmas of Sailor's Creek. But to the Federal cavalry gathering on the hills for any chance to pounce that Thursday, the enemy wagons rumbling in the distance with no visible infantry
support presented prime saber fodder.

CHAPTER 10
ATTACK OF THE "RED TIES"

While Crook's cavalry recoiled and the Confederates unwittingly allowed the crack to widen in their line of march, the bulk of the Union forces were closing in for the kill on their slow-moving enemy. With Crook's failure to dent the Rebel column, Sheridan began what would become a series of leapfrog motions with his three cavalry divisions. Crook was ordered to call off his attack, ride further west, and try to find a weaker point to assail the Confederate line.

Custer would strike the same general sector assailed by Crook and, if unsuccessful, would march past Crook's newest position and allow Devin's squadrons to attack. In so doing, the blue cavalry was bound to find a vulnerable spot to hit the wagons. But as Crook's horsemen regrouped, Sheridan's immediate problem was that Custer's and Devin's Divisions had not yet reached the field. The infantry was even more needed and the closest appeared to be Wright's VI Corps, which was somewhere on the roads behind Custer.[1]

Trying to buy time, Sheridan, who by now was on the scene after riding a portion of the way with Wright, saw that some guns of Captain Marcus P. Miller's 4th U.S. Artillery of Devin's Division were on hand, and sent them to shell the Rebel procession. General Merritt also had arrived on the field.

Custis Lee's Division of Ewell, meanwhile, had passed Holt's Corner and Kershaw's command had reached the road fork about midday [although Kershaw reported the arrival time of around 10 a.m.].

While the march was at a standstill, these Rebels either rested or fell into battle line to repel the sporadic enemy cavalry attacks that lasted from about 11 a.m. to 2 p.m., according to Ewell. The Southerners also had to deal with Miller's cannonading.

"[T]he enemy contented himself with shelling the trains and the road by which the troops passed," recalled Confederate Major William S. Basinger of the 18th Georgia Battalion. "But no one was hurt."[2]

Sheridan had a different perspective, writing that Miller shelled the column "with excellent effect."[3] Devin added that Miller "made great havoc in the train by his splendid service."[4]

Devin's First, or Michigan, Brigade under Colonel Peter Stagg was up by now and was flung forward by Merritt with permission by Sheridan who "felt so strongly the necessity of holding this large force of the enemy," Devin recalled.[5]

Stagg's troopers went in bravely, but had no better luck than Crook's boys at breaking the Southerners. Stagg was pushing at Ewell's Confederates when the two thousand one hundred men of Custer's First Brigade, led by Colonel Alexander C. M. Pennington, made their appearance about noon.

Roger Hannaford, one of Pennington's troopers, described the scene:

> moving thro' fields & bye roads in a nearly west direction...we could look away over to our right nearly 2 miles, and see a large wagon train moving...A mile or so farther, we came on the 2nd Cav[alry] Div[ision] [Crook's command], & from them learnt that it was indeed Lee's wagon train. A portion of their Div[ision] had attacked it, & had been repulsed...we soon came to a lot of their wounded...the effect of such a sight on a lot of men just going to attack the enemy is exceedingly bad.[6]

Custer himself was soon on the field and drew the personal attention of the Rebel General Kershaw before leading his blue squadrons west to attack the Confederates elsewhere. Kershaw's men were in battle line around Holt's Corner at the time.

Seeing Custer's personal guidon fluttering across the way, Kershaw called for his men to train their muskets on it. Kill Custer and the Rebels almost certainly would better their chances of escaping.

Kershaw, like most other Confederates who had faced Custer, knew he was pitted against a tenacious, aggressive, and utterly fearless warrior.

The daredevil 25-year-old Custer was as much known for his long, reddish-blond curls and custom-tailored uniforms as his reckless passion for cavalry combat. Custer feasted on military glory and always craved the headlines, but had the battle savvy and shrewdness to back up his vain strutting and posturing. This attitude and his often-gaudy appearance, however, did earn him the contempt of other officers, some of whom were simply jealous of his abilities. One of Meade's staff officers, Theodore Lyman, recalled that Custer was "one of the funniest-looking beings you ever saw, and looks like a circus rider gone mad!" Lyman went on to say that Custer's "coiffure [consisted of] short, dry, flaxen ringlets!...He has a very merry blue eye, and a devil-may-care style."[7]

Union cavalry Captain George Sanford offered this description of "Old Curly," as some of Custer's troopers called him:

> He was scarcely more than a boy in years, but was a man of tremendous energy and immense power. His great height and striking countenance made him a very imposing figure. His blue eyes, blond moustach[e] and great mass of blond curling hair falling almost to his waist gave him the appearance of one of the Vikings of old, and his fancy for startling effects was still farther indicated by his dress which I remember about this time to have consisted of an immensely broad "slouch" hat, a black velvet jacket heavily trimmed with gold lace, riding breeches of the same, and immensely long cavalry boots...One thing I have forgotten and that perhaps the most conspicuous article of his apparel—around his neck, loosely knotted, he generally wore a long flowing ribbon or cravat of brilliant red cashmere or silk. This streamed behind him as he rode, and made him a marked man a mile away.[8]

Because he did not carelessly expose his men for personal gain in battle, his troopers generally were devoted to him. Many of them adopted the scarlet kerchiefs like their boy general and were nicknamed the "Red Ties." Born in the Ohio hamlet of New Rumley in December 1839, Custer lived much of his childhood with his half sister and her family in Monroe, Michigan. He taught school in Ohio before entering West Point in 1857.

His tenure at the Military Academy was tempestuous. A slew of demerits kept him on the brink of expulsion for all four years there and he was under detention when he graduated, last in his class, in June 1861.

Immediately entering the service, he was a courier for Lieutenant General Winfield Scott before First Bull Run and later was a staff officer for George McClellan and cavalryman Alfred Pleasonton. During this time, the first lieutenant shone in all aspects of his duties, "distinguishing himself on a

**Union Brigadier General
George A. Custer**

Massachusetts Commandery, Military Order
of the Loyal Legion, and the
U.S. Army Military History Institute

number of occasions."[9] Some of his success likely is attributed to his study and admiration of Napoleon's Marshal Joachim Murat and the Frenchman's cavalry tactics.

Custer's shooting star ascended on June 29, 1863, when he catapulted from lieutenant to brigadier general of volunteers and was assigned a brigade command in Judson Kilpatrick's cavalry division. At a time when the Federal cavalry finally was coming into its own against its eroding Confederate counterpart, Custer excelled in fighting off Stuart's gray squadrons at Gettysburg. From there the Custer legend steadily heightened, as he became a keystone of the Union horse.

A hard hitter cut from the same cloth as Sheridan, Custer steadily became a favorite of the cavalry commander based on his excellent operations in the Shenandoah campaign against Early.

Kershaw's infantry tried to draw a bead on Custer and loosed a ragged fire. Custer's horse was shot from under him and a bullet in the face slew his flag bearer, but "Old Curly" was unhurt. Kershaw later recalled that he hesitated to try to kill "a man so brave, good and efficient" but admitted, "it was my only hope."[10]

Meanwhile, the halted Confederates at the head of Anderson's column either fell out by the road or were posted to guard against further enemy attacks as the wagon train passed them. With much apprehension, they watched Union troops hurrying forward ahead of them. Some of the Rebels, like Sergeant David E. Johnston, wondered what the hell their officers were doing while the enemy obviously was preparing a nasty surprise for them up the road to the west. He recalled later:

> Along our front and fully five hundred yards away we could see passing to our right, heavy bodies of the enemy, evidently bent upon getting ahead of us. Moreover, this must have been manifested to our commanding officers, who permitted us to remain idle for several hours and until the enemy made full preparations to attack us. That somebody blundered there is no doubt, as any enlisted man in the ranks could see. We should have moved on.[11]

Robert Lee was with Longstreet at Rice's Station late in the morning when he received word of the cavalry attacks on his wagon trains about three miles to the rear. Even though he was unaware of how black this dilemma really was, dispatches from other quarters were just as grim. Longstreet had learned that a force of about nine hundred enemy troops had been seen on the Farmville Road ahead of them. These Federals, in all likelihood, were on a mission to destroy the Appomattox River bridges in the area to prevent Lee from crossing, the Confederates believed. They guessed correctly, but did they have the means and muskets to stop it?

CHAPTER 11

UNION RAIDERS AT HIGH BRIDGE

When Longstreet arrived at Rice's Station with the advance elements of his corps before noon Thursday, he learned that Ord's Army of the James was threateningly close. "Old Pete's" Rebels immediately dug in behind light field works.

As his tired infantrymen labored with shovels and axes, Longstreet received the report about the enemy troops moving up the road to Farmville. He reasoned that their objective was to destroy High Bridge and its wagon span, both about four-and-a-half miles north of Rice's. It was imperative that these crossings be saved for Lee's army to survive. Longstreet initially was informed that the enemy force was all mounted, but most of it consisted of Union infantry.[1]

The Federal raiders from Ord's army indeed were intent on causing as much destruction as possible at High Bridge, in itself one of the most marvelous man-made structures on the continent. Built in 1852, it was approximately two thousand five hundred feet long and one hundred twenty-six feet high, pillared on 21 brick piers.[2]

"As Lee appeared to be aiming for either Danville or Lynchburg, Lieutenant-General Grant ordered me to cut the bridges in his front," Ord wrote.[3] If High Bridge and its wagon span could be destroyed or severely damaged, Lee might be trapped, or at least further delayed, on the south bank of the Appomattox.

Ord's strike force included two volunteer infantry regiments—Lieutenant Colonel Horace Kellogg's 123rd Ohio and the 54th Pennsylvania of Lieutenant Colonel Albert P. Moulton. Both regiments, a total of about eight hundred troops, belonged to Brigadier General John W. Turner's Independent Division of Major General John Gibbon's XXIV Corps.[4]

The marauders also included companies I, L and M of the 4th Massachusetts Cavalry, part of Ord's headquarters guard, led by cavalry Colonel Francis Washburn, who was in overall command of the expedition. Three days earlier, two guidons of the 4th had been the first Union banners to fly over the Confederate capitol as Ord's soldiers entered Richmond. The New Englanders faced a much more daunting task this day. Washburn's approximately 80 horsemen constituted "the only cavalry I had," Ord recalled.[5]

The troopers and the infantry left Burke's Station about 4 a.m. aiming at High Bridge, about 12 miles to the northwest. The Union force advanced slowly based on the pace of the infantrymen, who had had little rest in the army's pursuit of Lee. The march was further delayed by a stop for breakfast shortly after sunrise.

Longstreet was irritated that he had no cavalry to send after the raiders. The arrival of General Rosser and his undersized division of Virginia horsemen soon heartened him, however. Rosser had left the army procession with orders to picket and scout in all directions. But Longstreet informed the cavalryman about the enemy threat to the bridges and ordered him to follow and destroy them "if it took the last man of his command to do it."[6] The cavalry division of Colonel Munford was quickly sent to reinforce Rosser, giving the Confederates about one thousand two hundred troopers.

Ord soon learned that the raiders were being pursued by Rebel horsemen of unknown strength. "Apprehending that my bridge-burning party might meet a force of Lee's cavalry sent southward," Ord dispatched his chief of staff, Colonel Theodore Read, to warn Washburn and take command of the force.[7] About 9:30 a.m., Ord received word from Sheridan that Lee had evaded the trap at Jetersville. Ord sent another staff officer to caution Read and Washburn about this development and instruct them to take another route back to the army after their mission. The officer never reached the bridge burners and was instead driven back by enemy horsemen.[8]

Read, meanwhile, had joined Washburn and sent the cavalry about a mile further toward High Bridge on a reconnaissance. Washburn's troopers drove off a detachment of home guards near the span. It was just after midday when these horsemen were startled by gunfire to their rear where the Rebel cavalry had caught up to and collided with Moulton's and Kellogg's infantry. Encountering these Yanks, Munford dismounted his division to fight on foot while Rosser sent his two brigades off to the left to hammer the Union flank.

The blue cavalry, meanwhile, fell back to link with the infantry, which was now being assailed in a small strip of woodland. "When we reached the scene of the action the infantry was deployed and holding a fence just inside the woods," wrote Massachusetts Lieutenant Joseph H. Lathrop, "while beyond was a brigade of dismounted rebel cavalry engaging our infantry at short range."[9]

Read "rode along the front of his ranks, inspired them with all his own daring, and began the battle with an army in his front," Ord reported.[10] Read and Washburn briefly talked over the situation and "the chivalrous Washburn," as Ord described him, led a mounted charge against Munford's Southerners, who were coming towards them. Lathrop remembered:

> Forming the squadron on the brow of the hill we moved forward in column of fours, at a trot, until beyond the right flank of our infantry, and then, wheeling to the left, we charged into the woods. This charge was eminently successful, the enemy scattering in every direction, and we captured a number of them.[11]

Union Major Edward T. Bouvé wrote that Washburn's horsemen "crashed through three lines of advancing enemies, tearing their formations asunder as the tornado cuts its way through the forest."[12] Rosser's brigades quickly rode to the aid of their comrades and the blue and gray lines melded in a storm of hand-to-hand fighting with sabers, revolvers, and carbines.

Confederate Brigadier James Dearing and Colonel Washburn, who had attended West Point together, engaged in a personal duel on horseback. Their swords clanged together as they galloped past each other. Moments later, another gray trooper shot Washburn through the cheek and he toppled from his horse. Bleeding, dazed, and aground, Washburn was then sabered across the head by a Rebel horseman and mortally wounded. The 24-year-old Dearing then went after Read. In the act of firing his revolver at his adversary, Dearing himself was shot and gravely wounded, some accounts stating that he was accidentally hit by the gunfire of his own men.[13] Whether from Dearing's pistol or another enemy weapon fired at close range, Read was killed in the saddle, his body left on the field by the Federals.

**Confederate Brigadier General
James Dearing**

Author's Collection

The outnumbered 4th Massachusetts was quickly overwhelmed. "Some tried to cut their way out, but it was useless," wrote Lathrop, who was taken prisoner.[14] Ord wrote that "at last not an officer of that cavalry party remained alive or unwounded to lead the men, and not until then did they surrender."[15]

With the enemy cavalry taken, the Rebels turned their attention to the Union infantry, which held a position on a hill near a farmhouse and had apparently made little or no effort to assist Washburn and Read. On orders from Brigadier General John McCausland of Rosser's command, the 6th Virginia Cavalry and the 35th Virginia Cavalry Battalion charged the blue formation. Readying to join the charge, Colonel Reuben B. Boston of the 5th Virginia was "shot through the brain," but the troopers swiftly forced the Federal infantry off the hill.[16]

The 35th Virginia "Comanches" of Colonel Elijah White, meanwhile, had swung around the flank and were waiting for the fleeing bluecoats. The Union infantrymen offered little resistance and were captured. Ironically, many of them tried to escape in the direction of High Bridge and surrendered at their objective. The total haul for the

Rebels was about seven hundred eighty prisoners, an ambulance, six colors, and a brass band. The 4th Massachusetts lost its three company guidons, but the regimental flag was saved from capture by Color Sergeant Thomas Hickey, who burned it.

Southern trooper E. M. Boykin noted the contrast of the Yankees' fresh uniforms with the shoddiness of the Confederates:

> Their coats were so new and blue and buttons so bright, and shirts
> so clean, that it was a wonder to look upon them by our rusty lot.[17]

Among the blue dead was Captain John Goddard of the 4th Massachusetts. Goddard had been on leave, visiting his mother in Boston a few days earlier when news of the Federals' pursuit of Lee reached him. Not wanting to miss the action, he cut short his furlough and rode day and night to rejoin his unit. When the 4th trotted out of camp on the bridge-burning raid, Goddard was with it. "Better be killed than have a stain upon my honor in the hour of battle," he wrote in a letter home. Goddard was slain by a saber thrust early in the fighting. His sword and silk sash were recovered and sent to his mother.[18]

Indeed, all thirteen of the 4th's officers were killed, wounded, or captured. The cavalry battle had been especially vicious. "Several rebel officers with whom I conversed after their capture spoke of it as the most gallant fight of the war," wrote the 4th's Major Henry B. Scott in a postwar report. "The numerous saber wounds given and the great mortality among the officers is good evidence of this..."[19] Colonel Washburn was borne from the battlefield but would never recover. Sent home to recuperate, he died on April 22, unable to enjoy the brevet rank of brigadier general that U. S. Grant bestowed upon him as a result of the affair at High Bridge.

Critically wounded General Dearing was taken to a farmhouse where Rosser and Colonel White came to his bedside. He was especially close to Rosser since he commanded Rosser's old Laurel Brigade. Dearing grasped White's hand and with his other touched the general's stars on his own tunic. "Unable to speak above a whisper," Dearing told Rosser, "I want these to be put on his coat."[20] Dearing clung to life well after Lee's surrender but died at the Ladies Relief

Hospital in Lynchburg on April 23. He was the last Confederate general to die of war injuries.[21]

Despite thwarting the Union bridge burners, in the 15-minute combat, the Southerners suffered severely among officers. The losses included Dearing, Colonel Boston, Major John L. Knott of the 12th Virginia Cavalry who fell early in the fight, and Major James W. Thomson of the Stuart Horse Artillery who was shot in the neck and killed in the last charge. Rosser sustained a minor wound to the arm, and Confederate casualties overall were not recorded.

The little battle was a clear-cut Rebel victory and Rosser dispatched the good news to Longstreet, stating that he had "captured everything except a few cav[alry] that escaped by swimming the river."[22] Still, many of the Federals who were captured remained cocky, confident of final victory. A Union officer being led to the rear remarked to his Confederate guards, "Never mind boys, Old Grant is after you. You will be in our predicament in 48 hours."[23]

The conduct of Moulton's and Kellogg's infantry at High Bridge evoked different responses depending upon who was asked. The regiments "I regret to state were compelled to surrender during the day, having been surrounded by an overwhelming force of the enemy, not however, before making a gallant resistance," reported General Turner, the division commander.[24] "The men fought splendidly," wrote Lieutenant Colonel Andrew Potter of Turner's First Brigade, which contained the 123rd Ohio. "There was no thought of surrendering till the ammunition gave out, when they were compelled to yield and the whole regiment became prisoners."[25] Cavalry Major Scott had a very different opinion of the infantry regiments, writing, "It is generally conceded that their behavior was not creditable."[26]

Longstreet gave this assessment of the clash, paying tribute to the enemy as well as the Rebel cavalry involved:

> Reed's [sic] fight was as gallant and skillful as a soldier could make, and its noise in rear of Sailor's Creek may have served to increase the confusion there. The result shows the work of these remnants of Confederate veterans as skillful and worthy of their old chief who fell at Yellow Tavern.[27]

Grant was unaware of the outcome at High Bridge when he sent this dispatch to Ord:

HEADQUARTERS ARMIES OF THE UNITED STATES,
Jetersville, April 6, 1865-4.20 p. m.

Major-General ORD:

Send [Major General John] Gibbon with his two divisions to Farmington [Farmville], to hold that crossing. The VI Corps is also ordered. The colored division [troops of Major General Godfrey Weitzel's XXV Corps] will be sufficient to retain at Burkeville. The enemy is evidently making for Ligontown and Stony Point bridges. Indications are that the enemy are almost in a rout. They are burning wagons, caissons, &c.

U. S. GRANT,
Lieutenant-General[28]

Colonel Munford's actions were so conspicuous that a courier from Fitz Lee was dispatched to him during the night of April 6–7 with a promotion to brigadier general. But in the haze of Confederate defeat, Munford did not receive the commission before the war was over.

When Rosser rode to Rice's Station to give Longstreet more details of the battle, he was riding a shiny black horse and carrying a different sword on his side. Excitedly, he reined in at the Confederate bivouac, saying, "It was a gallant fight. This is Read's horse and this is his saber. Both beauties aren't they?"[29]

Neither the blue and gray fighting for High Bridge nor the combatants blazing away at each other along Sailor's Creek were aware of what was happening on the other battlefield this day. While simultaneous, the battles were independent yet equally as desperate; and both struggles did a great deal to sculpt the events of Palm Sunday, April 9, 1865.

CHAPTER 12

"EAGER FOR A TUSSLE WITH SHERIDAN"

Even as the High Bridge clash was unfolding, George Custer's horsemen were pounding west along the flank near the rear of Lee's army. Custer's Red Ties thundered past Pride's Church and crossed Little Sailor's Creek at Gill's Mill before turning north to puncture the Confederates' naked vein between Anderson and Mahone. They were quick to find and attack the sparsely defended Rebel wagon train that had passed into the opening. [These vehicles numbered several hundred, including some of Longstreet's artillery, but exact totals are unknown.]

The bluejackets rumbled across the spread of the Harper farm and slammed into the enemy file, with Pennington's brigade of Connecticut, New Jersey, New York, and Ohio troopers in the forefront. The assault occurred about 2 p.m. in the vicinity of Marshall's Crossroads, an intersection near the Marshall family farm where a dirt lane ran northwest from the Rice's Station Road about a mile west of Little Sailor's Creek.

Pennington's men "took off through the fields...on the gallop, gradually making for the train, yelling like Indians," a Yank recounted. "We soon flanked the train guard, who had been hastily drawn up in line to oppose us. This done, we came on the wagon train where there was not a single guard, or, indeed, often a man, for most of the drivers jumped off and ran away on our approach or ran toward us swinging their hats in token of surrender."[1]

Custer had found Sheridan's anticipated weak point in the Confederate caravan and the Union troopers flooded into the wound.

87

Pennington reported that his riders encountered only a few skirmishers while seizing about three hundred wagons, about eight hundred mules and horses, and 10 pieces of artillery."[2]

"General Custer succeeded in striking the enemy's wagon train at a point less strongly guarded than at others where it had been attacked," Merritt wrote, adding that Custer surprised and took a park of three artillery batteries.[3] The guns had belonged to the battalion of Lieutenant Colonel Frank Huger of Longstreet's Corps. Huger, a West Point classmate of Custer and the son of Confederate Major General Benjamin Huger, a former division commander under Robert Lee, was captured. Custer would later write that his breakthrough "secured a strong position in rear of that of the enemy's force engaging the VI Corps."[4] Unknown to him at the time Custer had, in effect, sprung a trap for three of the four corps of Lee's army. Merritt, who had assumed immediate cavalry command while Sheridan coordinated the infantry/cavalry operation, sent off a dispatch to Sheridan:

> General Custer reports being in rear of three divisions of rebel
> infantry. He has captured quite a number of prisoners and some
> artillery. The infantry should push in with vigor...I will send Devin
> in at once.[5]

Custer would sorely need Devin.

After resuming their march, Anderson's men had crossed Little Sailor's Creek and were approaching Marshall's Crossroads. In the corps' van, the Virginians of Brigadier General Eppa Hunton's command in Pickett's Division were resting on a hillside when they heard the snapping of small arms fire somewhere ahead of their line of march.

Unknown, to them, Custer's cavalry was breaking into the baggage train and artillery that had passed ahead of them earlier. The undulating nature of the hilly, heavily wooded terrain obscured their view of the attack.

Hunton's Brigade had been on duty elsewhere and had not been present when Pickett was routed at Five Forks. Still, these Rebels wanted revenge for that devastating embarrassment. The roar of gunfire to their front promised just that. These Rebs were "eager for a tussle with Sheridan...They felt that they were a match for the cavalry," wrote C. F. James of Company F, 8th Virginia Infantry, "and all along on the retreat they were hoping for a chance to wipe out the reproach of April 1."[6] James was delighted to see his brother, John, and another soldier, Thompson Furr, returning from a night of foraging. The excursion had been a success as they triumphantly were carrying a bucket of eggs, some fried chicken, and corn bread, which they had gotten in trade from a civilian for two army blankets. "It was timely relief," James recalled, "for we had not more than finished our breakfast when we were startled by the sound of pistol shots in our front. Looking up, we saw some ambulances and stragglers rushing down the opposite hill..."[7]

The Southerners soon learned that Union cavalry had cut the road between them and the rear of Longstreet's Corps. Very soon these Virginians would have their wish to "tussle" with Sheridan.

The Union high command learned of the escalating contact with the enemy near Sailor's Creek and moved with urgency to coordinate the kill. General Meade's chief of staff, Brigadier General Alexander S. Webb, sent a 12:40 p.m. message to generals Wright, Humphreys, and Griffin stressing the importance of a quick thrust at the stalled Rebel army:

> Major-General Sheridan reports that the advance of the enemy is checked. He urges an attack by all the infantry. The major-general commanding sends this for your information and feels that all will appreciate the rapidity of movement.[8]

At Jetersville, Grant sent this 2:05 p.m. message to Sheridan:

> From this point General Humphreys' corps could be seen advancing over General Vaughn's farm. The enemy occupied that place two hours ago with artillery and infantry. Griffin is farther to the right and has been urged to push on. He is, no doubt, doing so. Wright is pushing out on the road you are on and will go in with a

vim any place you dictate. Ord has sent two regiments out to Farmville to destroy the bridge, and is intrenching the balance of his command at Burke's Station. If your information makes it advisable for him to move out notify him and he will do so.[9]

Within minutes, Webb dispatched separate orders to Humphreys. Obviously Meade expected more drive and action from the II Corps:

> General Sheridan is in Deatonville with his cavalry. The V Corps covers well your flank and rear and Wright your left. You are therefore at liberty to push forward with your whole corps and to strike the enemy wherever you find him. The major-general commanding desires you to push on as rapidly as possible.[10]

Webb received conflicting information while composing the message and added a postscript:

> The enemy has Deatonville. Sheridan is on left of Deatonville. Sheridan will attack with three divisions at three points. General Meade says: "Push on without fear of your flanks."[11]

CHAPTER 13
"THE ROADS AND FIELDS SWARMED WITH THE EAGER PURSUERS."

Custer's Red Ties were securing and destroying the captured wagons when they were assailed by a strong mixed force of Confederates from Pickett's units and Bushrod Johnson's men from Anderson's Corps. Custer sent a rider to Devin detailing his predicament.

After the battle Custer, Pennington, and other Federal officers wrote that Custer's Division came under attack from Ewell's Southerners. Custer related that "two divisions of rebel infantry," under Custis Lee and Joseph Kershaw, "attacked my command with a view to recapturing their train."[1] Official combat accounts from Ewell, Custis Lee, and Kershaw offer no hint that they launched such a counterattack. Indeed, these Confederates were well behind, or east, of Anderson's Corps when Custer overran this segment of the wagon train.

Devin was passing to the rear of the point where Custer had speared toward the enemy procession when the courier from Custer reached him. "I received an urgent message from General Custer, stating that he had struck and captured part of the train and was hard pressed," he reported.[2] When he read this dispatch, Devin was edging his troopers to the west of Custer to take the next jump in Sheridan's cavalry leapfrog. Crook's battered division also was riding west. Both Devin and Crook were hoping to find an angle in which to drive another sledge into the Confederates' parade of torment.

Born to Irish immigrant parents in New York City, Devin, 42, was a former house painter who never spent a day at West Point. As a member of the New York state militia, he rose to become a lieutenant colonel of a

91

regiment and, when the war began, entered Federal service as a captain of New York cavalry. He was appointed colonel of the 1st New York Cavalry in November 1861 and experienced his battle baptism at Antietam. After Fredericksburg, Devin was given a brigade command and fought well at Chancellorsville and Beverly Ford. On the first day of Gettysburg, his horsemen helped stave off the Confederate advance, thus allowing the main Federal army to reach and occupy strong positions about the village. Devin participated in General Judson Kilpatrick's cavalry raid against Richmond in early 1864 and served under Sheridan in the Shenandoah later that year. Recovering from a minor wound sustained at Crooked Run, he was in action at Winchester, Fisher's Hill, and Cedar Creek. Less than a month before Sailor's Creek, Devin was promoted to brigadier general, to rank from the battle of Cedar Creek in October, and assumed his division command.[3]

If he was to aid Custer, Devin had only two of his three brigades, the Second of Colonel Charles L. Fitzhugh and the Third, or Reserve, under Brigadier General Alfred Gibbs. Left behind were Stagg's Michiganders and the section of Miller's horse artillery that had helped stymie the Confederates east of Sailor's Creek. They remained in position to further harass the Rebels there and link with Wright's VI Corps.

Among the Rebels Custer was battling were infantry of Hunton's and Terry's Brigades. A few minutes earlier, these Johnnies, including the 8th Virginia, had squinted against the sun to see Union horsemen darting about in their front. David Johnston of the 7th Virginia and his comrades had seen Huger's artillerymen marched away as prisoners while other Yanks chopped at the wheels of the captured cannon to temporarily immobilize them. Not waiting for orders from Hunton, who was somewhere to the rear of the column, the 8th Virginia went on the assault down the hill. Based on C. F. James' account, the blue squadrons retreated before this threat and Hunton soon assumed his place at the head of the brigade.

The Southerners roiled across a small stream and up the opposite hill before reaching some woods where they formed a battle line. To their front was a narrow clearing covered in broom sedge with more woods beyond. Skirmishers were posted minutes before "the cavalry appeared in heavy force in the woods opposite and bore down on us," James recalled, adding:

> They had gotten into the habit of riding over our infantry, and they evidently expected to ride over us. Our skirmishers emptied their muskets at them, and then dropped down into the thick broom-sedge to reload, while our main line fired over their heads at the advancing cavalry. The fire was too hot for them, and very few emerged from the woods.[4]

Hunton ordered a charge and his brigade surged forward. "It was an inspiring sight to see those nearly half-starved men move with quick step across that narrow field and into the woods beyond," James recounted, "and drive Sheridan's brag cavalry back..."[5] But the Southerners did not have the numbers or the firepower and their attacks were made in piecemeal fashion.

Devin had reinforced Custer by this time. "On joining him I found it necessary to bring up the division on a gallop and form on his right in order to hold the ground across Sailor's Creek and secure his captures," he reported.[6] "The enemy, concentrating, attacked [Custer's] Division in force, when the First [Devin] moved rapidly to his assistance, both divisions holding the enemy in check," General Merritt related.[7]

Two Virginia regiments in Brigadier General Henry A. Wise's Brigade charged and uprooted some Federals from a hilltop position. But Wise's division commander, Bushrod Johnson, who was not advised of the movement, did not send forward any support brigades and the attack withered. While Federal cavalry flooded into this main breach, other Union horsemen pried their way through a smaller opening between Johnson's Division, in column behind Pickett, and the upcoming elements of Custis Lee's units.

Ewell earlier had resumed his march to rejoin Anderson with still some three hundred wagons and ambulances behind his divisions. They were followed by Gordon, who remained involved in an ever heightening, fighting withdrawal.

Hearing intense firing ahead, Ewell crossed Sailor's Creek and met Fitz Lee. The cavalryman and the small remnant of his troopers not supporting Longstreet or Gordon had forded Little Sailor's Creek minutes before Custer checkmated the Confederate column.

Based on Robert Lee's earlier orders, Fitz had remained at Amelia Springs and conferred with infantry officers, probably from Gordon's Corps, about the army's route. Having rejoined the column further ahead, he and his accompanying gray horsemen now appeared to be netted with the bulk of the Confederates. "I was detained there some time, hoping an attack would be made to reopen the way," the younger Lee remembered.[8]

Fitz told Ewell that a substantial force of Union cavalry held the road, barring the advance of Anderson's Corps. The Yanks were in such strength that Anderson had halted about a mile ahead of them. Ewell rode forward to assess the crisis, while Custis Lee's Division was just approaching the creek and crossed with no opposition.

These Rebels quickly learned they were in imminent danger, however. The 18th Georgia of Crutchfield's Brigade was fording Little Sailor's Creek, bringing up the rear of Lee's Division. The Georgians' color-bearer was in the middle of the unit, "carrying the color-staff inclined upon his shoulder, when a spent bullet struck the staff, splitting it exactly in the middle and just burying itself in the crack," Major Basinger wrote.[9] The men realized that the round had come from their front, meaning that they likely had Yanks ahead of and behind them.

Meanwhile, the Confederates frantically trying to stem the lesser tide of cavalry sweeping between Johnson and Custis Lee and had some success. Officers, including Colonel Charles Venable of Robert Lee's staff, gathered some thirty to forty stragglers and hastily put them into line to fend off the assault. This very brief respite gave Johnson time to halt the rest of his units and deploy back along the road toward Custis Lee's Division. Lee was able to close up with Johnson's left.

"Sharp skirmishing continued on my left for some two hours, during which the men constructed temporary breastworks," Johnson wrote.[10] Pickett's Division, what was left of it, also fell in with Bushrod's embattled troops, retreating on the road to cover Johnson's right flank. General Gordon wrote of the Rebel desperation:

> The roads and fields swarmed with the eager pursuers and [R.E.]
> Lee now and then was forced to halt his whole army, reduced to

less than 10,000 fighters in order to meet these simultaneous attacks. Various divisions along the line of march turned upon the
Federals, and in each case checked them long enough for some
other Confederate commands to move on...[11]

But the break in the march was to have catastrophic consequences
for the Southerners. "The enemy's cavalry penetrated the line of march
through the interval thus left, and attacked the wagon-train..." Robert
Lee wrote in an April 12 report to Jefferson Davis. "This caused serious
delay in the march of the center and rear of the column, and enabled the
enemy to mass upon their flank."[12]

Without placing direct blame, Lee thus recognized that the opening caused by the delay of Anderson's course was the incubus of defeat
at Sailor's Creek.

When he continued his march to link with Anderson, Ewell had
made another error. He allowed a breach to develop in the line between
the rear of Custis Lee's column and Kershaw's van. Kershaw's infantry
still were deployed around Holt's Corner when Custis Lee moved ahead
toward the stream. But the Federals did not, or could not, make an effort
to exploit this opening.

Ewell then made a decision that would further dissect Lee's army.
"The trains were turned into a road nearer the [Appomattox] river, while
I hurried to General Anderson's aid," he wrote.[13] In plainer words, Ewell
diverted the wagons behind his corps onto the Jamestown Road fork
while he rode ahead and crossed the creek to ascertain what was happening to Anderson. The side route taken by the train wound to the
northwest before bending sharply to the southwest past the James S.
Lockett farm and then to a point where Big Sailor's Creek and Little
Sailor's Creek branched to the south. The wagons creaked onto the
Jamestown Road as another appearance of blue cavalry, probably some
elements of Stagg's Brigade, caused Kershaw's Rebels to again have to
fall into a battle line to protect the train.

Anderson and Ewell had repulsed charges at several points along
the Rice's Station Road by now. But these assaults and the albatross of
the wagon train had delayed their march for at least three hours. And

Kershaw's Southerners had held their positions around Holt's Corner for approximately four hours, a critical delay in the retreat.

As the last of the vehicles trundled off in the distance, Kershaw's men fell back into ranks and prepared to close with Lee's Division. The head of Gordon's Corps appeared on the road before Kershaw moved forward. Units in the rear of Gordon's command were fighting the enemy as his troops tried to keep pace with the rest of the escaping army.

Based on his account, Kershaw did not know that Gordon would follow the wagon trains. He presumed that Gordon was behind him when he headed after Lee's Division.

Gordon apparently was never advised that the wagons were to take the road fork to the north. Not receiving orders to either follow Ewell's men or continue to guard the portion of the train ahead of him, Gordon did what he had been doing all day: he turned onto the road behind the wagons.

Amid the engulfing crescendo of musketry, Ewell found Anderson west of Little Sailor's Creek, and they conferred about how the situation should be handled. They were facing at least two divisions of blue cavalry in their front, Anderson estimated. The strength of the enemy to their rear could only be guessed as well, but it was substantial.

According to Ewell's account, Anderson suggested two options: the Rebels could unite their two corps and attempt to cut their way through, or they could move to the right, or north, through the woods and try to reach the Jamestown Road.

Ewell recommended the latter choice, but "as he [Anderson] knew the ground and I did not, and had no one who did, I left the dispositions to him."[14] Anderson opted to try to clear the road before him and couriers rushed to the rear to set Ewell's troops in motion to support this action.

The generals still were talking when a large body of Federal troops appeared in Ewell's wake and began deploying to attack. The Union VI Corps had caught up with its quarry!

Custis Lee's Division was across Sailor's Creek and near the crest of a hill on the opposite bank when the Yankees emerged from the woods. Quickly, Anderson told Ewell that he would attack the cavalry in his front if Ewell's men could hold off this threat from behind.

The most startled Confederates were of Kershaw's Division. Instead of seeing their comrades in Gordon's Regiments, they suddenly had enemy infantry, in addition to the several pieces of Federal artillery, at their backs. "I was not informed that Gordon would follow the wagon train as he did, and was therefore surprised...to find that my rear was menaced," Kershaw later wrote.[15] At the time, Kershaw only knew that Custis Lee's troops ahead of him had halted and that he was being threatened from the rear as his division neared Little Sailor's Creek. He had less than two thousand men, including three brigades and a dismounted battalion of cavalry.

Confederate Lieutenant General Richard H. Anderson

Author's Collection

Kershaw ordered Humphrey's Brigade, led by Colonel William H. Fitzgerald, and the cavalry, the 24th Virginia under Lieutenant Colonel Theophilus Barham, to take positions at the Hillsman farm and cover the creek crossing. The bulk of his troops reached the far side of the stream as the musketry fire intensified behind them.

Ewell had about three thousand men total. Some accounts state that it was closer to six thousand, but his corps had been decimated by "the fatigue of four days' and nights' almost constant marching, the last two days with nothing to eat."[16]

Robert Lee had spurred Traveller east from Rice's Station in the early afternoon, trying to find out what was happening to the rear echelons of his army. He had received scattered and scanty information of fighting but had not heard from Anderson, Ewell, or Gordon with any solid intelligence. At various times during the retreat, he had come dangerously close to the front lines, putting his own safety aside to exhort his troops. This Thursday was no different. General Gordon related:

> General Lee was riding everywhere and watching everything, encouraging his brave men by his calm and cheerful bearing. He was often exposed to great danger from shells and bullets...[17]

In one sector a group of Union cavalrymen spied Lee and rode after him. The danger ended, however, when artillery Colonel Thomas H. Carter trained a gun on the bluecoats and repelled them with a few shots. Reaching a ridge at a point overlooking much of the creek valley, Lee joined Brigadier General William P. Robertson's cavalry who was watching a battle between Gordon's Corps and Union troops [apparently the II Corps] on the far side of the stream. Lee dismounted and took out his field glasses to identify some white objects he saw in the distance.

"Are those sheep or not?" Lee asked a captain who was near him.

"No, General, they are Yankee wagons," the officer replied.

Lee again peered through his glasses.

"You are right; but what are they doing there?"[18]

Lee tried to decipher what this meant. He had received no word from Anderson or Ewell for several hours. They had been in ranks in front of Gordon! And the fact that the enemy's trains were up was a foreboding sign to say the least.

The Confederates of Bushrod Johnson's Division and the remaining units of George Pickett's command would be the sword point of Anderson's desperate attempt to punch out of the Union cavalry roadblock. Many of these Southerners already had been hotly engaged with the bluejackets of Custer and Devin.

Johnson, 47, was an Ohio-born 1840 graduate of West Point who had fought in the Seminole and Mexican Wars. He resigned from the army in 1847 to become a teacher and served in the state militias of Kentucky and Tennessee, rising to the rank of colonel. Johnson joined the Confederacy as a colonel of engineers and was promoted to brigadier general in January 1862. Captured at Fort Donelson, he escaped and

returned to duty in time to be seriously wounded at Shiloh. After
his recovery, he led his brigade in
the Kentucky campaign of 1862,
at Stones River and Chickamauga
and in the Knoxville campaign.
Transferred east, Johnson was
commissioned major general in
May 1864 and remained with the
Army of Northern Virginia for the
war's duration. His division saw
much combat in the Petersburg
siege.[19]

**Confederate Major General
Bushrod R. Johnson**

Author's Collection

Johnson had just been in-
formed of the successful assault of
General Wise's pair of Virginia
regiments when a courier galloped
up to him. "About this time, General Anderson sent a staff officer
to say to me that, as we appeared to be driving the enemy, I should
advance my whole command," Johnson recalled.[20] But the war cyclone's
sudden swirl of events apparently was too much for Johnson to be spurred
to immediate action. Wise's men had charged without orders from him
and this action seemed to unsettle Johnson for the rest of the battle.

The Federal cavalry seemed to be everywhere, bedeviling him at
other points on his line. Johnson was uncertain whether to maintain his
position or form the entire division and attack to the west. Stating his
plight, Johnson sent the messenger back to Anderson and "awaited a
repetition of the order, as I gave the staff officer to understand I would
do."[21] Johnson did place three of his brigades, under Brigadier Generals
Wise, William H. Wallace, and Matthew W. Ransom, into a battle line
when another rider arrived from Anderson with orders for Johnson to
hasten his movement.

To their front, these Confederates faced squadrons of blue cavalry
and saw the smoke and flames of many of the wagons seized by Custer
spiraling skyward.

This was 40-year-old Pickett's last hurrah. In chivalric dazzle nearly two years earlier he had ridden along the bristling infantry of his division forming the phalanx of Lee's attack against Cemetery Ridge on the third day of Gettysburg. The legendary assault is known in popular history as "Pickett's Charge," even though the Virginian commanded only three of the eleven brigades involved and was conspicuously unaccounted for while the onslaught was in progress.[22] An 1846 West Point graduate, Pickett was brevetted twice for bravery in the Mexican War and served on the Texas frontier and in the Washington Territory just prior to secession. As a Confederate brigadier he performed well in the Peninsula campaign and was seriously wounded at Gaines' Mill. Appointed major general in October 1862, he saw action at Fredericksburg and obviously played a key role in Lee's Pennsylvania invasion.

Like George Custer, Pickett was renowned for his curly ringlets of hair cascading to his shoulders. He perfumed them as well as his beard. Regarding the horrendous charge that bears his name, Pickett placed much blame for its failure on the support troops, claiming that they had done little or nothing to assist him. Included in his bitter indictment were three brigades of General Dick Anderson's Division.[23] This criticism only aggravated the raw wounds from the attack's failure and further alienated Pickett.

After Gettysburg, Pickett's Division was detached from the rest of the Army of Northern Virginia for some nine months as Pickett found himself in the backwater command of the Department of Virginia and North Carolina. For all intents, Lee had shelved him, at least temporarily. The inactivity ended for Pickett in late January 1864 when he joined in an unsuccessful strike against Union forces at New Bern, North Carolina. Angered and frustrated by this defeat, Pickett bloodily vented his ire on a group of pro-Union North Carolinians who had been captured while serving with the Federals at New Bern. Many of these 53 men had been in state militia units when the war began and Pickett thus considered them Confederate deserters. Enraged to see them now wearing Yank blue, Pickett had most of them hanged or shot, including 25 in one day, the largest single execution of the conflict.[24]

Despite the notoriety of this incident, which would haunt him infinitely, Pickett earned his greatest war glory in May 1864. With a scrap force, he aggressively stalled a Union expedition of some 12,000 troops under Major General Benjamin Butler at Bermuda Hundred, ending Butler's threat to Richmond. Pickett suffered a nervous collapse shortly afterward at a time when his division was being readied to return to the army at Petersburg. The general rejoined his command about two weeks later and the soldiers settled into their earthworks. Through the rest of 1864 and into late winter 1865, Pickett's Division, now consisting of about six thousand five hundred men, saw little heavy fighting in the siege. Thus, in late March, Lee decided to again trust Pickett with a vital task—guard the South Side Railroad on the Confederates' right flank and hold, at any cost, the road junction at Five Forks. From March 29–31, heavy formations of Union troops menaced this sector of Lee's lines. With a strong enemy presence so near, Pickett likely made the worst mistake of his career on April 1 when he chose to attend the shad bake, hosted by cavalry General Rosser, well behind the Five Forks position. Fitz Lee was also at the gathering.

When Sheridan's hosts descended on the Rebels late that afternoon, the front-line Confederates were surprised completely and rapidly overrun while their commanders savored their fish dinner. Pickett tried to reach the front but was quickly caught up in the gray mass of fugitives from Five Forks. Only at Sailor's Creek five days later did he have the remotest chance to salvage his reputation.

With Pickett, Johnson eventually pushed forward a battle line but could not make any headway against Custer and Devin. The attack was over in about five minutes.[25] Anderson and Ewell had ridden forward to check on the progress of Anderson's attack. Even as they did so, the VI Corps battle lines were nearing Little Sailor's Creek, but Ewell seemed more concerned with what was happening on the road ahead than the assault on his two divisions.

The general was either extremely composed about the dilemma or did not fully realize what was transpiring as the enemy seemed about to surround them. Lieutenant Colonel R. T. W. Duke of the 2nd Battalion of Virginia Reserves happened upon Ewell, Custis Lee and several other mounted officers and heard Ewell remark: "Tomatoes are very good; I wish I had some." In his haste, Duke was tempted to laugh at this comment, but the day was far from humorous.[26]

Within minutes one of Anderson's staff officers galloped up to the generals. The news was not good. Anderson's troops had failed to make the breakthrough. Anderson later wrote that "The troops seemed to be wholly broken down and disheartened. After a feeble effort to advance they gave way in confusion..."[27] Ewell and Anderson then parted to tend to their embattled commands. "General Anderson rode rapidly toward his command," Ewell recounted. "He wheeled his horse and started back to his beleaguered corps, intent on trying to salvage the other option to strike toward the Farmville road."[28] In a letter to his wife, Ewell later confided, "Anderson was badly whipped."[29]

The door to the west was shut to the Rebels, and Anderson ordered his men to begin digging in along the Rice's Station Road.

Chapter 14

"The Little Stream Bawled Peacefully at Our Feet."

The bluecoats fanning out from the road behind Kershaw's Rebels belonged to the Union VI Corps' Third Division of Brigadier General Truman Seymour. The division was at the head of the corps' advance, its point being the Second Brigade of Brigadier General J. Warren Keifer. These Yankees and the rest of the VI Corps had left the Jetersville area and followed the cavalry for some distance before crossing Flat Creek and turning more to the north just south of Deatonville.

The gods of war, fate, or chance had placed the 40-year-old Seymour on this field at this time and it was altogether fitting. The son of a Methodist preacher, Seymour was a West Pointer from Vermont who was in the Union garrison at Fort Sumter at the war's opening salvo. Thus it was an unnoticed measure of closure, not only for Seymour, but also for the Union, that he was among the Federals about to strike the last enormous maul blow of the conflict. An 1846 West Point graduate, Seymour fought well as an artillery officer in the Mexican War and in the Seminole Wars of 1856–58. Stationed in Charleston in April 1861, Seymour was brevetted major for his gallantry during the bombardment of Fort Sumter. He was promoted to brigadier general of volunteers the following spring. Seymour commanded a brigade in the Peninsula campaign and performed very capably at Malvern Hill, Second Bull Run, South Mountain, and Antietam. He led the ill-fated attack against Battery Wagner near Charleston on July 18, 1863, in which the famed 54th Massachusetts Infantry, U.S. Colored Troops, was decimated. Seymour was seriously wounded in this battle but recovered to taste defeat again at Olustee, Florida. He returned to the Army of the Potomac and was captured at the Wilderness, ironically by Confederate Second Corps troops under Ewell. Released after about three months in Rebel hands, Seymour returned to lead his division in the Shenandoah Valley, the Petersburg fighting and the chase for Lee.

It was about 3 p.m. when Seymour's column linked with the Union cavalry menacing the enemy trains. With expected hustle, the Yank infantry hurried ahead over the remaining few miles toward Sailor's Creek. Arriving at Holt's Corner they marched cross-

**Union Brigadier General
Truman Seymour**

U.S. Army Military History Institute

country to close with the Rebels brought to bay at the Hillsman farm. Seymour's men were "pushed to the utmost to get up in time," Captain Harwood reported.[1]

Sheridan ordered Seymour to sweep the Confederates from the road ahead. From a ridge to the west, Sheridan had a bird's-eye view of blue "cavalry on the high ground above the creek and south of it, and the long line of smoke from the burning wagons."[2]

Indeed, from his own accounts, Sheridan already had an idea of the enemy's deployment. "A cavalryman, who in a charge cleared the enemy's works and came through their lines, reported to me what was in front. I regret that I have forgotten the name of this gallant young soldier," Sheridan wrote days after the battle.[3]

This intelligence had come from Trooper William A. Richardson of the 2nd Ohio Cavalry who had been engaged in one of the charges against Anderson and had incredibly ridden through the Rebel positions, including Ewell's troops, to find Sheridan. With Richardson's information, Sheridan was better able to synchronize his offensive.

Keifer's 122nd Ohio was immediately thrown forward to sting the gray rearguard and two companies of the 110th Ohio scampered into position to guard his right flank. The remainder of the command was posted in two lines facing the creek. Seymour's First Brigade, under Colonel William S. Truex, was formed in column of regiments behind Keifer with orders to support him.

In the distance, Keifer saw enemy troops and wagons moving on the Jamestown Road from Holt's Corner. He ordered the bulk of his skirmish line, composed of the 110th Ohio reinforced by the 9th New York Heavy Artillery, to pursue these Southerners. These regiments were under the overall command of Lieutenant Colonel Otho H. Binkley of the 110th Ohio.

Two Rebel guns posted in a patch of woods opened on Binkley's advance with grape and canister and the 9th New York cannoneers of Lieutenant Colonel James W. Snyder were ordered to try to silence them. Twice, the Union artillerists advanced and forced the gray gunners to limber and retire. The 9th's Major William Wood was wounded severely in the face during this clash. "The men were completely exhausted, having marched some eighteen miles, and receiving no rest before entering into action," Snyder reported, "if they had been fresh, we should have captured the battery without any doubt."[4]

The 122nd Ohio of Lieutenant Colonel C. M. Cornyn also took aim at the Confederate artillery. Based on Cornyn's account, his men were poised to overrun the Rebel battery, but had to pause when a force of blue cavalry blocked their way while preparing to charge. The delay gave the Confederates time to haul off the guns.

Seymour hurled the rest of Keifer's men and Truex's brigade against Kershaw's rearguard, fighting on the main road with their backs to the creek. Formed in this Union battle line were Keifer's 138th and 67th Pennsylvania Volunteers and the 6th Maryland Volunteers. Truex's units were the 14th New Jersey, 106th New York, several companies of the 151st New York, the 87th Pennsylvania, and the 10th Vermont.[5]

Like most of the Union regiments, the quick, grueling march had exacted its toll on these Yanks and considerable straggling had depleted their strength. After brisk skirmishing, the Federals secured a stretch of the road, but the stubbornness of the Confederate resistance compelled

Wright and Sheridan to hold up Seymour's men for reinforcement by Wright's First Division under Brevet Major General Frank Wheaton, which was racing toward the battlefield.

———————

By this time Ewell had positioned the bulk of his corps in a defensive line looking across the creek. The Rebs were arranged in a perimeter sliced by a little ravine leading almost at right angles toward the stream, which was about three hundred yards in their front. Custis Lee held the corps' left with Kershaw on the right. Tucker's Naval Battalion was in the center of the line, connecting the divisions. The Confederate line generally faced toward the northeast. Lee's command and most of Kershaw's troops were posted behind rising ground that gave them some protection from artillery fire. Ewell had no cannon of his own, all being with the wagon train.

Shortly after it crosses the creek, the Rice's Station Road cuts sharply to the southeast, which meant that about half of Ewell's Corps was looking over the road toward the stream. On his far right Kershaw placed the brigade of Brigadier General Dudley M. DuBose in the edge of some woods with DuBose's right resting along the road. DuBose's Georgians were entrusted to hold the right flank of Ewell's position, but there was nothing to the right of these men but open country and woods. The four Georgia regiments of Brigadier General James P. Simms were stationed to DuBose's left, with their backs to the road and a short distance ahead of the rest of Kershaw's Southerners.

Simms, 28, was a prewar lawyer in his hometown of Covington, Georgia, and had led Georgia troops from the Seven Days' battles to Fredericksburg, Gettysburg, and in the Shenandoah where he performed admirably at Cedar Creek.[6]

A scattering of brush pines in their front mingled with their lines and shielded these Confederates, who looked across the creek through some swampy bottomland to the cleared fields beyond. The center of Ewell's line, however, was open ground and the Naval Battalion lying prone there would pay for their exposure. Commodore Tucker, 52, was a Virginian who had logged a 35-year career in the U.S. Navy, including duty in the Mexican War, before his state seceded in 1861. He commanded the Confederate steamer *Patrick Henry* during the epic sea battle between the U.S.S. *Monitor* and C.S.S. *Virginia* in March 1862. A week after this duel, Tucker and his crew were among Rebel seamen who hauled heavy guns ashore from their vessels and fought off a Union naval assault at Drewry's Bluff.[7] Promoted to captain, Tucker was flag officer of Confederate naval forces in Charleston and when that city was evacuated in early 1865, returned to Drewry's Bluff.

Tucker's men were in line just behind the rest of Custis Lee's Division. Tucker was fighting his first land battle and added an old salt's flavor to his orders. "To the starboard, march!" he bellowed to his sailors and marines, who replied in unison, "Aye, aye, sir!" A Rebel officer rode forward and offered to help Tucker, but was quickly turned down. "Young man," Tucker replied. "I understand how to talk to my people."[8]

The rest of Custis Lee's line consisted of Barton's Brigade of Virginians, stationed to Tucker's front left, and Crutchfield's artillerymen serving as infantry. Crutchfield's units were deployed on either side of Barton. To Barton's left were the 18th and 20th Virginia Battalions of Heavy Artillery under Colonel James Howard. To the right were the 10th and 19th Virginia Heavy Artillery, led by Colonel John W. Atkinson, the Chaffin's Bluff Battalion, and the 18th Georgia Battalion.

"We had been marching under most distressing conditions," artillery Captain Thomas Blake of the 10th Virginia remembered. "More than half of our men had staggered or fallen by the wayside from sheer exhaustion, but those whose endurance and grit had brought them thus far were ready to face any foe."[9] "I reconnoitered the enemy's position, which was a good one, the road being on a ridge," Union engineer Captain Harwood related.[10]

Silently, the Rebels crouched in their defenses, watching the lines of blue infantry attack Kershaw's rearguard. Humphrey's Brigade and the dismounted troopers were obviously outmanned, being driven back to the creek and now enduring artillery fire. Bolstering the blue infantry was a section of guns from Battery E of the 5th U.S. Artillery under Lieutenant C. H. Carroll which was ordered into line about 4 p.m. and commenced a hot fire. When the cannoneers received no Confederate shelling in reply, they became bolder, closing to within eight hundred yards of Kershaw's defenders and began a heavy shelling. Carroll's artillerists were severe in their running bombardment of the Southerners as Kershaw's units retreated through the swamp and over the creek to rejoin their division.

Meanwhile, Humphreys' II Corps had kept up its zealous pursuit of Gordon's Confederates. Reaching Holt's Corner about 4:30 p.m., Humphreys' infantry turned onto the Jamestown Road after Gordon.[11]

This sector of the battlefield was now clogged with Union artillery, cavalry, and elements of two infantry corps, causing some disruption among the troops. While his rearguard was being pummeled, Kershaw had earlier ridden to find Ewell and determine what was going on ahead of him. He met Ewell and was told of the Federal cavalry impeding Anderson. Ewell also instructed Kershaw to hold off the enemy while Anderson tried to clear the road ahead. Carroll's gunners toiled away for about an hour before ceasing their fire. As the cannon smoke lifted and the echoes of gunfire died away, a silence smothered the battlefield. Confederate Colonel Peter A. S. McGlashan recalled:

> The little stream bawled peacefully at our feet. The tender flowers
> of spring were showing above the grass. The hum of insects and
> the strange silence all around seemed to cast a drowsy spell over
> the men, and I could see them gradually sinking to the ground and,
> pillowing their heads in their arms, fitfully dreaming.[12]

The tranquility was short lived. While Union infantry readied for the expected assault, Ewell's Confederates suddenly had to deal with another deadly threat. Into the fields to their front, the five batteries of the VI Corps Artillery Brigade of Captain Andrew Cowan [minus Carroll's section] galloped and unlimbered. Most of the Federals wheeled to a stop near the Hillsman house and readied their pieces.

Sheridan and Wright had decided to pin down the Rebs with even heavier cannon fire while they waited for Wheaton's Division. They knew the Confederates had no artillery to retaliate.

"Their line extended in a semicircular form," Union Captain Harwood wrote, "the convexity toward us, encircling the hillside upon which they had taken position, which was densely timbered." He also noticed the one open area "of about 100 yards width" where the sailors and marines of Tucker's Naval Battalion could be plainly seen lying down.[13] Morris Schaff, a Northern correspondent, watched the proceedings from a hill:

> The Confederates could see the regiments pouring into the fields
> at double quick, the battle lines blooming with colors, growing
> longer and deeper at every moment, and batteries at a gallop com-
> ing into action in the front. They all knew what it meant...Batteries
> right and left of the Hillsman house opened on Ewell's line, a rapid
> destructive fire.[14]

Cowan's cannoneers and their 20 guns began blasting the make-shift Rebel defenses about 5:15 p.m., even as Custis Lee's men still were taking their posts and digging in. "Before the line was formed, and while the greater part of the troops were yet moving to their position, the enemy opened fire with case, shells and canister," Basinger reported.[15]

At a range of about eight hundred yards, the shelling was horrific, deafening, and deadly. The Chaffin's Bluff Battalion, composed of gray artillerymen from the Richmond defenses, was hard hit by the bombardment. In their jaunty scarlet caps and trim many, if not all of these soldiers, led by Major Robert Stiles, were enduring their first real combat, other than serving as skirmishers on the march. [Basinger had been placed over Stiles' unit the previous day after Major W. H. Gibbes was transferred to another artillery unit. Thus, Basinger commanded the 18th Georgia and the Chaffin's Bluff troops in Crutchfield's Brigade.]

Both battalions reached their assigned posts in the line, but the conformation of the ground was such that they could not see any other of their units beyond their little command. This being said, it must have appeared that the entire Union army was descending on these Rebels, but Custis Lee rode along the artillerymen's line, telling Basinger that he could feel secure about his flank because Kershaw's Division was in place beyond a thicket.

The sight of the battalion's unfurled Rebel flags must have attracted the attention of the Union artillerists who directed a rapid and accurate fire on Basinger's position. The major remembered the shelling and especially the gallantry of the Chaffin's Bluff troops.

Both battalions dressed up to their colors with as much steadiness and formality as if on parade...There was something surprising in their perfect steadiness and order. By this time many casualties having occurred, and the enemy's fire becoming remarkably accurate and severe, the troops were directed to lie down in their places. But not withstanding this precaution, many of Major Stiles' command were killed and wounded. The 18th Georgia suffered not at all, as they lay in a slight depression of the ground. I do not think I had a man hurt by artillery during the engagement."[16]

Basinger's Georgians, posted on the extreme right of Crutchfield's Brigade, had proudly joined the Confederate military as the Savannah Volunteer Guards in 1861 and were designated as the 18th Georgia Battalion. The two hundred fifty Guards had served in relative inaction along the Georgia-South Carolina coast until May 1864 when they received orders to report to Virginia. Exultantly, they had joined the Army of Northern Virginia, only to find themselves with scarce fuel, scant rations, and severe duty. Almost a year since arriving at the front, the surviving 85 Georgians remained staunch Confederates willing to follow Robert Lee to the last. Many of them did just that at Sailor's Creek.

"We were in an open field and knew that we would be attacked," recounted a young Confederate in Crutchfield's Brigade. "The enemy began the attack by shelling us from the woods, while with our hands and bayonets we threw up what fortification we could."[17]

The Yanks "opened an accurate and deadly fire, we having no guns with which to reply and thus disturb their aim," Stiles related. "My men were lying down and were ordered not to expose themselves...A good many had been wounded and several killed..."[18] Stiles was pacing behind his prone artillerymen when a 20-pound Parrott shell ripped the line in front of him, nearly cutting one of his men in half. Stiles wrote that the luckless Reb, a recruit named Blount, was hurled "bodily over my head, his arms hanging down and his hands almost slapping me in the face as they passed."[19]

Cowan's short-range and intense cannonade continued for about half an hour with the Rebels curled low and enduring the hellish pounding. Tucker's Naval Battalion suffered most from the bombardment.

"From our commanding position three or four batteries were brought up to bear on this exposed position of their line," Union Captain Harwood reported, "which was cut up terribly by our plunging fire of shell and case-shot."[20]

"We had no artillery and could not return their fire," wrote Virginian Thomas Blake, "and as they were beyond the effective range of our rifles, they could indulge in their artillery practice without let or hindrance."[21]

With Seymour's First and Second brigades already aligned to attack, General Wheaton's troops of Wright's Corps arrived on the field during the bombardment. Wheaton's lead unit was the Third Brigade of Colonel Oliver Edwards which had received orders about 3 p.m. to rush as quickly as possible. With some difficulty due to the changing combat conditions, Edwards aligned his regiments into a battle line on the left of the road. Wheaton's Second Brigade, under Colonel Joseph E. Hamblin, hastened forward to form on Edwards' left. Wheaton had only two of his three brigades with him. The brigade of Brevet Brigadier General William H. Penrose was somewhere to the rear, guarding the Federals' wagon train.

Wheaton's men had been marching and countermarching since dawn. A short time earlier, however, they had heard the growl of guns as they crossed Flat Creek and were revitalized by the prospect of battle.

Blue troopers along the road to Little Sailor's Creek reported no gray infantry in their front and that Reb cavalry was retreating, but the First Division still was spoiling for a fracas.

Wheaton related:

> I never saw troops press on more eagerly or show greater desire to meet the enemy. By the time the head of my column had reached the vicinity of Little Sailor's Creek we found the Third Division deployed...(along with some II Corps troops on the right.) Although the division had been pushing forward with the greatest haste, much of the march over plowed fields and rough ground, and the troops greatly fatigued, they double-quicked into position with the greatest spirit upon finding themselves in the presence of the enemy.[22]

The 31-year-old Wheaton was a pure Rhode Island Yankee but he had relatives well seated in Rebeldom's hierarchy. His father-in-law was Samuel Cooper, the ranking general officer and the adjutant and inspector general of the Confederate military. His mother-in-law was the sister of Senator James M. Mason of Virginia. Serving as a Confederate commissioner, Mason was one of the principals in the Mason-Slidell Affair, which almost resulted in war between the United States and England. Wheaton had seen action on the Indian frontier as a first lieutenant in the 1st U.S. Cavalry before the war. He was lieutenant colonel of the 2nd

**Union Major General
Frank Wheaton, Postwar**

U.S. Army Military History Institute

Rhode Island at First Bull Run and was commended for his service at Williamsburg in the Peninsula campaign. Promoted to brigadier general in November 1862, Wheaton assumed command of a VI Corps brigade and was in combat at Fredericksburg, Chancellorsville, the Wilderness, and Petersburg. In division command by late 1864, Wheaton was instrumental in stopping Jubal Early's thrust toward Washington and also had fought under Sheridan in the Shenandoah.[23]

Wright also sent word to his Second Division, under Brigadier General George W. Getty, to hurry forward in case they were needed and, at least to support the artillery. Getty's men had been the blue iron of Cedar Creek, holding their ground against Early's waves long enough so that Sheridan's ride saved the army. They also had been stalwarts in the battles for Petersburg.

About a third of a mile in their front, Wright's assembling brigades could see the main Confederate position of Ewell's Corps on the ridge behind Little Sailor's Creek and amid some trees. In the Rebel line, Kershaw's retiring rearguard was hustled into the defenses on the left of the road and Simms' men were moved further to the right so that

Fitzgerald's troops could take position on Simms' left and to the right of Basinger's 18th Georgia.

The Union infantry would have to charge down a slope of furrowed fields, cross the swampy bottom and the creek, and bog into the mire on the other bank. Then they would have to struggle up the hill to reach the Rebels. Some of Kershaw's snipers crawled in near the stream between the lines to contest any Federal initiative. Spring rains had swollen the creek over its banks, the flood adding to the muck on both sides. The stream itself was two to four feet deep.

Union Colonel Oliver Edwards

U.S. Army Military History Institute

After what must have seemed like infinity to the Johnnies, the Union shelling suddenly slackened about 6 p.m. Then the cheering lines of Federal infantry emerged from the cannon smoke, tramping across the fields toward the creek and the Confederate line. Sheridan conferred with General Wright about how the VI Corps should approach the enemy positions. "I saw him [Sheridan] make a gesture with his palm turned to the front that said unmistakably that whatever opposed us on the hill opposite was to be pushed away," a Federal officer recalled.[24]

The surviving Confederates on the ridge raised their heads to see the gore about them and the blue lines coming toward them. Major Stiles remembered the scene:

> In a few moments the artillery fire ceased and I had time to glance about me...I had seldom seen a fire more accurate, nor one that had been more deadly, in a single regiment, in so brief a time. The expression of the men's faces indicated clearly enough its effect upon them. They did not appear to be hopelessly demoralized, but they did look blanched and haggard and awe-struck.[25]

Essentially, the contest on this part of the field would pit Wheaton against Kershaw *and* Custis Lee with Seymour also attacking Lee and overlapping the latter's left flank. Looking from the Federal positions, Wheaton was on the left and Seymour on the right, nearest to the II Corps.

W. L. Timberlake, the Georgia infantryman, and his comrades saw the two Union VI Corps divisions forming for the all-out onslaught:

> In full view on the valley's eastern brink, the corps was massing into the fields at a double quick, the battle lines blooming with colors, growing longer and deeper at every moment, the batteries at a gallop coming into action front. We knew what it all meant. The sun was more than halfway down, the oak and pine woods behind them crowning the hill and laying evening's peaceful shadows on Ewell's line and on Sheridan's; its long afternoon beams glinted warmly and sparkled on the steel barrels of the shouldered arms of moving infantry.[26]

"We threw ourselves prone upon the ground, which was covered with a growth of broom sedge and a few small bushes, mostly pine," Captain Blake wrote. "Our line of battle was long drawn out, exceedingly thin. Here we rested, awaiting the attack, as the enemy had been following closely behind us."[27]

Wright was committing about seven thousand well-equipped and -supplied men, almost all veterans, to the assault. Ewell had substantially fewer defenders, perhaps less than half, most of whom were famished, physically spent and in rags. Against arguably the Army of the Potomac's finest troops, Old Baldy stood with Kershaw's fighters and a patchwork of sailors, marines, artillerymen and untried militia.

Kershaw had earlier received word by courier that Anderson was beginning his attack "and hoped to be successful if I could hold out a few moments longer. Sending him [Anderson] an encouraging reply, I continued to resist the enemy for some time, hoping to hear... that the way was open."[28] The South Carolinian had no way of knowing that Anderson's offensive already was ruined and that he soon would have thousands of enemy cavalrymen bearing down on his soldiers from behind.

CHAPTER 15

"THE GRANDEST CAVALRY CHARGE OF THE WAR"

At the edge of some woods Union General Wesley Merritt looked up across a sloping field to watch hundreds of Confederate soldiers toiling to build a long line of breastworks along the Rice's Station Road. All about him was the martial panorama of Sheridan's three cavalry divisions, some 10,000 men, forming to destroy this enemy. These Yankee troopers had blunted Dick Anderson's feeble breakout attack to reopen the road for the Rebels. Now, as Anderson's infantry entrenched about eight hundred yards away, Merritt was readying for a titanic cavalry charge against them to coincide with Wright's assault on Ewell.

The Confederates were knocking down fence rails, stacking rocks, chopping trees, and piling them together as a haphazard defensive work took shape along Anderson's position. The road cut provided some additional cover for these Southerners. "Here we hurriedly tore away an old worm fence, piling up the rails to make some protection against rifle balls," related Sergeant Johnston of the 7th Virginia.[1] Longstreet was somewhere ahead, but the road was blocked and there was a wasp nest of Yankees between these Rebs and any help from him.

Merritt, 30, had been a cavalryman since his graduation from West Point in 1860. One of eleven children, he was born in New York City but his father, an attorney, had moved the family to a farm in St. Clair County, Illinois, when Merritt was seven. The youngster seemed destined to follow his father in the legal profession but his acceptance to the Military Academy in 1855 greatly altered his life. Entering the army as a lieutenant of dragoons, Merritt served in Utah before becoming

aide-de-camp to Brigadier General Philip S. Cooke, commander of the
Army of the Potomac's cavalry, in 1862. He was on the staff of Major
General George Stoneman, Cooke's successor, in the same capacity. As
a captain, Merritt led a reserve cavalry brigade in Stoneman's botched
raid during the Chancellorsville campaign. Promoted brigadier general
in June 1863, he headed a brigade at Gettysburg and fought in all of the
major engagements leading to Sailor's Creek.[2]

Merritt proved to be just as stout a fighter as Custer, but without the
flamboyance. Unquestionably they were rivals, their contests for grandeur
boiling highest in the Shenandoah battles of 1864. After Cedar Creek, Merritt
questioned the number of enemy guns taken by Custer, stating that Custer
had exaggerated in his report. Merritt declared that Custer's accounts were
"without foundation in truth," but the matter was never resolved.[3]

Anderson's makeshift perimeter faced south and west and was less
than a mile southwest of the Little Sailor's Creek crossing tenuously
held by Ewell in the face of the oncoming VI Corps rush. The two
Confederate corps were virtually back to back. In effect, the commands
of Ewell and Anderson formed the sides of a "V" with an open-ended
apex facing slightly to the northeast near the Marshall farm.

Because of the suddenness of how this battle unfolded, however,
the Rebels had done nothing to plug this hole of several hundred yards
in their center. If the Federals had had a force of division strength or
more to push through this gap between Anderson and Ewell, attacking
west across the Marshall spread, the war quite possibly could have ended
this day at Sailor's Creek.

Anderson, 43, was another Southern general whose rise was due
more to attrition among Lee's more capable lieutenants than his individual leadership and battle prowess. While Lee described Anderson as
a fine officer, he harbored concerns about the Carolinian's supposed
bouts with the bottle based on their prewar frontier service together.
Born in October 1821 near present-day Sumter, South Carolina, Anderson was in the West Point class of 1842, which also included future
Confederate generals James Longstreet, Alexander P. Stewart, Earl Van
Dorn, and Daniel Harvey Hill.[4]

Brevetted first lieutenant in the Mexican War, Anderson resigned his captaincy in the 2nd U.S. Dragoons in March 1861 to enter Confederate service. Commissioned a major of Confederate infantry, Anderson was present for the Fort Sumter bombardment and on July 18, 1861, was promoted brigadier general in command at Charleston. Anderson was assigned to a brigade in Longstreet's Division on Virginia's peninsula in early 1862, fighting at Williamsburg, Seven Pines, and the Seven Days' battles before being named a major general on July 14.[5] This advancement did not come before Lee, in his low-key style, advised President Davis about Anderson's drinking. "I know little of General Anderson personally except as captain of dragoons," Lee wrote. "He was a favorite in his regiment and was considered a good officer. I am told he is now under a pledge of abstinence which I hope will protect him from the vice he fell into."[6]

Wounded at Antietam while directing his division, Anderson recovered in time to see action at Fredericksburg, Chancellorsville, and Gettysburg. When Longstreet was critically wounded in the throat and right shoulder by friendly fire from other Confederates at the Wilderness on May 6, 1864, Anderson was temporarily placed in command of Longstreet's First Corps. Based on Lee's orders but much to his credit, Anderson made a vigorous and successful overnight march on May 7–8 to beat an anticipated Union attack on the crossroads town of Spotsylvania Court House. Lee had guessed correctly and Anderson was able to hold his ground before fierce Federal assaults until he was reinforced.

After the Wilderness struggle, Colonel Moxley Sorrel, one of Longstreet's closest staff officers, wrote that Anderson "had shown commendable prudence and an intelligent comprehension of the work in hand. He was a very brave man, but of a rather inert, indolent manner for commanding troops in the field, and by no means pushing or aggressive...He seemed to leave the corps much to his staff..."[7] Sorrel also wrote of Anderson, "His courage was of the highest order...His capacity and intelligence excellent, but it was hard to get him to use them."[8]

Longstreet, having known Anderson since their cadet days on the Hudson, [and both from South Carolina] influenced Anderson to fight his hardest and most efficient, according to Sorrel. Anderson was appointed lieutenant general with temporary rank from May 31, 1864, and continued to lead the First Corps until Longstreet's return to duty in October. Anderson's Corps, also known as the Confederate Fourth Corps, was organized shortly afterward so that Anderson would have a command in keeping with his rank. It consisted of the divisions of Bushrod Johnson and Major General Robert F. Hoke and four artillery battalions.[9] Hoke's four brigades of about six thousand five hundred troops were transferred to North Carolina on December 20, leaving Anderson with only Johnson and a few scattered units to help man the Richmond-Petersburg trenches. Anderson's small corps put up a sturdy resistance to Federal thrusts at Hatcher's Run and along the White Oak Road on March 30–31, 1865, but was thrown into retreat the next day when the bluecoats grabbed Five Forks.

Anderson would make his fight on the Rice's Station Road with Bushrod Johnson's Division holding his right flank and Pickett on the left. Johnson would meet the enemy with Brigadier General Matthew W. Ransom's Brigade of North Carolinians facing west, perpendicular to the rest of the division. Ransom's command was linked on the left by the brigades of Brigadier Generals Young M. Moody, William H. Wallace, Henry Wise, George H. Steuart, William R. Terry, and Eppa Hunton.

Brigadier General Montgomery D. Corse's Virginians had the unenviable task of holding the extreme left of Anderson's position with nothing to his left but undefended woods and fields. Kershaw's equally exposed right flank was somewhere to the northeast, but Corse's men had no way of knowing this. Corse, 49, was a civilian soldier and banker from Alexandria. He had led Virginia militia in the Mexican War and in secession had fought the Federals from Blackburn's Ford to this desolate place. His red badge of courage had been won at Antietam where, as colonel of the 17th Virginia, he had been seriously wounded and lay on the battlefield behind Union lines before being rescued. As a brigadier under Pickett, his brigade had been on duty in Virginia at the time of Gettysburg. Undismayed in being left out of Lee's drive into

Pennsylvania, Corse and his men had fought as well as any of the Confederate units defeated at Five Forks.

Ransom and Moody's men were holding an intersection where a lane turned off the Rice's Station Road and led north toward the Appomattox. In actuality, Colonel Martin L. Stansel led Moody's Brigade since Moody had been ill since the Confederates left Petersburg.[10]

Poised against Anderson's Johnnies from left to right and aimed almost due north, the Union cavalry consisted of Crook, Devin, and Custer's divisions. In the same order, the brigades were commanded by Colonel J. Irvin Gregg, General Davies, Colonel Charles H. Smith, Colonel Charles L. Fitzhugh, Brigadier General Alfred Gibbs, Colonel Alexander C. M. Pennington, and Colonel Henry Capehart, with Colonel William Wells going in behind Capehart. After their bloody check in the battle's opening dance, Crook's cavalry had ridden further west, across country and parallel to the Confederates' march. Now Crook "found the enemy strongly posted on a high eminence, behind temporary breastworks."[11]

Crook ordered Gregg to dismount his Second Brigade and seize the road, which Gregg was able to accomplish, pushing Ransom's North Carolinians back among a section of their wagon train. Colonel Smith's Third Brigade, also on foot, ran forward to the right of Gregg while Davies' command, mounted, remained posted in a field in front of the Rebel works. The Federal horsemen tried several unsupported frontal attacks on Anderson's infantry, inflicting and taking casualties with little else to show for their initiative. Rebel C. F. James of Hunton's Brigade described the scene:

> An open field was in our immediate front, leading down to a long stretch of woods beyond. Over this field the cavalry charged time and again, now on horseback, now on foot; but each time they advanced, they recoiled before the well directed musketry fire that greeted them.[12]

In one of these assaults, a group of blue troopers spotted Pickett and two of his aides and rode for them. But a small squad of Confederate infantrymen recognized the general and "risking their own lives, rallied to our assistance and suddenly delivered a last volley into the faces of the pursuing horsemen, checking them but for a moment." Pickett wrote to his wife. "But in that one moment we, by the speed of our horses, made our escape. Ah, my darling, the sacrifice of this little band of men is like unto that which was made at Calvary."[13]

David Johnston of the 7th Virginia wrote of this episode:

> These reckless [Federal] troopers pushed up after the General until close enough to our men, who fired upon them, emptying every saddle. This incident is given to show...how desperate was this prolonged game of death.[14]

"In front of our regiment was a plain open field where the enemy had a good line of rifle-pits," reported Major Robbins of the 1st New Jersey in Davies' Brigade. He received orders from Davies to attack, and expected "the whole line would charge at the same time." It was not to be. "I moved on their line of works at once; the troops on my right, instead of charging the enemy, were being pushed back," Robbins wrote. "The regiment acted splendidly, but it was impossible for us to make any impression on the enemy's line." Indeed, at least some troopers on either side of Robbins had plunged forward and also were forced back due to the ferocity of the Confederate resistance. "The fire from the enemy was terrible," Robbins wrote. "Lieutenants [Thomas H.] Ford and [James S.] Metler and many of the men were wounded; horses were dropping fast."[15]

With no support, the New Jersey troopers wheeled and galloped to the safety of their original line. Robbins reported that he later discovered "the order for the regiment to charge was rather premature." In an April 14 report, Davies glossed over the misunderstanding, writing that the 1st New Jersey made a "very spirited and dashing reconnaissance of the position...which was of great assistance..."[16]

Once he had manhandled Ransom's Confederates and ensured that his troopers had a firm hold on their roadblock ahead of Anderson, George Crook felt certain his brigades were where they needed to be for the final great charge. "After these arrangements were made, a general assault was made," he reported.[17]

The cavalry thrust against Anderson and the VI Corps attack on Ewell were to be made at the same time. Robbins recounted that "a simultaneous charge was made by the VI Corps and the cavalry. This was probably the grandest cavalry charge of the war."[18]

Certainly this was one of the last colossal spectacles of the conflict. Sabers clanking, bugle calls ringing, and horses snorting and pawing, the thousands of Union cavalrymen reined into formations. These bluecoats were intent on a brutal ride to victory over the hell-bound butternuts arrayed up the hill. The cocking of muskets, excited shouts of officers and the oaths of sweating, dirty soldiers hauling freshly chopped tree trunks up to the roadside filled the air for Anderson's Confederates. Over their gun barrels they eyed the enemy massing in seemingly endless numbers across the field and along the tree line below. Squads of blue horsemen jangled here and there with colorful guidons fluttering among the glint of carbines and bridles.

Bugle shrills echoed up the hill, and the blue cavalry suddenly broke toward them as if energized by a single spark. The earth trembled from the punishment of infinitely pounding hooves. Along a front of about a mile the cavalry powered forward and the immensity of such a sight sent the first panicky chills up the spines of many of the Johnnies. But the wolfish "Rebel yell" shrieked from the gray line as the pageantry swirled toward a savage end. The Confederates fired a sporadic volley and a few of the Federals tumbled from their saddles while the mounts of others crashed to earth, launching their riders headfirst. Yet the incoming blue tide appeared unstoppable and the fire from their Spencers was like a swarm of deadly bees stinging the Confederates.

"We were behind the rails, close to the ground," recalled Sergeant Johnston of the 7th Virginia. "The enemy, armed with repeating rifles, when within seventy-five yards or so opened upon us, filling the air with balls, and coming at us. Every man who raised his head above the rails gave his life for the venture." Johnston saw a nearby captain peer over the defenses and fall backward, dead. "A sandy haired man of my regiment at my elbow met the same fate. He was from Orange County and never knew what hit him."[19]

Davies' Brigade charged in a line of the 24th New York, 10th New York, and the 1st New Jersey with the 1st Pennsylvania as support. "The charging regiments behaved admirably, keeping their line perfectly...," Davies recalled.[20]

Davies "made one of the finest charges of the war," wrote Crook, the blue horsemen and dismounted troopers barreling over the grim gray line, the Southerners resisting desperately.[21] Yipping Yank riders leapt their mounts over the Rebels' stacked logs and fence rails and the gray defenders began to break in confusion and panic. Horses thudded violently into Confederates unable to get out of their path, sending them flying.

The rapid fire of the Yanks' carbines and other small arms mingled with the crackle of the Southerners' muskets to create a hell of zipping lead and yelling soldiers. The agonized cries of wounded men and the higher-pitched screams of horses that had been hit crowned the battle chorus. A New York trooper noted the "Confederates fought heroically, but were out-matched by the determined Federals, who saw victory and home but a short distance ahead."[22]

Merritt had concentrated Custer's troopers to overlap or flank Pickett's position and the Red Ties stormed over the fields to add to their day's glories. Terry's troops massed with Hunton's Brigade to stifle this Yankee threat. Terry had been severely wounded in the Petersburg fighting and replaced by Colonel Titus V. Williams, who quickly sent word to Pickett that "the enemy was gathering in great numbers in the woods to turn his flank, and that he could not hold his position."[23]

During a brief lull in the fight, David Johnston of the 7th Virginia looked behind him to see enemy cavalry to the rear. One of the Yanks galloped to the regiment's color-bearer and at saber point seized the flag. "Such was the character and bravery of the men we had to fight," Johnston later wrote.[24]

About a dozen Union troopers dashed around the end of Corse's Brigade holding down the end of Anderson's left flank. These Federals then attacked, "charging down in the rear of our line, shooting and yelling like demons," James wrote. "It was their last charge." The Rebels quickly killed these cavalrymen, one of whom was "knocked from his horse" by a corpsman who crushed the Yank's head "with a stretcher."[25] But the Confederates in this sector, as elsewhere in Anderson's battle line, simply did not have the stamina, firepower, or numbers to cope with this Union juggernaut.

The 8th Virginia of Hunton's Brigade had been in its post only a short time when Pickett ordered a retreat. "During all these hours in which we had been holding the cavalry at bay, the Federal infantry and artillery had been coming up," wrote C. F. James. These Union units now occupied the hill, to the left and rear of Anderson's line, where Hunton and others of Pickett's command had been resting when the battle opened. "To remain where we were meant certain destruction or capture," James continued. "Our only hope was in retreat."[26]

Custer's Third, or "Virginia Brigade" of Colonel Henry Capehart, drove home its charge against Pickett's demoralized regiments. The brigade had earned its nickname from the rest of the Third Division because it was composed of two regiments and one partial regiment of West Virginia troopers. It also contained the 1st New York. One of the West Virginians later wrote that this was "one of the hardest cavalry fights of the war."[27]

Other Union cavalrymen watched in admiration as Capehart's command moved to the attack. One Third Division horseman related:

> As they came on in double line we could see them plainly...The fire as they neared the rebel line was terrific, opening gaps in their lines, but if a horse was shot & the rider unhurt he would jump up [and] take his place, firing as he went. "Never was such a charge seen," was the universal comment; as they emerged from the woods they began firing, keeping it up steadily, their gait was a slow walk...there was not another Brig[ade] in the Cav[alry] Corp[s] that had such trained horses, they kept in line almost as well as on parade, forward they move, never once checking, not even wavering, pouring their deadly fire as they go, at last when almost into the enemy's line, the word is given to charge & like a bullet...they are away into & over the enemy's breastwork with a rousing cheer in which we now join...for we had been spell bound with admiration at their coolness & bravery & splendid discipline.[28]

"The bugles sounded the charge, and forward up the face of that ridge swiftly swept that grand cavalry command with an irresistible

With the smoke of burning Confederate wagons in the background, General Custer and his cavalrymen prepare for another charge against the Rebels in this drawing by artist Alfred R. Waud.

force...," related one of the West Virginians. "The rebels rose and fired a terrific volley...but they fired too quickly and too high, and before they could reload most of our brigade had leaped the works and were among them...The scene at this time was fierce and wild, but the saber, revolver and Spencer carbine of the cavalry were too much for the bayonet, and the musket that could not be quickly loaded."[29]

George Custer's brother and aide-de-camp, Lieutenant Thomas W. Custer, was riding with Capehart's boys. Spurring ahead of the blue ranks, the lieutenant soon found himself battling a Confederate color-bearer in a death struggle. As they grappled, the Southerner fired a pistol at Custer's face from only a few inches away. The shot sent a ball slicing through Custer's cheek and exiting behind his ear. His face spattered with blood and powder, Custer was hurled backward by the impact but retained his seat in the saddle. Swaying momentarily, Custer managed to draw his revolver and kill his foe with a single shot. As the Rebel slumped from his horse, Custer seized the banner, belonging to the 2nd Virginia Reserves, and, waving it in triumph, galloped back to his lines.[30]

Despite his wound, Tom Custer was eager to tell his older brother about his latest exploit, especially since he had captured another Confederate flag three days earlier in a running fight with Rebel cavalry at Namozine Church.[31] Riding to the rear with his new trophy, the lieutenant continued to wave the enemy banner, prompting a New Jersey officer to shout at him: "For God's sake, Tom, furl that flag or they'll shoot you."

"Armstrong, the damned rebels have shot me, but I've got their flag," Tom called to his brother. The general was relieved that his sibling was alive, although grievously wounded, it appeared. George Custer's color-bearer had been killed a short time earlier by a bullet that ripped through the soldier's face and neck. Tom's injury looked to be similar and the boy general was somewhat rattled when he saw his brother coming toward him, blood reddening his head and tunic.[32]

Custer ordered Tom to steer to the rear and have his wounds treated. In his combat fever, the lieutenant ignored the general and asked for someone to take his flag while he returned to battle. Infuriated, Custer shouted for Tom to be arrested and taken to a field hospital.

Private Daniel A. Woods, of the 1st West Virginia's Company K, fought his way forward and captured the flag of a Florida infantry regiment. In the process, he earned a Medal of Honor.[33]

Sergeant Francis Marion Cunningham of the 1st West Virginia rode in the climatic charge on the back of a "fine, fleet-footed" but badly wounded mule. Although named for the South Carolinian Francis Marion, the patriot "Swamp Fox" of the American Revolution, Cunningham was a Union man sure, serving his second enlistment in the regiment's Company H.[34]

"During the afternoon we had made a number of charges, some of which were repulsed, with severe loss of men and horses," he wrote in a postwar account. "I had two horses killed under me." Finding the mule, Cunningham galloped back into the fray leading only three men, all who remained available from his company. In moments, Cunningham and his troopers were in the faces of a swarm of gray infantry posted behind a fence. "The mule jumped the fence, carrying me in among the Rebels where they were pretty thick," Cunningham recalled. "I had some lively work on hand, and a good deal of trouble with about three of the Rebel color guard before I got within striking distance of the colors of the 12th Virginia Infantry. I then had a lively set-to with the color bearer. The poor fellow fought bravely for his colors but the mule and I were too much for him."[35] Like Private Woods, Cunningham's capture of the enemy flag garnered him a Medal of Honor.

Anderson's defensive perimeter dissolved in a mass of disheart-ened and overmatched Confederates streaming to the rear, some run-ning in panic while others retreated in clots of fighters, firing at the Yankee horsemen who rumbled all about them. One of Davies' New Yorkers remembered how the Southerners "lost all formation and went across the country scattering like children just out from school, our boys chasing up and gathering them in."[36]

Bands of gray infantry did not surrender their positions so easily, but it was a hopeless effort. Virginian David Johnston recalled:

In a moment began an indiscriminate fight with clubbed muskets, flagstaffs, pistols and sabers. In a few moments all was over. We had met the enemy and we were theirs. This final struggle was most tragic. We were now marched out and surrounded by a cor-don of cavalry.[37]

"The enemy was driven from his breast-works in great confusion," General Custer wrote in his battle report. "Thousands of his men were captured on the spot, others surrendered after a short pursuit."[38]

Some of the Federals risked their lives by riding after the Rebels and calling for them to give up. These Yank horsemen soon found themselves in the rear echelon of Ewell's Corps, which was heavily engaged against Wright. Artillery Captain Thomas Blake of the 10th Virginia was taking aim at Federal infantry on the slopes west of Little Sailor's Creek when he was startled by one of Custer's troopers who came in from behind him:

> A young cavalry officer rode in among us and begged us to surrender, telling us that we were entirely surrounded and that further resistance would be useless. It was so gallant an act that no one attempted to molest him.[39]

During this mammoth cavalry assault, Union Lieutenant William Hughes, leading Robbins' second battalion, was grazed in the head and toppled from his saddle. The wound proved minor, but Hughes still had to make his way to the rear to receive medical treatment. A sight in the nearby woods suddenly elated him. The Confederates had tried to hide two cannon in the forest because they had been unable to pull them away during the Federal attack. Hughes collected some dismounted troopers and a mule team to haul off his battle prizes. Two other light field pieces were captured in Robbins' charge. Davies reported a booty of seven hundred fifty prisoners, two guns and two flags. Some three hundred captured Rebs were "inadvertently turned over to another command by the officer in charge," Davies added.[40]

Terry's Brigade, along with Hunton's 8th Virginia, headed toward the rear in good order. Behind them, the rest of Hunton's regiments and the brigades of Corse, Steuart, Wise, Wallace, and Moody were melting away before the enemy tidal wave. Emerging from a lane in the woods, C. F. James caught sight of General Pickett and his staff riding out of the trees. To James' left was a throng of Union cavalry gathered about some burning wagons. Some seven hundred yards to their front, the shaken Confederates spied "a large and dense woods, extending we knew not how far, offering us the safest, if not the only refuge," James said.[41] They would have to cross an open field to get there, however.

At the quick-step, Terry's men headed toward the woods. Behind them, they heard the clatter of gunfire, indicating that some units of Hunton's and Corse's commands still were holding out. James recalled:

> Our situation was extremely critical. A large body of victorious cavalry was but a short distance behind us, and would soon be after us...But as long as we kept in good order and showed no signs of panic or flight, they did nothing but cheer and fire at long range.[42]

An officer on foot led the Rebs across the open ground toward the tree line. "The question which was uppermost on every man's mind was, 'Can we reach yonder woods before the cavalry head us off?'" James remembered. Fate turned on short notice. A servant brought the Confederate officer, whom James misidentified as Terry, his horse and the officer quickly mounted. Terry's Brigade and the 8th Virginia, which was in the lead, were about halfway across the field at the time. Based on James' account, the officer, who in all likelihood was Colonel Williams, galloped to join Pickett, "leaving our regiment and his own men under the command of his regimental officers."[43]

Almost immediately, Terry's soldiers became demoralized. They crowded in behind the 8th Virginia eventually breaking ranks as panic seized them. Emboldened by this scene of turmoil, the Union cavalry attacked. With the enemy horsemen bearing down on them, the Rebels broke into a run to reach the woods. The head of the column streamed into the forest before the cavalry hit, but the rear elements were not as lucky. Yells, screams, carbine and revolver fire echoed in the forest as the 8th Virginia ran through the underbrush. Behind them, many of Terry's men had been engulfed by a wave of blue troopers, fighting, giving up, or dying. A number of the Rebs smashed their muskets rather than have them fall into enemy hands. Captain Archer Campbell of the 18th Virginia was killed while trying to surrender.

The 8th Virginia's commander, Major William N. Berkeley, guided the regiment about one hundred yards into the woods before he stopped, in pain and gasping for air. Berkeley could go no further. An ankle wound at Gettysburg still slowed him, limiting his endurance to march on foot. He had sent his horse to the rear when the battle began. "Not being able to make a good run, his safety was in surrender," James said of Berkeley. "He released us all from his authority, saying that if we did not wish to surrender we could go. There was an immediate scattering of the head of the regiment..."[44]

Confederate General Corse found himself facing a Yankee trooper who chanced upon him and two staff officers in the midst of the climactic Union charge. Private W. T. Bateman of the 1st New Jersey Cavalry was among the personal escort for General Crook. When Crook allowed these men into the fray, Bateman raced into a thicket and was surprised when he "came across the rebels," the general reported.[45] "He [Bateman] saw three of them mounted, in a little ravine, and ordered them to surrender. General Corse threw up a white handkerchief and came up toward him. He then told his aide to give up his pistol, which was in possession of one of them."[46] Bateman then herded Corse and the other officers to the rear and turned them over to the division provost marshal.

Eppa Hunton, the Southern brigadier, also was among those netted by Merritt's troopers. The 42-year-old Virginian had been a prominent commonwealth attorney and an ardent secessionist in 1861. Dogged by bad health, he nevertheless led the 8th Virginia Infantry, as its colonel, through the Gettysburg campaign in which he was wounded. Promoted to brigadier general in August 1863, he led his brigade to Sailor's Creek. Yank cavalrymen accompanied Hunton away from the battlefield. But Hunton's chief adversary in the coming months of his captivity would ironically be another who wore the stars of a Confederate general at Sailor's Creek.

**Confederate Brigadier General
Montgomery D. Corse**

Author's Collection

**Confederate Brigadier General
Eppa Hunton**

Author's Collection

CHAPTER 16
"A TIGER AT BAY"

The Union VI Corps battle lines stretched beyond Dick Ewell's position in both directions and Cowan's artillery resumed a shielding barrage of canister for the attackers. "A concentrated artillery fire was directed upon the enemy's center," General Keifer reported, "under cover of which the troops advanced..."[1]

"After a thorough shelling, to which we had no artillery to reply and no cover except a scanty fringe of small timber, the Union infantry in heavy column advanced on our thin line," related J. S. McNeily, one of Kershaw's veterans.[2] The Federals assailing Ewell were hot and tired from their arduous, 18-mile march to catch up with the graybellies, but the thrill of coming action galvanized them.

Wheaton's two brigades—Edwards' and Hamblin's—trudged forward in a single battle line on either side of the road. On Edwards' right was Truex's Brigade of Seymour's Division, which already had tasted combat and was returning for another round. Truex and Edwards, therefore, formed the bind between the two Federal divisions.

The lay of the land was such that Seymour's Division had to cover more ground than Wheaton to reach the creek. And Wheaton's line charged before Seymour, meaning that the infantry assault would be a piecemeal affair not performed in unison.

"I moved...without waiting for the Third Division," Edwards noted in his battle report.[3] The 6th Maryland, which also had been bloodied earlier, formed up behind Wheaton. "We then formed for the grand charge in rear of the First Division," wrote the Marylanders'

Lieutenant Colonel Joseph C. Hill. "The command forward was given, and we plunged into the swamp, driving the enemy before us."[4]

"We commenced one of the finest charges in which it was ever our lot to participate," wrote Colonel Andrew N. McDonald of the 106th New York in Truex's Brigade. McDonald's boys trod "gallantly and steadily forward, forgetting all the pains of blistered feet and cramped and stiffened limbs in the excitement of the coming contest."[5] "Our movement toward the creek was in plain view and down a perfectly cleared field for more than one-quarter of a mile," Wheaton remembered.[6]

Some of the Confederates still were digging in when they saw the Union infantry poised before them. "The enemy began the attack by shelling us from the woods, while with our hands and bayonets we threw up what fortifications we could, and awaited the charge," recounted one of Ewell's men. "In a little while a large body of infantry emerged from the woods and came right toward us at double quick."[7]

The 82nd Pennsylvania of Colonel Isaac Bassett in Edwards' ranks stumbled into the "deep, difficult swamp and almost impenetrable under-growth and forest" taking casualties as they stormed toward the Rebel defenses.[8]

Lieutenant Colonel Elisha Hunt Rhodes of the 2nd Rhode Island Infantry in Edwards' Brigade was committing a number of raw troops to their baptism by fire in this charge. Included in these rookies was Lieutenant George B. Peck in the newly recruited Company G. Peck related:

> We were on the crest of a hill, where we halted for some minutes.
> A second glance towards the left revealed a farmhouse [Hillsman's]
> in the distance. I noted its bearings, feeling sure a field hospital
> would speedily be established there, and ere long I might need to
> visit it.[9]

Rhodes began the day leading about four hundred men, but almost half of them had been left along the route as guard details at points the Federals considered important. The Rhode Islanders emerged from a wood and heard firing off to their right and front. Rhodes quickly noticed a nearby gathering of officers, including Sheridan, Wright, Wheaton, and Edwards. Rhodes recalled the encounter:

I rode up and saluted and was told that in our front was a small stream called Sailor's Creek and that on the opposite side Gen. Ewell's Rebel Corps was guarding Lee's wagon train, and that our Cavalry had cut them off and we were to attack.[10]

His regiment had supposed to be used in a support role, but soon found itself formed on the left of the 49th Pennsylvania as the Union line expanded around the Rebels' flanks. As Rhodes galloped back to his regiment, he was met by one of his line officers, Captain Charles W. Gleason. "Colonel, are we to fight again?" Gleason asked. Rhodes answered that they were. And he never forgot Gleason's reply. "Well," said he, "this will be the last battle if we win, and then you and I can go home. God bless you Colonel." I replied: "God bless you, Captain. I hope to meet you after the battle."[11]

Also in Edwards' Brigade was the 37th Massachusetts of Captain Archibald Hopkins, which had been posted behind the 2nd Rhode Island and moved to the left of that unit when the order to advance was given. The 5th Wisconsin of Colonel Thomas S. Allen was also in Wheaton's onslaught. "I pushed ahead...down the hill and across the swamp into which the men plunged recklessly, some of them up to their arm-pits," Allen recalled.[12]

Fingers curled around triggers, the Confederates of Kershaw and Custis Lee squinted at their targets and waited until the Yankees were in range. They had orders not to open on the enemy until told to do so. "Their infantry then appeared in solid formation, division front, and moved steadily forward," recounted Captain Thomas Blake of Crutchfield's Brigade. "They reached the creek which we had so recently crossed, waded through as we had done, dressed up their line, and continued their advance toward the rising ground where our men lay."[13]

As the long blue ranks neared the creek, the Southern skirmishers flamed into action, sending a sleet of bullets into the Union formations. Charging toward the quagmire, Wheaton's infantry were greeted by fierce musket fire from the Confederates as they reached the fringe of the swamp. The Northerners waded into the muck and reached the stream as Rebel bullets zipped into the water or tore into blue uniforms.

"At the command 'Forward,' we proceeded steadily (notwithstanding a severe fire of musketry, by which I sustained some loss) across the open ground until we arrived at the creek, where some little delay took place, it being difficult to cross in some parts," observed Lieutenant Colonel John Harper of the 95th Pennsylvania in Hamblin's Brigade.[14] General Wheaton remembered:

> Reaching the creek, instead of finding it like most of the streams we had passed that day, it was discovered to be a swamp, varying in width from 40 to 100 yards, and traversed by several streams, the water in many places above the shoulders of the troops. I was ordered to attack, and none but good troops, knowing that there was no second line behind them, would so gallantly have dashed into and crossed this difficult swamp and stream, while from the moment they reached its edge they were under the enemy's severe musketry fire.[15]

The 2nd Rhode Island drove on through the fields and underbrush, taking casualties. Colonel Rhodes dismounted and sent his horse to the rear, preferring to lead his men on foot. Rhodes related:

> Arriving at the creek we became exposed to the enemy's fire, but pushed on through the swamp, which in many places was so deep as to destroy the ammunition of my men. The Rebels opened upon us as soon as we reached the river, but we jumped in with the water up to our waists and soon reached the opposite side.[16]

"The colonel's clear voice sounded 'ATTENTION!'...Descending the hill, 'Prepare to cross a marsh!' was passed along the line," related Lieutenant Peck of the 2nd Rhode Island.[17] Allen's 5th Wisconsin also was rocked by the storm of musketry, men slumping into the ooze. With their blood reddening the mud and weeds, these troops toiled to the opposite side of the branch where they reformed their line. Allen threw out two companies as skirmishers and they ran toward the Rebel positions. Sixteen of them fell to gray marksmen perched on their left flank.

A dense hedge beside the creek stymied some of the Rhode Islanders. Peck's company filtered on either side of the obstruction while the lieutenant tried to fight through the greenery. Spreading it apart with his hands, he beheld "a stream of muddy water a dozen feet wide. Visions of New England brooks at once rose before me." Peck yelled to his men to follow him as he struggled through the bushes and vines and leaped toward the creek, expecting to land in knee-deep water. He sank over his sword belt in the branch and his boots were sucked into the mud: "Thoroughly startled at the idea that perchance I had jumped into a Virginia quicksand, I seized hold of the farther bank and held on tightly."[18]

Emerging on the opposite bank, some of Wheaton's officers began to realign their units at the base of the hill, the creek crossing and enemy fire having caused some disarray among the excited troops. Edwards' Brigade, however, was reassembling in an area where the hill had only a slight slope, meaning that they were still targets for butternut riflemen. The Confederates sent a hurricane of bullets into the center of Edwards' ranks and an enfilading fire that was just as heavy.

With Edwards' men under bloody duress, Hamblin's Brigade had to relieve the pressure. The best way to do this was to continue the assault. Hamblin "was ordered to charge at once up the steep hills and into the enemy's line in the woods," Wheaton reported. "This movement was brilliantly executed under a galling fire..."[19] Rather than remain sitting ducks, Edwards' Yanks also stormed up the slope toward the Southerners in their front.

"After crossing...the line was reformed, and advanced to the foot of the hill upon which the enemy was posted," recounted Colonel Harper of the 95th Pennsylvania in Hamblin's Brigade. "Here we halted, by order, for a short time, during which the line was put in good shape for the charge. Very soon the order to advance was given..."[20]

Like the rest of the Union assault force, the 37th Massachusetts of Captain Hopkins in Edwards' Brigade had plowed through the swamp and across the creek. At the base of the hill, the men had reformed before plunging up the slope. By now all of Seymour's Division was across the creek and attacking up the smoky ridge as well.

Despite the masses of enemy troops having established a foothold on the western bank, the Rebels of Custis Lee and Kershaw continued to deluge them with intense musket fire. "I had a splendid blue-barreled Enfield and plenty of the best English ammunition," recalled the Rebel

Private Timberlake. "I saw and did some good shooting that evening. I was slapped on the back and complimented by an officer..."[21]

Heading up the hill the Federal infantry encountered another problem. While the center of their lines advanced up a fairly open slope, denser undergrowth and rougher terrain slowed their flanks. Thus the Union center, composed of Edwards' troops, made speedier progress and soon found themselves well ahead of their comrades in confronting the dug-in Confederates.

A Federal artillery round that fell some 30 yards short of their line unnerved Peck's Rhode Island company. Peck wrote:

> It was amusing to see the men, naturally disturbed and irritated, shake their fists and hurl maledictions at the blunderers. A second shot just cleared our heads, but the third struck half way up the hill on our front, and the fourth reached the enemy's lines. At the same time the bullets began to fall as hailstones around us, and twigs from the hedge just passed covered the ground like snow-flakes....[22]

As he moved forward Peck watched other Yanks fighting up the slope:

> Every imaginable position was assumed, from the half erect to an apparent attempt to tunnel the hillside... Suddenly, "Whit!" sped a ball by my right ear; involuntarily I imitated those I had been ridiculing, and thereafter stooped about two inches lower. All this time, while the leaden missiles were as thick as mosquitoes in early autumn, I saw not a grayback, nor yet a rifle flash.[23]

Hopkins' New Englanders "reserved their fire with noteworthy coolness until we were within a few rods of the enemy, who were formed in two lines of battle on the crest of the hill," the captain noted. Pressing the attack, the bluecoats were cheered by one of their sergeants who, lying severely wounded under a tree, urged them on. The Yanks then "opened with rapid volleys, advancing all the while with a yell. The enemy, unable to stand our fire, gave back slowly at first, and soon disappeared from our front, leaving several prisoners and a caisson in our hands," Hopkins wrote.[24]

Kershaw, meanwhile, prepared to repulse the enemy's renewed charge. His men, as well as Custis Lee's units, were now ordered to hold their fire until the blue ranks got closer. For a few minutes, this sector of the battlefield was deathly quiet [despite heavy firing from other quarters] as the Rebels bit into cartridges and the sounds of ramrods rattled in musket barrels.

"General Kershaw gave strict orders to hold fire until the enemy was within 50 yards and to aim low," wrote Captain Charles Stevens Dwight of his staff.[25] As the Northerners edged up the final few yards, everything was "still as the grave," Georgia Major Stiles recalled.[26]

The 2nd Rhode Island fired and dropped three times to reload as they climbed the hill toward Custis Lee's men. "Now, close on them! Go for them!" officers shouted as the Rhode Islanders reached the crest.[27] Other Federal infantrymen had instructions to hold fire until within two hundred yards of the Rebels. As they came on, some of the bluecoats fluttered white handkerchiefs at the Southerners as a sign that they should surrender.

Ewell's Johnnies replied with lead. The Confederates suddenly blasted away, pouring a withering but uncoordinated hurricane of bullets into the oncoming blue waves. Among the Rebs, Major Stiles remembered that his raw troops performed coolly as the Union battle lines closed with them at a walk:

> *Ready!* To my great relief, the men rose, all together, like a piece of mechanism, kneeling on their right knees and their faces set with an expression that meant—everything. *Aim!* The musket barrels fell to an almost perfect horizontal line leveled about the knees of the advancing front line. *Fire!* The earth appeared to have swallowed up the first line of the Federal force in our front. There was a rattling supplement to the volley and the second line wavered and broke.[28]

Recalled R. S. Rock of Crutchfield's staff:

> We reserved our fire until they were about forty yards from us, and there opening on them they soon turned and fled. Soon it seemed that Grant's whole army was coming from the woods.[29]

"As soon as our skirmishers had retired, they (the enemy) were received with a general discharge from our whole line, which speedily threw their first line into confusion, killing and wounding considerable numbers," Major Basinger wrote.[30]

The Rebels' point-blank, deadly reception caved in a section of Wheaton's line, primarily the 2nd Rhode Island and the 49th Pennsylvania, which staggered and gave way. These troops had been among those of Edwards' Brigade that had moved up the hill ahead of the rest of the blue regiments. Suddenly, the center of Wright's assault was in jeopardy. "For a short time there was a temporary reverse, owing to a portion of the line of the First Division breaking," a Maryland officer noted.[31]

"The attack by the infantry was not executed exactly as I had directed, and a portion of our line in the open ground was broken by the terrible fire of the enemy...," recounted Sheridan in his battle report.[32]

Elisha Rhodes had reorganized his green regiment after the stream ford and was advancing "up a slight hill towards a piece of wood, the Rebels retreating from our front" when hell came to earth. Some 50 paces from the woods, the Yanks were surprised when "a Rebel officer stepped out and shouted: 'Rise up, fire!' A long line of Rebels fired right into our faces and then charged through our line...getting between us and the river," Rhodes related.[33] The lanky Captain Gleason lurched over dead when a Minié smacked into his head and First Lieutenant William H. Perry also was killed. "Poor Gleason...he was a gallant fellow, and I thought the world of him," Rhodes wrote later.[34] The regiment's Rhode Island flag was captured and Rhodes' line disintegrated, the men scrambling back to the swamp and creek.

The Confederate fire also devastated the 49th Pennsylvania of Lieutenant Colonel Baynton J. Hickman. "After getting within twenty yards of the woods the enemy got upon our left flank and had then a fire in front and flank, compelling us to fall back," Hickman reported, his only description of the setback.[35] Colonel Edwards, the brigade commander, wrote that Hickman, like the 2nd Rhode Island, "was also thrown into disorder, but soon rallied."[36]

The Rebel volley was so lethally effective that the Chaffin's Bluff Battalion, sensing confusion and disarray among the advancing Federals, charged without orders, fixing bayonets as they ran down the slope. Two other units of Crutchfield's Brigade, the 10th and 19th Virginia heavy artillerymen, joined in the hodgepodge assault, racing downhill. "The big column hesitated and then with a Rebel Yell the thin line charged them," Captain Dwight recalled.[37] Major Stiles was swept up in the impromptu charge:

> The revulsion was too sudden. On the instant every man in my battalion sprang to his feet and, without orders, they rushed, bare-headed and with unloaded muskets, down the slope after the retreating Federals. I tried to stop them, but in vain, although I actually got ahead of a good many of them. They simply bore me on with the flood.[38]

"When they had advanced to within thirty or forty paces of our line, the order was given to charge," recounted Captain Tom Blake of the 10th Virginia artillery. "In a moment we were all on our feet, yelling like demons and rushing at them."[39] These Virginians apparently believed they were acting alone, the broken nature of Ewell's line obscuring their view of other Rebels as they surged forward in this spur of the moment attack. A number of the Confederates fixed mud-caked bayonets as they charged, having minutes earlier used them to dig in.

"Such was the eagerness of Major Stiles' men, that upon perceiving the enemy's hesitation, they sprang up from their recumbent attitude and rushed upon them...," Major Basinger remembered.[40]

Blake was shocked that the Federals did not immediately annihilate the relatively few Confederates in this desperate push. "It has always been a mystery to me why they did not then and there wipe our little band from the face of the earth," he wrote. "It may have been that the very audacity of our charge bewildered and demoralized them."[41]

Stiles encountered his battalion color-bearer moments before an artillery round killed the soldier. The major reached for the flag, but the dead man's brother grabbed the staff. This Rebel was fatally shot through the head seconds later. Another member of the color guard snatched the banner and was dropped by enemy fire. Stiles found himself holding the blood-spattered flag with dead and wounded Confederates twisted on the ground around him and bullets whizzing. "I did not see why I should continue to make a target of myself," he wrote. "I therefore jammed the color staff down through a thick bush, which supported it in an upright position, and turned my attention to my battalion..."[42]

Cannoneers of the 10th Virginia endured a volley from Wheaton's men as the Yanks tumbled back toward the creek. "We followed them to the edge of the stream, into which they plunged, and kept up a merciless fire on them at short range as they crossed," Thomas Blake recounted.[43]

"The enemy, seeing little chance of escape, fought like a tiger at bay, but both Seymour and Wheaton pressed him vigorously...," Sheridan related, but "Seymour's left [actually Wheaton's right] was checked" near the road. "Here, the Confederates burst back on us in a counter-charge, surging down almost to the creek..."[44]

Rhode Islander Lieutenant Peck had been close to the summit when he was caught up in the retreat. Grudgingly, he also descended the hill, "As I did not care to present any Confederate with either sword, watch, or revolver, and could offer but slight resistance, when single-handed..." Peck was in exodus when he "noticed thirty or forty 'secesh' on a projecting knoll, enjoying a comfortable little target practice."[45]

A Union officer watching the action from near the Hillsman house was as shocked as any of the other Federals in seeing the blue infantry-men running back toward the creek. He wrote:

> Suddenly the brave Union line breaks into scattered fragments, which flow tumultuously down the hill before an unbroken gray line which charges furiously upon and after them...The rebel yell rises exultant from their swift pursuing line. There is nothing between it and the artillery but the fugitives...[46]

While Wheaton's men were trying to ward off the Rebel counterthrust, Seymour's Division was attacking after suffering heavy fire as it trudged through the creek and swamp in front of Custis Lee's defenses. Truex's Yanks plunged "through mud and water to their hips, and under a severe fire from the enemy by which many lives were lost."[47]

"The stream in front of us was edged with marsh waist deep; through this the command handsomely advanced" even as the Union

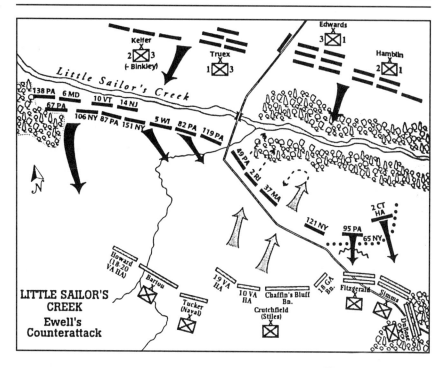

Keller
2 ⊠ 3
(+ Binkley)

Truex
1 ⊠ 3

Edwards
3 ⊠ 1

Hamblin
2 ⊠ 1

Little Sailor's Creek

138 PA 6 MD
67 PA
10 VT 14 NJ
106 NY 87 PA 151 NY
5 WI 82 PA 119 PA

N

49 PA
2 RI
37 MA

121 NY
95 PA

2 CT
HA
65 NY

Howard
(18,20
VA HA)

Barton

19 VA
HA

10 VA
HA

Chaffin's Bluff
Bn.

18 GA
Bn.

Fitzgerald

Simms

Tucker
(Naval)

Crutchfield
(Stiles)

DuBose

**LITTLE SAILOR'S
CREEK**

**Ewell's
Counterattack**

The Appomattox Campaign

artillery continued its deadly work, General Seymour observed.[48] A number of Federals, holding their rifles and cartridge boxes high, fell on both sides of the creek and in the water. McDonald's 106th New York absorbed a galling fire and 12 men were hit and crumpled either on the spongy banks or in the creek. Others sank up to their hips in the mire. The New Yorkers then moved rapidly to the right and added their weight to the pressure being exerted on Custis Lee's extreme left flank. Reforming his line, Truex "advanced to the crest of the hill, driving the enemy before them."[49]

The 121st New York of Colonel Egbert Olcott in Hamblin's Brigade was nearing the Rebel line and had bagged a number of prisoners when the 49th Pennsylvania and the 2nd Rhode Island collapsed to their right. Thus left exposed, the New Yorkers and Hopkins' Massachusetts boys quickly found themselves threatened in the flank by Crutchfield's Rebels. Olcott quickly changed his front, forming a battle line on the road. His maneuver under heavy fire later drew Hamblin's praise and a recommendation for promotion. But the battle at hand occupied all present.

Further down the road near the creek a portion of the 37th Massachusetts was struggling to hold its ground. These veterans under Captain Hopkins had been startled after their initial success in crossing the creek. As his soldiers exulted over their captures, Hopkins had been surprised to see that he was unsupported on either flank, this due to the effect of the Southerners' telling volley and the disorganization accompanying the Union attack up the hillside.

Hopkins was taking measures to connect with Hamblin's Brigade when movement in the distance caught his eye. "I noticed what seemed to be a heavy column of the enemy moving by the flank around our left," he wrote. Hopkins ran to the threatened part of his line and, "with a few well directed volleys," drove the Rebels "out of sight again."[50]

These Federals were not yet out of harm's way. The Confederates, some of Crutchfield's men, had used a ravine to scramble almost totally out of sight of Hopkins' soldiers and menace his rear. "We had barely time to face about when they charged us...," the captain recalled, "and a desperate hand-to-hand fight with swords, pistols, and bayonets ensued." But strength of numbers and the firepower of the Federals' Spencers forced the Southerners to recoil. "We did not give them an inch of ground and they were finally forced back into the ravine," Hopkins wrote.[51]

Amid this torrid action on the hillside, Colonel Crutchfield was killed, although first-person accounts vary about the circumstances. Some state that he either led the charge of his command or was caught up in its momentum. Others detail how he had ridden to find Custis Lee and receive orders. Again there are conflicting stories, a few depicting how he never made it to Lee—falling under heavy fire with a fatal bullet wound to the head.

In an April 25 report, Custis Lee stated that Crutchfield "was killed after gallantly leading a successful charge against the enemy."[52] Still more records relate how Crutchfield reached Ewell and Kershaw and pleaded that he had lost most of his guns due to the muddy roads, marauding cavalry or teams unable to pull their loads. Captain Dwight of Kershaw's staff described the latter scenario in which Crutchfield was conferring with the generals when he died. The gathering of officers attracted the attention of enemy artillerists who opened fire. Based on Dwight's account, Kershaw told the men to scatter, but Crutchfield was hit in the right thigh by a shell that knifed through his horse and left leg before exploding a short distance beyond. Crutchfield and his mount collapsed in a heap as other Rebels rushed to his aid. Dwight wrote that Crutchfield's dying words were "Take my watch and letters for my wife. Tell her how I died at the front."[53]

**Confederate Colonel
Stapleton Crutchfield**

Virginia Military Institute

R. S. Rock, one of Crutchfield's orderlies, gave his version of how the Virginian fell:

> We fought hand to hand in that fearful and unequal struggle, and just before the white flag was hoisted, we saw our beloved Col. Shot and mortally wounded, and there were few of us to surrender.[54]

Major Basinger, who wrote a detailed report about the brigade's battle conduct for Custis Lee after the war, did not mention Crutchfield's death.

The exultant Confederates who had charged down to the creek were now being cut down by a concentration of Federal infantry and cannon fire. Thomas Blake saw the color sergeant of the 10th Virginia artillery slump with a fatal gunshot and the battalion adjutant, Lieutenant Sam Wilson, collapse with a shattered leg. Blake dashed to grab the flag and was decked by a spent ball that smacked him in the shoulder.[55]

A Yank officer wounded in the side when the Johnnies charged, hobbled back across the creek and had to bob away from the maws of Union guns roaring at the Rebels. With some bitterness about the setback, he later described how he had "stepped not half a dozen paces when a shell shrieked by, taking my benedictions to friends across the flood."[56]

Major Stiles made his way back up the hill and found Custis Lee, explaining that he had not ordered an attack and that he would bring his men back to the line on the hilltop where they had the best cover from enemy fire. According to Stiles, Lee doubted that he could reform his battalion, but the major stumbled back down the slope to give it a try. With some difficulty, Basinger, Stiles, and other officers halted the eager Rebs and restored their line, artillery ripping them as they retreated up the hill. Stiles led some of his men through a gully to reach their previous position and avoid the Union shelling.

Captain Blake organized his surviving cannoneers and ascended the slope, littered with dead or wounded from both sides. He recalled the sight of one slain young Rebel in particular:

> In going back over the ground I came across the body of a handsome young fellow, only about seventeen years old, a new recruit, who had been with my company but a few weeks. He had fallen with his face to the foe.[57]

As they had since the early stages of the battle, Captain Cowan's blue gunners wrecked these Confederates. With the Southerners scurrying back to their works were some Federals who had been captured in the counterattack. Escaping blue and gray both sought safety from the incoming canister.

A Pennsylvania rifleman was among prisoners who dropped into a trench within the Confederate position. "We were scarcely down when the rebels came tumbling in and filled the ditch, nearly smothering me," he remembered. When the shelling ended, the Johnnies ordered these captives out of the gully. The Pennsylvanian recalled the macabre scene about them: "Then we saw a sight I will never forget. Men were lying in every direction, heads shot off and arms and legs scattered and bleeding."[58]

Of the Rebel countercharge, Sheridan related:

This audacious and furious onset was completely broken, though
the gallant fellows fell back to their original line doggedly, and not
until after they had almost gained the creek. Ewell was now hemmed
in on every side...[59]

And Elisha Hunt Rhodes was able to rally most of his command in
short order and rejoin Wheaton's assault. Lieutenant Peck was not among
the Rhode Islanders. After coming down the slope, he was on the creek
bank when he felt a dull blow near his left hip. Peck was able to walk
with the aid of his sword as a crutch and headed to the rear.

The temporary Confederate success did little to disrupt Edwards'
regiments—the 119th Pennsylvania, the 82nd Pennsylvania, and the 5th
Wisconsin—that were attacking to the right of the point where
Crutchfield's Rebs punched through.

The retreat of the 49th Pennsylvania had exposed the 119th Pennsylvania to a "severe flank fire...which
caused a temporary panic, which
was at once corrected and the line
established," reported Major W. C.
Gray of the 119th.[60]

Colonel Isaac Bassett's 82nd
Pennsylvania came under heavy
small arms fire from their left and
"confronted the enemy within 50
yards of his position."[61] The Pennsylvanians unleashed a torrent of
musketry which "the serious loss or
vast number of the enemy's dead in
our immediate front afterward in-
dicated." Private Charles Desota of
the 82nd's Company K scrambled
forward to retrieve a Confederate
battle flag amid the carnage.[62]

Union Colonel Isaac C. Bassett
Roger D. Hunt Collection
U.S. Army Military History Institute

Major Basinger's Savannah Volunteer Guards, the 18th Georgia, were posted facing generally to the northwest with the battalion's right resting on the road, a dense pine copse on the other side. They had resisted the urge to join the mad dash of Crutchfield's charge on their left, but now found a strong enemy force moving through a pine thicket to reach the Georgians' flank and rear. The woods' thickness impeded the Union force, allowing Basinger, who was on the Guards' right flank at the time, to take action. With the Yankees only about 40 yards away, there was no time for deliberation

**Union Brigadier General
Joseph E. Hamblin**

Roger D. Hunt Collection
U.S. Army Military History Institute

and Basinger apparently did not even attempt to alert Stiles' haggard Virginians as to his intent. Instead, he ordered the Guards to change front to face this new threat. As the Georgians obeyed, the Federals loosed a volley, killing several of the Rebels. Basinger's command "took position in a wide and shallow gully at the road-side."[63]

Seeing that he was outnumbered and about to be overrun, Basinger ordered bayonets fixed and attacked. The hand-to-hand fighting was bloody and to the finish as Basinger's 85 men speared into Hamblin's infantry, which included Olcott's New Yorkers and the 65th New York, which was serving as skirmishers.

Rebel Captain Gilbert C. Rice was overpowered by an adversary in a Confederate uniform, "a spy of course," Basinger related.[64] Rice's assailant was of greater size and strength and, throwing the Georgian to the ground, pressed a revolver to his breast and shot him. Lieutenant William H. King avenged Rice by killing the disguised Federal with a head shot at close range. King instantly was fatally wounded himself. Lieutenant William D. Grant snatched a Union flag from its bearer, but was cut down as he tried to deliver the banner to Basinger.[65] "Through the extraordinary gallantry of the men, the attack was entirely successful," Basinger remembered. "Many of the enemy were killed with the bayonet, and the rest were driven off in disorder."[66]

The surviving Georgians limped back to their original positions, but the charge had all but destroyed the battalion.

"I hope I did not commit an error in taking this course," Basinger would write after the war. "The safety of the brigade was at stake. If my brave fellows had flinched or given way, the enemy would have thrown himself on our flank, and the general loss must have been much greater than it was."[67]

Despite these heroics, the Federal infantry was hardly slowed in its ascent and Basinger's Rebs soon would find themselves facing these same bluecoats again.

CHAPTER 17

"I SAW MY LIFE PRESERVED MANY TIMES."

Blue cavalry boiling up behind them suddenly threatened Kershaw's Rebels, already hard-pressed by Federal infantry in their front. The enemy horsemen, initially appearing to the rear of Simms' Brigade, were a violently blunt signal to Kershaw that Anderson's attack had failed and that Anderson was in serious trouble. Before this threat materialized, Kershaw's veterans had remained in their rifle pits and fired dead-aim at Hamblin's Yanks rampaging up the slope from the creek. Simms' men were involved in a live-or-die fight on their front and flank against these Federals.

With Hopkins' Massachusetts men, Olcott's New Yorkers had made a tooth, fang and claw stand to help contain Crutchfield's counterattack, allowing the rest of the brigade to concentrate on assaulting Kershaw. The 95th Pennsylvania of Lieutenant Colonel Harper and the 2nd Connecticut Heavy Artillery Volunteers of Colonel James Hubbard, assigned to Hamblin as infantry, battled their way up the hill, cheering as they went. Harper's line was momentarily staggered by Confederate musketry before the Pennsylvanians, bolstered by Olcott's Regiment, closed in on the Rebs. Also pressuring Kershaw were the Connecticut artillerymen and bevies of Sheridan's troopers who were riding down on him from the west.

Assailed from every direction, Simms' Georgians tried to find an alley of escape, but were surrounded. The confusion of trying to retreat under these conditions was incomprehensible and Simms surrendered. "That officer attempted to extricate his command, but found it impossible to do so without confusion, as he was attacked on all sides," Kershaw reported.[1]

Harper's Pennsylvanians continued up the hill in their attack on the position held by Colonel Fitzgerald's Confederates. "With a cheer...the men pressed forward, and, after a stubborn contest, forced the enemy to retire in confusion, capturing many prisoners, who were ordered to the rear," Harper related.[2]

Ewell had ridden close to Custis Lee's defensive line on the left when he suddenly encountered a strong line of Yankee skirmishers advancing from his left rear. "This closed the only avenue of escape, as shells and even bullets were crossing each other from front and rear of my troops, and my right was completely enveloped," Ewell stated.[3]

Some soldiers of the Union 6th Maryland, including Lieutenant Colonel Hill, had been among Federals taken prisoner by the Southerners when Wheaton's infantry had earlier given way. The situation now changed with the wholesale quandary in the wilting Rebel positions. "Owing to the cavalry getting in the rear of the enemy, we succeeded in escaping, capturing our captors and bringing them into our lines," Hill related.[4]

Seeing the plight of Simm's command, Kershaw's other units began to pull back. Fitzgerald's Brigade was broken up, and Union horse and infantry soon smothered General DuBose's Georgians. "We punished them severely and stood our ground until so close that an officer who rushed to clutch our colors was killed" by a Reb private, related J. S. McNeily of Kershaw's Division.[5] But Artillery Sergeant Wesley Gibbs of the 2nd Connecticut seized an enemy battle flag to earn a Medal of Honor. Kershaw kept some riflemen in his rear to skirmish with the Federals behind him and slow them in coming after his fleeing division. The flight was short-lived, as Kershaw soon found nothing but Federals coming toward him. McNeily wrote:

> In falling back we moved away from the road, thinking the cavalry would pursue down it, not knowing, though our commanders did, that they had already guns around and formed across the road behind us. In this way, every man looking out for himself, we became scattered, but all drifting to the bag of the net.[6]

General DuBose was among the Confederate prisoners bagged by the Yankees. The 30-year-old Tennessean had been a lawyer before the war. His most notable battle service before Sailor's Creek had been as colonel of the 15th Georgia Infantry in General John Hood's Division which lost heavily at Gettysburg.

Harper's Pennsylvanians edged into the woods and the shallow trenches vacated by Kershaw's soldiers minutes before. Landing more prisoners, these Yanks proceeded to an open field about half a mile distant where they joined with Merritt's cavalry. General Kershaw had only retreated about four hundred yards to the west when he saw that

> all who preceded me had been taken by the Yankee cavalry who were in a line of battle across the road. I then directed the men about me and the members of my staff to make their escape in any way possible. I discovered afterward that but one succeeded, as the enemy had completed the circle around our position when General Anderson's line was broken.[7]

In the melee, a cavalryman in the 2nd Ohio, Corporal Larimer Smith, seized Kershaw's headquarters flag and with it, a Medal of Honor. Kershaw was captured by enemy horsemen moments later. His withdrawal left the flank of Custis Lee's Division laid bare for attack. J. S. McNeily was bandaging the shattered wrist of a Rebel officer when Kershaw's line crumpled. Blue soldiers were bearing down on him when McNeily ran to catch up with his retreating comrades.[8]

Topping a hill, McNeily beheld an interesting sight. A lone blue-coated horseman was holding his brother, Captain W. P. McNeily, the regimental commander, and a color-bearer at pistol point. The Federal was demanding the latter's flag. The Yank had just been handed the standard when he spotted McNeily taking in the situation.

"For an instant he was puzzled. Knowing he would risk a bullet if he rode away, he decided to try on a bluff," McNeily recalled. The Union cavalryman, resplendent with a red sash around his waist and aboard a handsome mount, confidently dashed toward McNeily, calling on him also to surrender. "Feeling a complete master of the situation," McNeily defiantly replied, "My gun is loaded, you d——n fool." McNeily's hard eye spooked the Yankee, who wheeled his horse and galloped away.

McNeily fired his musket, killing the officer's charger and sending the Federal flying over the horse's nose-diving head. The Confederates recovered their flag, dropped by the stunned officer, and continued their withdrawal.[9]

Like much of the rest of Kershaw's Division, squads of blue cavalry coming up from behind quickly confronted these soldiers.

"We had not gone a hundred yards before the cavalry, coming from the direction we were going, were on, or rather, all around us," McNeily wrote. He added that the Rebs in his sector were "holding them off all right" when a staff officer from Kershaw came up with news of the division's surrender.

The pitiful remnant of Fitz Lee's cavalry had stayed within the Confederate perimeter as the trapped portion of the army began to crumble. All the horsemen left to him were a few hundred Virginians and North Carolinians of Rooney Lee's scrawny division. Unlike a Stuart or Bedford Forrest, who likely would have dismounted their troopers to deploy as infantrymen, Fitz Lee did little, other than a reconnaissance, to save the deteriorating situation around him. Perhaps, under the confused circumstances and outnumbered so greatly by Sheridan's cavalry, as well as the engulfing blue infantry, there was nothing else that he *could* have done.

With the divisions of Ewell and Anderson nearing a bloody breaking point, Fitz Lee and an escort were scouting the Jamestown Road taken by the wagon train and Gordon's Corps. He soon determined that this route could be used to extract the embattled Southerners, reasoning that the "nature of the ground, wooded and much broken, would have kept the cavalry from harassing them sufficiently to retard their progress until the arrival of their infantry."[10]

Fitz Lee sent a staff officer to find Anderson and Ewell and inform them of this possible line of escape but it was too late. "The halt, allowing time for the accumulation of the enemy's troops, proved fatal," he wrote.[11]

Kershaw's end made Custis Lee's right flank an Achilles' heel for his already faltering division. Union cannon rounds were shrieking into the Confederate positions and a shell fragment mortally wounded Lee's aide-de-camp, Lieutenant Robert Goldsborough. Described as "one of the handsomest young fellows in the army," Goldsborough died in his first engagement since being recently exchanged after spending almost two years in a Federal prison. He had been captured at the battle of Brandy Station in June 1863.[12]

Major Basinger had scarcely reassembled what remained of his Georgia battalion when Custis Lee rode up. Based on Basinger's account, Lee told him that other troops had been sent to guard against other assaults from the flank and rear.

"They probably never reached their destination," Basinger wrote of these reinforcements to Lee after the war, "for in a very few minutes another but smaller body of the enemy came on over the same ground. Supposing them to be some of our own troops giving way, I took my men out to rally them and discovered they were enemies only when within a few paces. I attempted, as our only recourse, to repeat the attack which had just terminated so well..."[13] These Federals belonged to Hamblin's Brigade, primarily Olcott's 121st New York, which the Georgians had battled earlier. They commenced a murderous fire into this Confederate nest.

A death duel was nothing new to Basinger's family. The major's uncle, William E. Basinger, had been a U.S. Army lieutenant in 1835 when he was among troops of Major Francis L. Dade's command ambushed and wiped out in the most famous battle of Florida's Seminole wars. Thirty years later the enemy was different, but history seemed ready to repeat itself for the nephew at Sailor's Creek.

Basinger tried to renew his assault, but the Union troops were too numerous and too close. The Rebs were "over powered by superior numbers, though fighting to the last, all the rest of the command were killed, wounded or taken. Sergeants [Richard] Millen and [Simeon] Morton stood to the last before their colors, keeping at bay a party of about fifty men, and were the last to fall."[14]

Basinger himself did not escape injury. A bullet shattered his sword in his right hand and another smashed his revolver and slightly wounded him in the left hand. "Another hit my belt buckle and another pierced my coat just above the belt. I saw my life preserved many times."[15]

Finally Basinger waved his handkerchief in surrender:

Union Colonel Egbert Olcott
U.S. Army Military History Institute

> As I did so, the enemy, hitherto sheltering themselves behind the trees, rushed into the road, and fired upon my wounded who lay in the gully...It was with great difficulty they could be induced to cease from this barbarity. I mention this closing incident as one more of the numerous atrocities which indicated the relentless spirit in which the war was waged against us.[16]

Private Warren C. Dockum of the 121st New York seized the 18th Georgia's flag, inscribed with "Victory or Death," and later was venerated with the Medal of Honor. One of Dockum's comrades, Private Benjamin Gifford, took another Rebel standard and also earned the medal. Although not recorded, Gifford's prize may have been another flag carried by the Georgians and presented to them in 1862 by the "Ladies of the Savannah Volunteer Guards."[17] Dockum's heroics, however, were disputed by the Confederates, who claimed their banner was not captured until all of its defenders had fallen to Yankees firing from the cover of nearby trees. Only then did any of the Federals "dare to touch them."[18]

The 18th Georgia Battalion lost 30 killed, including those who later died of their injuries, and 22 wounded, or 61 percent of the number engaged. Those of Crutchfield's other artillerists still standing couldn't decide whether to fight on or give up. "We now realized we were utterly powerless and were forced to surrender, though a few of the young fellows, with their fighting blood up, crowded around me and insisted that we could 'whip 'em yet,'" Captain Thomas Blake related.[19]

By now, what remained of Custis Lee's Division was surrounded. Lee recounted that "to prevent useless sacrifice of life the firing was stopped by some of my officers, aided by some of the enemy's, and the officers and men taken as prisoners of war."[20] Included in the roundup of gray captives with Custis Lee was General Barton. For the 35-year-old Virginian, this was the second time he had been a Union prisoner of war, having earlier been taken at Vicksburg in 1863. After his exchange, he had commanded a brigade under Pickett, but had clashed with the latter after the operations at New Bern, North Carolina. Barton had been relieved of command at Drewry's Bluff in May 1864 [although his regimental commanders repeatedly requested his reinstatement] and did not receive another assignment until the fall, when he was given a brigade in the Richmond defenses.[21]

General Ewell already was in Union hands, having surrendered a few minutes earlier with a cluster of Northerners claiming credit for his capture.

Custis Lee's capitulation also resulted in contradictory reports from the victors. Captain Hopkins of the 37th Massachusetts wrote that Lee gave up his sword to Private David D. White of his command. Lee then formally surrendered his blade to Lieutenant W. C. Morrill of the 37th who wore it, said Hopkins. Disputing Hopkins was Colonel Olcott of the 121st New York who stated that Private Harris S. Hawthorn of his regiment captured Lee. Based on Olcott's version, Hawthorn was the first Yankee to confront Lee and escort him to the rear where the private reported to the colonel. Hawthorn was one of the Federals ordered to accompany Lee to General Wheaton's headquarters. Hawthorn appeared before a VI Corps judge advocate on April 14 and gave a sworn statement describing his role in Lee's capitulation.

Regardless of who captured Custis Lee, General Keifer summed up the battle in a few paragraphs:

> The enemy was soon routed at all points, and many general officers and many thousands of prisoners threw down their arms and

The Last of Ewell's Corps by artist Alfred R. Waud. Of this sketch, Waud wrote, "This was quite an effective incident in its way the soldiers silhoutted [*sic*] against the western sky—with their muskets thrown butt upwards in token of surrender, as our troops closed in."

surrendered...Flight was impossible, and nothing remained to put
an end to the bloody slaughter but for them to throw down their
arms and become captives.[22]

Keifer had been through some of the hottest combat of the afternoon, emerging unscathed. Yet he would face death at the muzzles of
many Rebel muskets before the day was done.

CHAPTER 18

"I CAN'T SURRENDER."

Tucker's Naval Battalion had ferociously stood its ground all day. Even as Ewell's line melted on either side of them the Confederate sailors and marines maintained their formation and kept up a steady, rapid fire. With the battle hopelessly lost, the command was still holding its position. Yet after Crutchfield's countercharge, which temporarily blunted the Federal assault in their sector, the marines and seamen were ordered into a patch of thick woods in a gully between the creek's ridges. Squads of victorious Union troops surged westward on either side of them, but Tucker's men remained resolute and calm.

As dusk settled, the Federals suddenly noticed this hostile den of Johnnies still clinging to their position. The news was relayed to General Keifer who twice tried to signal the Confederates secreted in the thicket, but to no avail. Finally, he decided to ride forward himself and determine if indeed there were Rebels in those woods. Keifer had barely entered the trees when he blundered into Tucker's battle line, many of the Southerners hidden only by underbrush. Within point-blank range of Rebel riflemen, Keifer tried to bluff his way out of a lethal situation. He shouted, "Forward," and some of the shadowy gray forms instantly complied, passing the order down the line. In the half-light, they believed Keifer was a Confederate officer. Having fooled the Johnnies to this point, Keifer wheeled his horse and tried to flee, but the tangled scrub kept him from a clean escape.

The enemy marines were upon him when he and his horse entered a cleared area where the Confederates realized that he actually was a

Yankee. Some raised their weapons to shoot him, but Tucker and marine Captain Simms used their swords to divert musket barrels of Rebels taking aim at Keifer. With this reprieve, the general was able to gallop to safety lying along his horse's neck. Keifer reached his command and soon returned to the woods under a truce flag. He met with Tucker and explained the hopelessness of further resistance. Tucker earlier had received word that Ewell had surrendered, but "refused to believe it," a Confederate sailor wrote. "The brigades of infantry on either side of him had ceased firing, but with the remark, 'I can't surrender,' he ordered his men to continue the engagement."[1]

The battle resumed as Hopkins' New Englanders and Olcott's New Yorkers had come up by this time and joined Keifer's Ohioans in renewing their assault. The Rebel W. L. Timberlake described the shocking and climactic insanity between these Federals and the mixed force of Confederates, including Tucker's tars and the artillerymen:

> Near the end the 37th Massachusetts had the fiercest literally savage encounter of the war with the remnant of Stiles' battalion and the Marines. I was next to those Marines and saw them fight. They clubbed muskets, fired pistols into each other's faces and used bayonets savagely.[2]

"A severe conflict ensued as the lines of the opposing forces came together," reported Keifer. "A number of men were bayoneted on both sides."[3] Enduring the fire and cold steel carnage swirling all about him was Major Stiles, who later wrote of this Confederate last stand:

> By the time we had well settled into our old position we were attacked simultaneously, front and rear, by overwhelming numbers, and quicker than I can tell it the battle degenerated into a butchery and a confused melee of brutal personal conflicts. I saw numbers of men kill each other with bayonets and the butts of muskets and even bite each other's throats and ears and noses, rolling on the ground like wild beasts. I saw one of my officers and a Federal officer fighting with swords over the battalion colors, which we had brought back with us, each man having his left hand upon the staff. I could not get to them, but my man was a very athletic, powerful seaman, and soon I saw the Federal officer fall.[4]

Stiles earlier had cautioned his men about wearing captured Union clothing that might confuse their comrades in battle. Some ignored his warning with tragic results. "I saw a young fellow of one of my companies jam the muzzle of his musket against the back of the head of his most intimate friend, clad in a Yankee overcoat, and blow his brains out..." Sandwiched between other Southerners, Stiles vainly tried to use his sword to deflect the boy's aim, but his blade had been snapped in the fighting and he could not strike the rifle. "I well remember the yell of demoniacal triumph with which this simple country lad of yesterday clubbed his musket and whirled savagely upon another victim," he recalled.[5]

**Union Brigadier General
Joseph Warren Keifer**

Roger D. Hunt Collection
U.S. Army Military History Institute

Private Charles A. Taggart of Hopkins' Regiment ran forward and surprised a group of Confederates. He fired into the thick of the butternuts, snatched a flag, and sprinted toward the Union lines. With Rebels in pursuit, some Federals mistook him for an enemy standard-bearer leading a charge. Taggart was wounded slightly, but made it back to his lines with the banner.[6]

Men on both sides sagged in bloody heaps, brained by muskets, shot at point-blank range, or skewered with sword or bayonet. A Confederate officer described the madness as "one promiscuous and prolonged melee" in which the enemies seemed "bent on exterminating each other."[7] But the Yanks held their hard-won real estate.

The gully used by the Confederates to attack the rear of Hopkins' regiment minutes earlier quickly became a butcher's pen for massed Rebel survivors. The Massachusetts soldiers "swept the whole length of their line with such a terrible raking fire that they were unable to reply and soon gave token of surrender," recalled Hopkins.[8]

The Federals stopped shooting but, according to the captain, the Southerners resumed fire, fatally injuring Adjutant John S. Bradley and wounding several other men. "We immediately opened again with redoubled energy, and in a few minutes they surrendered in earnest," Hopkins reported. About four hundred Rebs were taken and sent to the Union rear.[9]

Hopkins added that after the battle the bodies of more than 80 dead Confederates were found strewn in the ravine.

There were rare moments of humanity. With his musket ready, a Yank corporal came face to face with a Rebel officer, and called for the Southerner to surrender. Hopkins described what happened next:

> The officer refused and the corporal fired, shooting him through the body. As he fell, the corporal bent over him and told him he was sorry he had to shoot him, and that he was a Christian, and, if he wished it, would pray for him. The officer eagerly assented, and the corporal knelt by his side...and offered a fervent prayer for the parting soul of his dying foeman, hostile no longer. When he had finished, they shook hands, and the officer gave the corporal his sword as a memento, and asked him to write to his wife and tell her what had befallen him.[10]

Realizing that his command had ceased to exist, Stiles tried to flee on foot, but was captured moments later. "Thus ended my active life as a Confederate soldier, my four years' service under Marse Robert, and I was not sorry to end it thus, in red-hot battle, and to be spared the pain, I will not say humiliation, of Appomattox," he wrote.[11]

Minutes later, a Rebel navy lieutenant brought Commodore Tucker a second message telling of Ewell's capitulation. With Keifer's entreaty and the apparent reality that Ewell was a prisoner, Tucker "followed the example of the infantry" and surrendered.[12]

A Confederate sailor wrote:

> He [Tucker] had continued the fighting fifteen minutes after they had lowered their arms, and the naval colors were the last to be laid down. The bravery of the sailors [and marines] was observed along the Federal lines, and when they did surrender the enemy cheered them long and vigorously.[13]

"They fought better and longer than any other troops upon the field," Keifer later said of the Naval Battalion in a letter to his wife. He also acknowledged that Tucker "knocked up the muzzles of the guns nearest to me and saved my life. I succeeded in escaping to my lines unhurt."[14]

Some of the Yanks were surprised to see these Rebels wearing naval uniforms. "Good heavens!" remarked one Federal. "Have you gunboats up here too?" Remembered another bluecoat, "Although sailors themselves, yet Sailor's creek had no charms for them."[15]

The battle conduct of Tucker's Brigade awed General Wright of the VI Corps. He wrote in a report of the action:

> I was never more astonished. These troops were surrounded—the First and Third Divisions of this corps were on either flank, and some three divisions of Major-General Sheridan's cavalry in their rear. Looking upon them as already our prisoners, I had ordered the artillery to cease firing as a dictate of humanity; my surprise, therefore, was extreme when this force charged upon our front; but the fire of our infantry...the capture of their superior officers, already in our hands, the concentrated and murderous fire of six batteries of our artillery within effective range, brought them promptly to a surrender. The position was won, the right of the rebel army was annihilated, and the prisoners secured were counted by thousands.[16]

"The rebel Marine Brigade fought with most extraordinary courage," Keifer recalled, "but was finally cut off and captured." He added that Commodore Tucker and about 27 other Confederate navy or marine officers surrendered to him.[17] Tucker later told a fellow officer that Sailor's Creek had been his first land battle and that he "supposed everything was going on well" before he was forced to lay down his arms.[18] Keifer estimated that the Naval Battalion prisoners numbered about two thousand. Confederate marine historian Ralph Donnelly, however, put the total much lower, writing that Tucker's command likely consisted of a total of three hundred to four hundred marines and seamen who surrendered.[19]

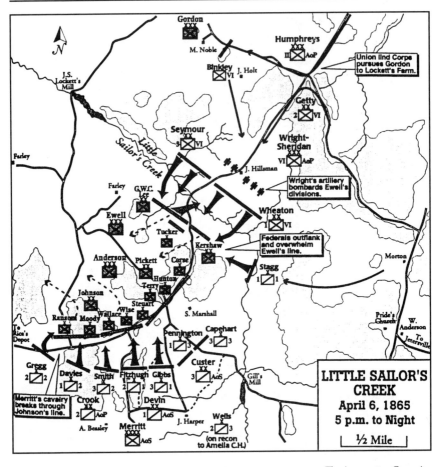

The Appomattox Campaign

Other Union officers singled out the Rebel tars in their reports. "A brigade of Southern marines stubbornly continued the fight," wrote General Wheaton. The aggressiveness of the 121st New York and 37th Massachusetts Volunteers, however, "compelled them to speedily recognize our victory."[20] General Seymour of the VI Corps said, "The Confederate Marine Battalion fought with peculiar obstinacy and our lines, somewhat disordered by crossing the creek, were repulsed in the first onset."[21] A few years after the struggle, Keifer and Tucker met again, and the general returned the commodore's sword surrendered at Sailor's Creek.[22]

Sheridan's cavalry rumbled through the woods and over the fields, rounding up mobs of Ewell's and Anderson's Confederates or snap firing at other Southerners who had not lost their pluck despite the rout. Rebel C. F. James and a few comrades were among the men in flight after Anderson's line fell to pieces. He recalled:

> I had held on to my big navy revolver, and we did not mean to surrender to any one or two pursuers...Twice, as the bullets whistled by us, we stopped to surrender, thinking that the cavalry was upon us, but seeing that they were occupied with stragglers in our rear we pressed on deeper into the forest...We were running, not from the Federal cavalry, but from Federal prisons, which we knew were more to be dreaded than battle with Sheridan's men.[23]

Near sundown, James made his way across Sailor's Creek and rejoined the fractured remains of the Confederate army. Also among the running Johnnies were Private W. S. White and others from the Richmond Howitzers. These cannoneers waited until after dark and then buried their remaining guns. White wrote:

> It was now apparent to all that we could hold out but a few hours— men and horses were utterly worn down by fatigue, loss of sleep and hunger. Thousands were leaving their commands and wandering about the devastated country in quest of food, and they had no muskets.[24]

General Wright was in a battle heat when he dispatched a message to Meade at 5:45 p.m.: "I am in the immediate presence of the enemy, and am rapidly driving them. Everything is favorable."[25]

Meanwhile, Fitz Lee and his gray horsemen had not found the escape route in time to save Ewell and Anderson. And Lee preserved what was left of his cavalry to fight another day by a hard ride toward Rice's Station where he linked with Longstreet's Corps. Behind him, Fitz left the legions of Anderson, Ewell, and Gordon in crimson tatters.

CHAPTER 19
CLASH AT THE LOCKETT FARM

The advance of Grant's army struck Ewell upon one road and my command upon another almost simultaneously.
—Confederate Major General John B. Gordon,
Reminiscences of the Civil War

The sun was dropping rapidly, shrouded in black powder smoke when the Union II Corps finally brought Gordon's Confederates to bay. The rival corps had been battling since morning as Gordon forlornly tried to keep the Yanks from capturing Lee's main wagon train. The running fight had covered 14 miles or so with the Federals sweeping over several partially entrenched positions defended by the delay-minded Rebels.

Ironically, the foes in this cockfight were the Second Corps and II Corps of their respective armies. In their rearguard role the Rebels, composed of the divisions of Major General Bryan Grimes and Brigadier Generals James A. Walker and Clement A. Evans, had resisted doggedly all day despite being outnumbered and outgunned.

Each of these generals was a seasoned and reliable commander who had been with the Army of Northern Virginia [even before its official establishment] since the war's onset.

Walker was a 32-year-old Virginian who, as a senior at Virginia Military Institute in 1852, had challenged then professor Thomas J. Jackson to a duel after a clash of words in the classroom. Jackson declined the contest of honor, but the issue resulted in Walker's expulsion. Walker later graduated from the University of Virginia and when he entered the Confederate service was under the command of old Jackson himself at

Harpers Ferry, Virginia. Their earlier difference was buried by then. Walker would later lead Jackson's storied Stonewall Brigade and was its commander when he was seriously wounded and the unit all but destroyed at Spotsylvania.[1]

Grimes, 36, was a North Carolinian who graduated from the University of North Carolina in 1848. A member of the state secession convention, he joined the Confederacy as major of the 4th North Carolina Infantry. He fought at Seven Pines, Mechanicsville, Antietam, Fredericksburg, Chancellorsville, the Wilderness, and in the Shenandoah Valley. Grimes' February 15, 1865, promotion to major general was the last such appointment made in Lee's army.[2]

Evans had taken over John Gordon's old division when Gordon was promoted to corps command in late 1864. The 32 year old was born in Stewart County, Georgia, and had been an attorney, judge, and Georgia state senator before the war. Destined to be wounded five times in the conflict, he enlisted in the 31st Georgia Infantry in 1861 and had seen combat from the Peninsula campaign to this day at the Lockett farm.[3]

All three of Gordon's division leaders had fought wisely stubborn in trying to delay and punish the Yanks behind them. Every natural barrier—a stream, rise, or valley—turned into a makeshift Confederate outpost, Gordon's men holding as long as possible to allow the wagons and the rest of the army to outdistance their pursuers. Grimes shuffled his brigades from front to rear to hold off the Union attacks.

But the Union II Corps continued shoving hard after the Rebel wagons and Gordon, breaking connection with Wright's VI Corps in the process.

Gordon recalled:

> Indeed, not only was my command in almost incessant battle as
> we covered the retreat, but every portion of our marching column
> was being assailed by Grant's cavalry and infantry.[4]

Amid the day's fighting, a green Massachusetts lieutenant was separated from his infantry regiment. He stumbled forward through the woods and weeds and, in moments found himself face-to-face with Gordon and his staff officers. Shakily, the officer called on the Rebels to surrender. Unruffled by the intrusion, Gordon calmly said: "Young

man, you must have made a mistake and I would advise you to go
back to your friends."[5] The lieutenant beat a quick retreat.

Close-in fighting continued on
the Jamestown Road, taken by the
wagon train and Gordon's corps
from Holt's Corner, and in the fields
and woods on each side of it. This
route snaking toward the confluence of Big and Little Sailor's
Creeks twisted to the northwest for
about two miles, bending sharply
to the southwest past the Lockett
farm and then descending into the
creek valley to the Double Bridges.
Before reaching the Lockett home-
stead, another road forked to the

**Confederate Major
General Bryan Grimes**

Author's Collection

north and crossed the creek further upstream at Perkinson's Saw Mill.

From a signal station, Humphreys sent this message to General
Meade at 4:40 p.m.:

> I have driven the enemy ever since I came in contact with
> them, and have all the time moved almost as fast as troops could
> move in line if they were not in the presence of the enemy. The
> officers and men are doing everything possible. I hope soon to
> take their artillery and break into their trains. Gordon's corps is
> guarding it, according to all statements of prisoners. The enemy
> retreats so rapidly that it is very difficult to overtake them.[6]

Confederate John Methvin of Evans' Division had been granted permission from an officer to get some branch water during a rare lull in
the fighting. Methvin, whose brother had given him some meal at Amelia
Springs earlier in the day, quickly built a small fire and prepared some
of the meal to make a hoecake. The Georgian baked his cornbread and
did not wait for it to cool before heading back to his regiment, carrying

his makeshift canteen skillet on a forked stick. Hearing the wagon train grinding along off to his north, Methvin climbed a boulder-strewn hill and happened upon a dead Federal lying face down. The Yank had been shot in the breast, and Methvin relieved him of his Enfield and a packet of 10 cartridges from his belt. Methvin then found a comfortable rock and settled down to cool and eat his bread. "Soon after taking my seat I discovered just down east of me a heavy column of Yankees moving along the ravine and concluded to take a shot at them as they were so thick I could not miss a man..." Methvin fired off several shots before he turned and saw a line of blue pickets coming up behind him and about 150 yards away. These Yanks unleashed a volley and bullets splattered against the boulders around him, but Methvin was unhurt. "I fell off the rock on the opposite side," the Reb related. "I was in such a hurry to move I forgot my pan of bread and I did not go back for it either."[7]

Pierce's Union brigade of the Third Division was heading the II Corps assailment on Gordon. Near dusk, his troops emerged from thick woods to see the Confederates digging in on high ground at the Lockett farm about half a mile from the creek. Obviously, Gordon was trying to cover the wagon train's crossing.

"About sunset, the enemy made a determined stand behind some slight breast-works on the main road"; Pierce reported, "owing to a bend in the road, my brigade was brought parallel with it."[8]

"The road turned abruptly to the left and ran there parallel to the breast-works which covered it and close in their rear," wrote de Trobriand, the division commander. "The rear part of the enemy's train was close by, and their only chance of escape was in the holding of the breast-works."[9]

The Confederate force "was found entrenched, covering the crossing," observed Brevet Captain Charles W. Howell of the Union engineers.[10] "The stream at this place was about twenty feet in width and from two to three feet in depth, impassable for artillery and trains, except over a narrow, rickety bridge; it was bordered on either side by a soft bottom land about 100 yards in width, with a hilly, open country gradually rising beyond."[11]

The II Corps artillery under Union Major John G. Hazard had kept up its flying battle with the Rebels since the enemy wagon train had first been seen near Amelia Springs. Now Hazard's cannoneers saw the Confederates "in a strong position, trying to cover the crossing of his train over Sailor's Creek."[12] Battery M of the 1st New Hampshire Artillery under Captain George K. Dakin and Captain A. J. Clark's Battery B of the 1st New Jersey Artillery unlimbered to the right of the Third Division. They opened fire on two enemy batteries in the distance, causing them to make a hasty withdrawal. The battery of Captain J. W. Roder, 4th U.S. Artillery, was soon posted to the left of the Third Division and added its firepower.

Gordon had little choice but to make his stand here. Many of the Confederate wagons had become stuck in the ooze of the creek's swampy bottomland, creating a traffic jam. The easternmost of the flimsy Double Bridges, built for farm herds and civilian buggies rather than the flight of an army, simply collapsed, stranding the Confederate procession.

"The bridge across Sailor's Creek had broken down and hundreds of our wagons were detained," recalled one of Gordon's men. "The enemy were pressing us hotly."[13]

"When about half our ordnance and wagon train had crossed the bridge [it] broke in and we had to stop," related a Georgian in Evans' Division. "The Federals who were pursuing us closely soon learned our condition and crowded our troops; we quickly resented it and a bloody conflict there ensued."[14]

General Grimes related that along Sailor's Creek "we made the final stand of the day, the wagons becoming blocked up at the bridge crossing this stream." Grimes added that he received orders from Lee to hold the ridge at the Lockett house "until he could have artillery put in position on the opposite hills over the creek parallel with those I occupied."[15]

Wading into the quagmire, Rebels were frantically trying to free some of these vehicles when the first elements of Humphreys' main force arrived on the field.

The Union troops "struck my command while we were endeavoring to push the ponderous wagon-trains through the bog, out of which the starved teams were unable to drag them," Gordon later wrote. "Many of these wagons, loaded with ammunition, mired so deep in the mud that they had to be abandoned."[16]

"The line of battle was formed on Locket[t]'s Hill, which sloped gently down from the line to the creek" about one hundred fifty to two hundred yards behind the Southerners, remembered Rebel Carlton McCarthy of Cutshaw's artillerymen.[17] The road ran through the middle of Cutshaw's position and crossing it was "a hazardous experiment, as the enemy, thinking it an important avenue, swept it with musketry."[18]

Rooney Lee's cavalry, that had assisted Gordon through the flight, already was gone, ordered back to Fitz Lee.

The oncoming Federals quickly realized the plight of their cornered foe. "Upon arriving in the vicinity of Sailor's Creek, at about sunset, the enemy were found strongly posted, on a commanding ridge of ground, covering the crossing of the creek, evidently determined to make a fight in order to gain time for the crossing of his train," wrote General Miles, of Humphreys' First Division.[19]

The 25-year-old Miles already had earned a reputation as one of the army's hardest fighting generals. Born on his family's farm near Westminster, Massachusetts, in August 1839, Miles moved to Boston at age 17, working days as a store clerk and attending night school. He also learned military matters from a former French army colonel.[20] After the war erupted, Miles was commissioned a first lieutenant in the 22nd Massachusetts Volunteers and fought at Seven Pines, Antietam, Fredericksburg, and Chancellorsville. In the latter battle, he suffered the third of four war wounds and later would be awarded the Medal of Honor. He led a II Corps brigade at the Wilderness and Spotsylvania and was commissioned a brigadier general of volunteers in June 1864. During the Petersburg siege, Miles attained division command, was wounded for the fourth time, and appointed major general of volunteers after his gallant conduct at Reams' Station.[21]

Now with Gordon finally pinned down, Miles ordered forward his First Brigade under Colonel George W. Scott. These Michigan, Pennsylvania, New Hampshire, Massachusetts, and New York troops were followed closely on their right flank by the Third Brigade, New Yorkers led by Colonel Clinton D. MacDougall.[22] Massachusetts, New Jersey, and

New York troops of de Trobriand's Third Brigade under Colonel Robert McAllister joined General Pierce's units in the attack.

Watching on the ridge, the Confederates braced for the assault. Carlton McCarthy recalled that he saw some of his comrades "hauling out of their pockets a mixture of corn, salt (their paltry rations), caps, and cartridges, and, selecting the material needed, loading. They were getting ready to stand."[23]

Blue skirmishers loped forward "confidently and in rather free and easy style" before a Rebel volley spurred them to cover. Another volley slowed them again. "Then came their line of battle with overwhelming numbers," McCarthy wrote.[24] The Yankees raised a cheer as they came on. Some of the gray cannoneers, untrained in infantry tactics, "dodged about from tree to tree, and with the deliberation of huntsmen picked off here and there a man," McCarthy recalled. "When a shot told, the marksman hurrahed, all to himself."[25]

**Union Major General
Nelson Appleton Miles**

U.S. Army Military History Institute

Colonel Cutshaw of the artillery command had a leg smashed by Union fire and was lifted from his horse and into a waiting ambulance. Taken to a house in the rear, he was later captured and the shattered leg amputated. Cutshaw was hit shortly after reporting to Major Douglas of Walker's Division. "His leg was torn off by a shell while we were watching the movements of the enemy," Douglas wrote. The major himself was sent sprawling from his mount shortly thereafter when a spent bullet slammed into a button on the breast of his tunic.[26]

Virginia Captain Asher W. Garber, of the Staunton Battery in Cutshaw's command, was staggered by an enemy bullet and called for a medic. In examining himself, however, Garber found the still-hot round in his pocket where it had struck the rowel of a spur he had put there the day before.[27]

Gordon's Southerners withstood one assault, but by about 6 p.m., the situation was grim indeed. Gordon was afraid that he was about to lose all of the wagons as well as having his command destroyed. Adding to his woes, Federal units of Francis Barlow's Division were seen a short distance to the north near Perkinson's Saw Mill, thus menacing his left flank. Yet Gordon remained mindful of Robert Lee, realizing that the commander in chief likely was being bombarded with inquiries and messages from every quarter. In spite of the near-collapse of his corps, Gordon sent a note to Lee that did not plead for help. Simply, it described the status of his force:

> I have been fighting heavily pressed all day. My loss is considerable and I am still closely pressed. I fear that a portion of the train will be lost as my force is quite reduced & insufficient for its protection. So far, I have been able to protect [the wagons], but without assistance can scarcely hope to do so much longer. The enemy's loss has been very heavy.[28]

"At last the enemy appeared in strong force on both flanks, while he pushed hard in front. It was useless to attempt a further stand," the Rebel McCarthy noted. Another Confederate described how "the enemy came upon our rear in great force and a 'sauve qui-peut' [every man for himself] engagement ensued."[29] The downfall of Ewell's Corps opened floodgates for even more Federals to assail Gordon's position from the south. A New Jersey soldier told how "The enemy made a spirited resistance, but were soon driven away from this position."[30]

Pressured in all directions, Gordon's soldiers finally broke about 6 p.m., fleeing the field in rout and suffering some one thousand seven hundred casualties out of about seven thousand men engaged. "General Gordon, seeing resistance was hopeless, gave us orders to save ourselves, showing us the way by galloping his horse down the hill and fording the creek," wrote Rebel Private Henry T. Bahnson.[31]

"The enemy pushed on rapidly, attacking us with very great pertinacity," recalled General Grimes. "We here repeatedly repulsed their assaults, but by turning both of our flanks they succeeded in not only

The Lockett House

Bullet holes still scar the walls of the Lockett House

dislodging but driving us across the creek in confusion."[32] Miles stated that Scott's troops "drove the enemy in perfect confusion into and across the creek..."[33]

A Rebel officer bawled to his men, "Boys, take care of yourselves!" Carlton McCarthy remembered. "Saying this, he planted himself against a pine, and as his men rushed by him, emptied every chamber of his revolver at the enemy, and then reluctantly made his way in company with several privates down the hill to the creek."[34]

A cluster of gray cannoneers fighting as infantry gathered at the base of the ridge with the creek behind them and saw Union skirmishers dashing about among the trees above them. A lieutenant in the Richmond Howitzers managed to stop them there, trying to rally for another stand. The Federals could be heard excitedly shouting for their comrades to ascend the hill and play hell with the Rebels and their trapped wagon train in the bottom beyond. McCarthy wrote:

> Their favorite expressions were, "Come along, boys; here are the damned Rebel wagons!" "Damn 'em, shoot 'em down!"[35]

Moments later, a Union battle line "in beautiful order stepped out of the woods with colors flying, and for a moment halted," McCarthy recalled. Marching in front of this formation, the enemy color guard, however, was too much for the Rebels to resist. They opened fire. "The color bearer pitched forward and fell, with his colors, heavily to the ground. The guard of two men on either side shared the same fate, or else feigned it," McCarthy said. This act of defiance enraged the Yanks arrayed on the crest. "Immediately the line of battle broke into disorder, and came swarming down the hill, firing, yelling, and cursing as they came," recalled McCarthy.[36]

A Union officer on horseback galloped close to McCarthy's group "and with most superb insolence mocked" the Rebels. The insult so angered the Rebel lieutenant that he ordered a soldier to shoot the Yankee. The Confederate's musket misfired, but another Johnny found the mark. The officer "at the shock of the bullet's stroke...threw his arms up in the air, and his horse bore him into the woods a corpse."[37]

Isolated pockets of resistance did not slow the Federals' descent on the wagon train and some of Gordon's men vainly used the vehicles for cover to stave off the attack. Hundreds of others ran through the stream bogs, waded the creek, and clambered up the west bank where Gordon tried to regroup. The fleeing graycoats were fired on at every step, including having to endure showers of canister from a Union battery.

The Federal infantry, meanwhile, had reached the wagons, and the battle sharpened again as the few Rebels there put up a feeble defense. McCarthy recalled:

> The crack of pistols and the bang of muskets was continuous. The enemy had surrounded the wagons and were mercilessly shooting down the unarmed and helpless drivers, some of whom, however, managed to cut the traces, mount, and ride away.[38]

"The scene among the wagons was one of pell-mell confusion," recounted a Confederate officer. "They were driving in lines, eight or ten abreast, across the field towards the stream..."[39]

Some Rebel teamsters unhitched horses and mules and tried to ride across the creek, but most were either shot or captured. The 17th Maine and the 57th Pennsylvania of Pierce's Brigade charged through the wagons in the ravine, crossed the stream, and ripped at the Southerners on the west ridge. Gordon later stated that even while he was making his stand, "the different divisions of Lee's lionhearted army were being broken and scattered or captured."[40] Lee later described the stand of Gordon's Corps to Jefferson Davis:

> Gordon, who all the morning, aided by General W. F. Lee's cavalry, had checked the advance of the enemy on the road from Amelia Springs and protected the trains, became exposed to his combined assaults, which he bravely resisted and twice repulsed but the cavalry having been withdrawn to another part of the line of march...the enemy, massing heavily on his [Gordon's] front and both flanks, renewed the attack about 6 p.m., and drove him from the field in much confusion.[41]

Even the toughest of the Johnnies, in Gordon's ranks and the others, took to their heels in this battle, some experiencing the bitterness of rout for the first time. "In all my service in the Army of Northern Virginia, I never ran until at Sailor's Creek," remembered Captain Frederick W. Colston. "I lost all my treasures of the war and narrowly escaped myself."[42]

Gordon's men who had reached the creek's far bank could not string together even the semblance of a battle line to try to halt the triumphant Yanks of de Trobriand's and Miles' divisions. Against the demoralized Confederates, MacDougall's infantry was among the bluecoats who forded the branch and drove off the hodgepodge force of Rebels defending the ridge, Miles reported. Under intense fire, MacDougall's New Yorkers charged, taking aim at a Rebel battery. These Yanks steamed into the confused gray mass, seized two guns and about one hundred forty wagons, MacDougall noted. Scott's Brigade crossed the stream and went into position with MacDougall.

Of Gordon's stand, de Trobriand wrote, "[T]his last effort was of no avail against the elan of our men, who would not be checked." In his division, de Trobriand credited Pierce's Brigade and the 120th New York Volunteers of Lieutenant Colonel Abram L. Lockwood in McAllister's Brigade with the capture of the stranded wagons.[43]

A skirmish line of gray cavalry had been posted to try to hold Gordon's last line in place but, seeing the extent of the rout, the troopers allowed the fugitives to pass. Some of the Federals tried to take the road behind the disorganized Southerners to snuff out their retreat. "Consequently, those [Rebels] who attempted escape in that direction had to run the gauntlet of a constant fusilade [*sic*] from a mass of troops near enough to select individuals, curse them, and command them to throw down their arms or be shot," Carlton McCarthy recounted.[44]

With his division routed, General Grimes found bluecoats quickly closing in on him:

> I galloped to the creek (the bridge being in their possession) where the banks were precipitous, and for protection from their murderous fire concluded to jump my horse in, riding him through the water...the bullets of the enemy whistling around me like hail all the while.[45]

Darkness, pure exhaustion, the exhilaration of a great conquest and a still hard-eyed enemy in their front dissuaded the II Corps Yanks from further offense. The 69th New York of Lieutenant Colonel James J. Smith had been skirmishers for Miles' Division all day. Now Smith rode among the scattered but conquering Yanks raising the devil and victory amid the captured Confederate wagons. Smith was trying to regroup his regiment and put other displaced New Yorkers into his formation. He had gathered about 75 men when General Miles approached and put him in charge of approximately two hundred fifty wheeled war trophies. General Pierce posted guards on another 56 wagons and ambulances.

"Such mules!" a Massachusetts soldier wrote of the pitiful Rebel teams. "[T]he skinniest, boniest animals that I ever saw retaining life. For a full week they had been on the go, night and day, with rare and brief halts for rest or food. Just before their capture they would seem to have gone down a long hill into a valley, a literal Valley of Humiliation as it proved, for there they were compelled to stay and surrender, either from inability to climb the opposite hill and get away, or else because there was not opportunity for them to do so before our forces came upon them."[46]

McCarthy was among the whipped Confederates filtering through the woods and valleys toward the west. He later described some of his companions:

> The men's faces were black with powder. They had bitten car-
> tridges until there was a deep black circle around their mouths.
> The burnt powder from the ramrods had blackened their hands,
> and in their efforts to remove the perspiration from their faces they
> had completed the coloring from the roots of the hair to the chin.[47]

"When the smoke had cleared away, there were many dead and wounded men found covering the ground," recounted Georgian John Methvin, who had scrambled back to his regiment after leaving his hoe cake to the Yanks. In his flight, Methvin arrived at the stream with bluecoats seemingly all about him: "I did not wait for ceremonies, but went into the creek up to my neck in water." Methvin escaped and rejoined Gordon's ruined corps.[48]

Meade sent a dispatch to Grant at 6 p.m. regarding the II Corps' success, unaware that Gordon's divisions were in the process of being dismantled at that very moment:

> General Humphreys reports that he has pursued the enemy three
> miles beyond Deatonville. Has captured one gun, and reports the

road literally strewn with tents, baggage, and camp equipage. He is still pushing on. No report from Griffin or Wright..."[49]

Even if Gordon had asked for support, there were no reserves to send to him. Longstreet, still unaware of the disaster behind him, had been dug in at Rice's Station for most of the day with the divisions of Major Generals Charles W. Field and Cadmus M. Wilcox covering roads leading to the bridges over the Appomattox. Wilcox's command was so undermanned that Major General Henry "Harry" Heth's Division was required to bolster it. This left only Mahone's Division, which Robert Lee himself was directing toward Sailor's Creek even as Gordon's Corps was being shredded.

CHAPTER 20

"MY GOD! HAS THE ARMY DISSOLVED?"

After determining that the "sheep" in the distance were Union wagons, Robert Lee tried to reach the Rice's Station Road on which the missing Ewell and Anderson should be moving. En route, he met Colonel Venable who told him that the army's wagons between the branches of the creek had been captured. At the time, Lee was talking to General Mahone of Longstreet's Corps. Hearing Venable's report, the commander seemed to wonder aloud: "Where is Anderson? Where is Ewell? It is strange I can't hear from them," Lee said. Turning to Mahone, he continued, "General Mahone, I have no other troops, will you take your division to Sailor's Creek?"[1]

Lee and Mahone rode toward the fighting with Mahone's Division marching behind them. It was late afternoon when the generals reached a rise dominating the valley of Big Sailor's Creek from which they had a panoramic view of the battlefield. They reined to a stop and Lee beheld the terrible vista before him. Hundreds of Rebels were rushing to the rear with no semblance of order. Regiments, brigades, and divisions had evaporated in the gunfire haze and battle din. This portion of his magnificent Army of Northern Virginia had ceased to exist as a combat arm.

Mahone described the scene and Lee's reaction:

The disaster which had overtaken our army was in full view... hurrying teamsters with their teams and dangling traces (no wagons), retreating infantry without guns, many without hats, a harmless

178

mob, with the massive columns of the enemy moving orderly on. At this spectacle General Lee straightened himself in his saddle, and, looking more the soldier than ever, exclaimed, as if talking to himself, "My God! Has the army dissolved?" As quickly as I could control my own voice I replied: "No, General, here are troops ready to do their duty."[2]

Lee immediately regained his poise and replied, "Yes, General, there are some true men left. Will you please keep those people back?"[3] Mahone galloped off to put his men into battle line, and Lee rode forward to try to rally the disorganized soldiers streaming toward him. He grabbed a battle flag, either from the ground where it had been abandoned or from a color-bearer, and held it aloft. It was one of the most dramatic moments of the entire conflict. The gray flood of men was upon him now. Some ran by without giving Lee a second glance. The wounded crawled, slowly staggered, or limped through the woods and over the fields. Other

Confederate Major General William Mahone

Author's Collection

Confederates saw their commander and stopped in their tracks, milling about Traveller as if the stately horse and rider were immune to the blue tsunami.

"His appearance raised a general tumult," wrote John Esten Cooke. "The dilapidated figures started up from the ground, shouting and gesticulating with hands clenched above their heads."[4]

General Lee!

There's old Uncle Robert!

"It was a stirring scene and a spirit of utter defiance spoke out in the voice of the men, with their dirty uniforms and emaciated faces full of wrath at having been 'scattered,'" Cooke penned. "They were certainly ready to fight again and hailed it as a piece of rare good fortune that 'old Uncle Robert' was there to lead them."[5]

Mahone deployed his infantry to repel the expected assault and returned to Lee, gently taking the flag from him. A soldier in Pickett's Division "ascended the hill...where Lee and Mahone were waiting and watching and soon [was] in the bosom of what remained of the Army of Northern Virginia.[6]

"An artist ought to have seen the old cavalier at this moment," continued Cooke, "sweeping on upon his large iron-gray, whose mane and tail floated in the wind; carrying his field glass half-raised in his right hand; with head erect, gestures animated, and in the whole face and form the expression of the hunter close upon his game. He rode into the twilight among the disordered groups, and the sight of him aroused a tumult."[7]

Riding along the line established by Mahone, Lee called for cannoneers of a battery galloping to the rear to unlimber on a nearby hill. An Irish sergeant among the artillerymen turned to his comrades and said, "Do ye hear, boys, 'tis the General himself that wants us."[8] These chivalric descriptions hardly set the tone of Lee and his army in the fading light of that Thursday.

Lee and Mahone conferred about the army's next move before Lee solemnly retired to Rice's Station and the relative safety of Longstreet's divisions. There he would have time, though precious little of it, to decide what course to take. Shocked and exhausted, he carefully examined the few options left to him. And Lee also reflected on the titanic events that had unfolded at Sailor's Creek that day, saying to his artillery chief, General Pendleton: "General, that half of our army is destroyed."[9]

A smattering of musket shots and thunderclaps of munitions erupted in the paling sunlight, but still the day refused to die, the battlefield illuminated by fires from the hundreds of flaming wagons. Patches of woods and fields also were ablaze, ignited by the battle's gunfire or from detonating ammunition. "I recall the glow of an evening sun, the mystery of a deep valley dimly seen through the trees to our right...our skirmishers pursued the enemy up the farther slope until the flashes of their rifles dotted the hillside, through the darkness like fireflies," remembered Union Colonel Thomas L. Livermore.[10]

"That long line of burning wagons, like a serpent of fire, stretched in graceful curves along the road, was a sight not to be forgotten," wrote Chaplain Samuel H. Merrill of the 1st Maine Cavalry.[11]

"It was terribly beautiful; the firmament in the direction in which the enemy retreated was one immense glow," remembered Trooper Hugo Mulertt of the 10th New York Cavalry.[12] "In a word, we had eight days of disastrous retreat, pushed to the extreme every hour of it," a Rebel surgeon from South Carolina, S. G. Welch, wrote to his wife. "At Sailor's Creek, we were compelled to abandon our wagons. They were captured and burned. What I hated most to lose was a case of the finest surgical instruments that had just run the blockade."[13]

Trying to escape, the Rebel W. L. Timberlake was overtaken by a blue cavalryman but the encounter was less than hostile. Timberlake related that the Yank reined in and asked, "'Johnny, are you hungry?' I said, 'That's a pretty question to ask a rebel.' His reply was, 'Never mind, that's all right. Have you a knife?'" When Timberlake said that he did, the Federal "turned his horse around, and I saw that he had a small ham strapped to the ring of his saddle. He said: 'Cut a piece of this meat quick because I am in a hurry.' I cut off a good slice, and he gave me a handful of hard-tack and said: 'Good-by[e], Johnny.' God bless that Yankee! He saved my life for I was nearly famished."[14]

Georgia Major Basinger was in a group of Confederate prisoners being marched down the hill that Ewell had defended. Stepping over corpses and smoking shell holes, Basinger was about to cross Sailor's Creek when he heard several Union soldiers discussing how a battalion of Georgians had inflicted heavy casualties on them and that one of the unit's officers was lying nearby, badly wounded. Basinger persuaded his guard to let him go to the Southerner and found that it was Lieutenant Frederick Tupper of the 18th Georgia who had been "impetuous as usual in driving the enemy back beyond the creek." The Georgians clasped hands for the last time; Basinger headed to a Federal prison camp and Tupper to die a few days later in a Union field hospital.[15]

Some of these Southern prisoners were bunched into a field surrounded by a temporary corral of rail fences and patrolled by blue sentinels. The Yanks humanely supplied these captives with wood to make campfires for the chilly night. "We were marched, or waded again, across Sailor's Creek and camped that night in an old field, wet, cold and hungry," Virginian Thomas Blake recounted. "We had received no food except what our captors had given us from their haversacks."[16]

Dark also brought on a torch-lit treasure hunt by many Federals, who gleefully plundered the hundreds of captured enemy wagons left on the battlefield and yet to be destroyed. Major Charles P. Mattocks of the 17th Maine saved an order book used by General Longstreet, an English double-barrelled shotgun and an ornate silver-plated bridle. Incredibly, many of the army wagons, carriages, buckboards, and other vehicles held immense troves of food which few, if any, of the starving Rebels ever knew they were guarding. Hungry Federals feasted on beef, boiled ham, bacon, onions, pickles, smashing in to barrels of applejack to sooth their thirsts.[17]

Other Yankees rummaged through the cargoes searching for souvenirs, which were numerous. In officers' trunks they found dress swords, other side arms, and belongings. One of the wagons contained a litter of puppies.[18] Some of the soldiers capered about their campfires wearing new Confederate uniforms they had salvaged. Others donned Rebel clothing as a matter of necessity to replace their own worn jackets and pants. Delavan S. Miller, a New York drummer boy from Watertown, described one Yankee who found personal effects of Rebel General Mahone and "dressed himself up in the coat, sash, etc. that had been worn by the distinguished Confederate."[19]

The battle-honed bluecoats of Miles' Division, II Corps, spent their evening playing high stakes card games. Among their pillage were several wagons containing a wealth of currency issued by the Confederate States Treasury.

General Miles remembered the scene:

A Monte Carlo was suddenly improvised in the midst of the bivouac of war. Spreading their blankets on the ground by the fires, the veterans proceeded with the comedy, and such preposterous gambling was probably never witnessed. Ten thousand dollars was the usual ante; often twenty thousand dollars to come in; a raise of fifty thousand to one hundred thousand was not unusual and frequently from one million to two million dollars were in the "pool." "Be prudent stranger!" "Don't go beyond your means, my friends!" "Ain't I glad I'm in *this* army!"[20]

Miles watched his raucously celebrating soldiers with a degree of solemnity. Some Yanks offered a wealth of Confederate greenbacks to disconsolate Rebel prisoners, many of whom either refused it or flung the money into the fires or the night sky. "They kept up the revelry during most of the night," Miles recalled, "though some were to make the soldiers' sacrifice on the morrow, while others were to witness the scene of final triumph."[21]

"We had in our Regiment about fifty Rebel officers prisoners," Elisha Hunt Rhodes recounted. "We set fire to the wagons which appeared to be loaded with potatoes and sorgham [*sic*] molasses, which our boys enjoyed."[22]

Maine Private John Haley was one of the thousands of Yankee stragglers who had fallen behind in the mad marching and countermarching to trap Lee. While he had been involved in the day's early skirmishing, he missed the main battle between the II Corps and Gordon's Confederates. Trudging through the cool night he happened upon some engineers from his corps and accompanied them to Humphreys' lines, reaching them about 10 p.m. Haley suddenly was immersed in a throng of Rebel prisoners milling about a large house just over Sailor's Creek where Humphreys had established his headquarters. Haley wrote in his April 6 diary entry:

> In the rear of the house are two thousand Rebel prisoners, among them General Ewell and several generals of lower grade. The prisoners go in and out as they please, seemingly more jolly than their captors. There is no fear of their escaping, for it is useless for them to return to their own army. With us, they have *something* to eat. As for going home, many are hundreds, even thousands, of miles from home and they are too weak to walk far. Destruction and

starvation on one hand, surrender on the other. Still many cling to General Lee with childlike faith.[23]

The floorboards dripped blood. In the basement of the Hillsman house, Lucy Hillsman, her mother-in-law, and the others huddled, listening to the groans and screams of the wounded men above them. The farmhouse had become a field hospital for the Union VI Corps, but dozens of men from both sides lay in and around the home. Army surgeons probed and sawed away, with amputated arms and legs being tossed out the windows.

J. S. McNeily was among butternuts from Kershaw's Division bunched into a makeshift prison pen. He was startled to see the red-sashed Yank officer, whom he had unseated from his horse with a rifle shot, checking and interrogating the captive Rebels. The Federal was looking in particular for the Johnny who had tried to kill him and McNeily stayed out of view. He recalled the incident years later:

> So I remained out of the light of the camp fire and quietly backed away, before I could be identified, into the deeper darkness, watching this kindly intentioned Yankee depart, leaving behind him a string of cuss words. I learned afterwards, and I mention it in his excuse, that in losing our colors he forfeited a claim to a ninety-day furlough."[24]

With a campfire illuminating them, these Confederates reverently unfurled their banner and consigned it to the flames. Color-bearer A. A. Trescott had hidden the standard in his jacket. McNeily remembered the solemn, impromptu ceremony:

"The end then came to the flag that had waved over the regiment at Gettysburg, Chickamauga, Knoxville, the Wilderness, Spotsylvania, Hanover, Cold Harbor, Petersburg, Berryville, Cedar Creek and Sailor's Creek."[25]

Chapter 21

"I Surrender Lieutenant-General Ewell..."

The circumstances of General Ewell's surrender are clouded and controversial, based on battle accounts. Ewell stated that he surrendered himself and his staff to a Union cavalry officer who approached down the road from the direction of Anderson's Corps. "Old Baldy" knew he was beaten and asked the trooper to send a dispatch to Custis Lee suggesting that he capitulate as well. "At my request, he sent a messenger to General G. W. C. Lee, who was nearest, with a note from me telling him he was surrounded," Ewell recalled. "General Anderson's attack had failed, I had surrendered, and he had better do so too, to prevent useless loss of life, though I gave no orders, being a prisoner."[1]

As to his captor, Ewell likely was referring to Captain Samuel Stevens of Company C, 1st New York Cavalry in Custer's Division. Stevens is reported to have taken Ewell and all his staff and Ewell is said to have presented him with his field glasses as a souvenir of the occasion. Custer backed this claim in an April 15 dispatch to Merritt, writing, "Lieutenant-General Ewell and six other general officers were captured...by my command."[2]

Union Brevet Major Hiram W. Day, however, told a different story. Day, inspector general for the First Brigade in Seymour's Division, recalled in an April 11 report that the enemy was being driven back when the Rebels showed a true flag near a house on the right of the advance of the 106th New York and about three hundred yards distant. Day signaled the development to Brevet Major Charles H. Leonard, the brigade's assistant adjutant general, who immediately ordered a cease fire. "Some men were ordered to move forward and gain information of its object," Day wrote of the truce flag, but, "Upon their advancing they received a severe fire from the enemy. At some distance to our right our lines were again immediately advanced, the enemy constantly falling back and returning but a feeble fire."[3]

Day reported that he was approached by a private "whose regiment and name I do not remember," saying that "General Ewell of the Confederate Army wished to surrender his forces." A cavalry unit then galloped past their right and slammed into the Rebel positions.

Union Colonel William S. Truex
Monmouth County Historical
Association, Freehold, N.J.
U.S. Army Military History Institute

"I at once called the attention of Major Leonard to the fact of the flag of truce and surrender," Day recalled. Leonard quickly rode forward onto the battlefield and was met by Major James W. Pegram, the inspector general on Ewell's staff. According to Day, Pegram told Leonard that he was surrendering the general and his staff and had "come in for that purpose with a flag of truce. Up to this moment, the firing on our left was kept up by our troops, but on word being passed down the line it ceased immediately," Day wrote.[4]

General Seymour's First Brigade commander, Colonel Truex, contributed other details of Ewell's surrender. Based on orders from Seymour, Truex had wheeled his brigade to the left to attack an exposed section of the Rebel line after closing with Ewell's defenders. His men were delivering a rapid and concentrated fire when a truce flag appeared near a house about three hundred yards away and to the right of his advance. "The command was immediately ordered to cease firing, but on moving forward to gain information, fire from the enemy at some distance to our right was again opened on me," Truex wrote in his report. "I again directed the brigade to advance. At this moment Major

Leonard...rode up to me with Major Pegram...the bearer of the flag of truce." Pegram, based on Truex's recollection, "said to me in person, 'I surrender Lieutenant-General Ewell and staff and his command.'"[5]

Mirroring Day's account, Truex noted that the brigade, along with other Union troops on his left, stopped firing as word of the surrender passed down the line. Pegram's entourage under the white flag consisted of "about 30 officers and enlisted men," Truex noted.[6]

Colonel Thomas Allen of the 5th Wisconsin added yet another twist. He reported that during the "general stampede" of the Rebels, Captain Henry Curran of his regiment saw "a general officer and staff making to the rear and left..." Curran sent a squad of soldiers forward to watch their movements. "These men soon got into their rear, when, seeing farther retreat useless, Lieutenant General Ewell surrendered himself and his staff. Ewell capitulated to Sergeant Angus Cameron, the squad leader, "remarking that he surrendered himself and five thousand men, and inquired for an officer; none being present at the moment he surrendered unconditionally.[7]

"Soon after, a squad of cavalry came up and claimed the prisoners and took possession of them." Allen went on to name Ewell's captors as Cameron, Corporals Charles Roughan, August Brocker, and John J. Cosat and Privates John W. Davis and H. W. True.[8]

"Rushing through the broad gap between Ewell and myself, the heavy Federal force soon surrounded the command of that brave old one-legged hero, and forced him to surrender," the Rebel General Gordon wrote.[9]

CHAPTER 22
"TOO UNEQUAL AND OVERWHELMING"

From his bivouac, Sheridan wrote to Grant at Burke's Station Thursday night, briefly describing the magnitude of the victory:

CAVALRY HEADQUARTERS,
April 6, 1865.

Lieutenant General U. S. GRANT,
Commanding Armies of the United States:

GENERAL: I have the honor to report that the enemy made a stand at the intersection of the Burke's Station road with the road upon which they were retreating. I attacked them with two divisions of the Sixth Army Corps and routed them handsomely, making a connection with the cavalry. I am still pressing on with both cavalry and infantry. Up to the present time we have captured Generals Ewell, Kershaw, Barton, Corse, De Foe [DuBose], and Custis Lee, several thousand prisoners, 14 pieces of artillery, with caissons, and a large number of wagons. If the thing is pressed I think that Lee will surrender.

P. H. SHERIDAN,
Major-General, Commanding.[1]

En route Sheridan's courier, Colonel Redwood Price, stopped at Meade's headquarters west of Deatonville and let him read the message. Meade was apparently greatly surprised by the immensity of the Sailor's Creek victory. He also was taken aback by the fact that none of

188

his infantry generals had notified him of the triumph and that Sheridan appeared to take sole credit for the rout. Of Meade's corps commanders, Humphreys was the first to send him word of what happened at Sailor's Creek.

Before receiving word from Sheridan, Grant did not know the extent of the victory. But culling details from the front, he was optimistic in a dispatch sent to Colonel T. S. Bowers at City Point on Thursday afternoon. Grant singled out the infantry divisions of Brigadier General Robert S. Foster and Brigadier General John W. Turner that had marched almost 30 miles the previous day to reach Burke's Station. Grant had ridden to the station from Jetersville late in the day.

At the time of the dispatch, Grant did not know that Turner's Ohio and Pennsylvania regiments had been destroyed during the High Bridge raid:

> These troops were sent out to Farmville this [Thursday] afternoon, and, I am in hopes, will head the enemy, and enable us to totally break up the Army of Northern Virginia. The troops are all pushing now, though it is after night, and they have had no rest for more than one week. The finest spirits prevail among the men, and I believe that in three days more Lee will not have an army of 5,000 men to take out of Virginia, and no train or supplies...[2]

In a 10 p.m. dispatch to Grant, Meade said:

> It is impossible at this moment to give any estimate of the casualties on either side or of the number of prisoners taken, but it is evident today's work is not going to be one of the least important in the recent brilliant operations.[3]

Grant sent this victory message to Meade at 12:10 a.m. on April 7:

> Sheridan and Wright have struck the enemy, captured a great many of the general officers, and from 10,000 to 12,000 men. Every moment now is important to us...[4]

Grant had not yet received Meade's 10 p.m. telegram, which did not arrive until 3:20 a.m. Friday. Both generals were getting reports from the front and the communications of the age did not allow for rapid responses. Thus, a succession of messages was passed between them essentially conveying the same information: a monumental Union victory had been won at Sailor's Creek. At City Point, President Lincoln learned of Sheridan's message to Grant and bluntly voiced his opinion in an 11 a.m. Friday dispatch to Grant:

> Gen. Sheridan says, "If the thing is pressed I think Lee will surrender." Let the thing be pressed.[5]

In effect, the battle annihilated the already decimated Army of Northern Virginia as a fighting force. This black Thursday of the Confederacy cost Lee seven thousand to eight thousand men, about one-third of the army that had left Amelia Court House the previous day. Eight Confederate generals were in enemy hands. Ewell's Corps no longer existed, having lost some three thousand four hundred of the approximately three thousand six hundred men engaged. Gordon had about three hundred dead or wounded and one thousand seven hundred captured. Anderson's casualties were two thousand six hundred out of his six thousand three hundred. Federal losses were one thousand one hundred fifty to one thousand one hundred eighty, depending on the source. Included in this toll were more than four hundred sustained by Wright, five hundred thirty by Humphreys and some one hundred seventy cavalrymen.

On no other battleground of the war had Lee's divisions endured such sacrifice based on the number of troops engaged. Union General Keifer may have put it best:

> It may truthfully be said that Sailor's Creek was not only the last general field battle of the war, but the one wherein more officers and men were captured...than in any battle of modern times.[6]

The Confederates had been even further reduced to a ragged rabble, many without weapons, which scarcely resembled the proud and cocksure legions that had marched to the front in the war's early months. No longer could Lee even consider any major offensive action, even against the weakest Union menace. Even before the Thursday nightmare, he had turned away to avoid battling the unknown size of Sheridan's cavalry and infantry at Jetersville.

With the horrendous losses at Sailor's Creek, Lee now could do little more than prod his dwindling, dirty columns toward the forlorn hope of a darkening western horizon.

There was little sympathy on the part of the Federals whom Lee had bested on so many fields. The blood of Union troops who suffered through the incompetence or wanton grossness of their commanders soaked the countryside from First Bull Run to Cold Harbor. Nothing but the trumpet of the Almighty could bring these men back from their graves. And nothing but the final bugle calls of victory, that eventually would resound from the woods and fields around Appomattox Court House, would end the violent madness. Thus, it was with a vengeful ferocity—as well as a deep-hearted homesickness and weariness of war—that Billy Yank swept after what was left of Lee's army.

These boys in blue were driven to avenge the setbacks, but their more fervent desire was to end the fighting and return home after honing a peace. And once the day's slaughters were done, some threads of civility were woven between the foes—Sailor's Creek was no different. "The infantry which we had so recently repulsed soon came up with smiling faces," recounted one of Ewell's surrendered Confederates. "They showed no resentment, but opened their haversacks and offered to share their hard-tack with us, saying: 'You Johnnies certainly did put up a good fight.'"[7]

In their brief conference on the battlefield, and during a meeting later that night, Robert Lee and Mahone worked out a plan possibly to save what remained of the Army of Northern Virginia. While Mahone's troops held off the enemy, Longstreet's other divisions were to march to Farmville that night and before daybreak Friday. As rearguard, Mahone would retreat across country before dawn and cross the High Bridge over the Appomattox. He was to hold this crossing of the South Side Railroad until all Rebel units were across. Confederate engineers were then to burn High Bridge and the planked wagon bridge just below it. Mahone's prewar expertise as a railroad construction engineer would aid him in ensuring the bridges' destruction, the Confederates believed.[8]

Lee's only hope was that he could outmarch the Yanks, as his men had done so many times before, and cross to the north side of the Appomattox. If the bridges were destroyed after him, his divisions might get some rest, at least for a few hours. Lee also received encouragement from another area. Commissary General St. John had reached Farmville and located the provisions the Confederates had sent up the line from Burke's Station. The eighty thousand rations of meal and about forty thousand of bread would be more valuable than gold for his men, many of whom had not been issued regular rations since Sunday. No doubt disheartened by the disaster that had waylaid his army this day, Lee had returned to Longstreet's lines at Rice's Station. Somehow, someway, he had to find a way out of this snare! Longstreet, however, was not informed of the Sailor's Creek calamity until sometime on Friday morning:

> I heard nothing of the affair at Sailor's Creek, nor from General Lee, until next morning. Our work at Rice's Station was not very serious, but was continued until night, when we marched and crossed the Appomattox at Farmville without loss...[9]

In his postwar memoir, Longstreet would write that while Ewell fought with "resolute coolness," the Union attacks were so battering that the "Confederate rear was crushed to fragments."[10]

Lee still was absorbing the dreadful events of the day when an officer approached him. John Wise, the messenger from President Davis, finally had found Lee after a harrowing journey by train, on foot, and by horse around and through the enemy lines. Wise knew that matters were extreme based on what he had seen of the retreating Confederates that day. Briefly encountering Mahone, the general had told him that the enemy had "knocked hell out of Pickett," that afternoon. Now he was in the presence of the army commander himself who was standing near a low-burning campfire of fence rails, dictating orders to his aide Colonel Charles Marshall. Wise introduced himself and explained his mission. "The enemy's cavalry is already flanking us from the south and east," Wise recalled of Lee's answer about his army's situation. "You may say to Mr. Davis that, as he knows, my original purpose was to adhere to the line of the Danville Road," Wise quoted Lee. "I have been unable to do so and am now endeavoring to...retire in the direction of Lynchburg." Wise then asked Lee if he intended to try to make a stand anywhere, to which the commander replied, "No, no; I shall have to be governed by each day's developments. A few more Sailor's Creeks and it will be over—ended—just as I have expected it would from the first."[11]

Lee suggested that Wise get some rest before beginning his return to Danville. Before leaving Lee, Wise asked if the general had any news about his father, Henry, who had been in the battle. "No, no," Lee answered. "At nightfall his command was fighting obstinately at Sailor's Creek, surrounded by the enemy...I fear they were captured, or—or—worse."[12]

Many of the Federals who fought at Sailor's Creek recognized the significance of their triumph. "This was a glorious day for the Army of the Potomac," recalled one of Sheridan's troopers.[13] "The troops felt the immense importance of success in this, the last battle fought by Lee's Army of Northern Virginia," wrote General Wheaton of the VI Corps, "and their marching and fighting was all that could be wished."[14] General Wright related:

> In this battle of Sailor's Creek the [VI] corps nobly sustained its previous well-earned reputation. It made the forced march which preceded that battle with great cheerfulness and enthusiasm, and went into the fight with a determination to be successful seldom evinced by the best troops, and by its valor made the battle of Sailor's Creek the most important of the last and crowning contests against the rebel Army of Northern Virginia. The corps has always fought well, but never better than in the assault at Petersburg, and at Sailor's Creek four days later."[15]

The Federals also acknowledged the superiority of Union firepower in deciding the battle. None were more grateful than Captain Archibald Hopkins whose 37th Massachusetts was involved in much of the heaviest combat. Hopkins' exhausted men had formed with a patchwork force of Olcott's 121st New York on their right to secure the sector after their holocaust with the Rebel Naval Battalion and Stiles' artillerymen. "It is a settled conviction of all engaged that had we not been armed with the Spencer rifle we should not have been able to maintain our position," Hopkins recounted, "but on the other hand, all would have been destroyed or captured."[16]

The Union artillery, with no opposing guns, played a huge part in the devastation of Ewell's Corps. Captain Cowan of the VI Corps artillery wrote:

> The natural position for artillery being good, a most effective fire was kept up until the enemy was routed. Prisoners stated that it was the most terrific fire that they were exposed to. So many killed and wounded from the fire of artillery has seldom been seen in this war in so small a space.[17]

Cowan's artillerists, meanwhile, came through the fight with only two men from Battery E being slightly wounded.

As he settled into the VI Corps camp that night, the weary engineer Captain Frank Harwood noted with topographical preciseness how the terrain had aided the Union columns in overtaking the Confederate army:

> It is to be observed that the pursuit during the day was greatly facilitated by the state of the roads, which were, as a general rule, in excellent condition; this I attribute to the rolling nature of the country, which was well drained by abrupt ravines, the roads being generally on the ridges.[18]

With the battle over, Wright sent his Second Division under General Getty, which had not been engaged in its support role, two miles to the front. Getty pushed skirmishers two miles further, but did not encounter any serious opposition. The First and Third Divisions of the VI Corps moved up on either side of Getty's position and bivouacked for the night.

The Union V Corps, which did not fight at Sailor's Creek, had marched and countermarched about 32 miles on Thursday. General Griffin's men had encountered only "small detachments of cavalry" during the day but had rounded up "about 300 wagons and many prisoners" for their efforts.[19]

Under guard, General Ewell was taken to Horatio Wright's head-quarters. The generals had been at West Point together and Wright was cordial. "I'm glad to see you, Ewell," he called as the Confederate dismounted. Ewell profanely fumed that he could not return the pleasure, but the moment passed quickly and they soon were talking over old times and the day's events.[20]

Ewell later recalled that Wright told him that some thirty thousand enemy troops were engaged against him at Sailor's Creek, including the two infantry corps and the cavalry divisions. Ewell's men did not face that many Yanks, but the total Federals involved in the Sailor's Creek battles was just under forty thousand. During their talk, Ewell told Wright that he had not intended to fight the VI Corps. He assumed that the enemy behind him was Sheridan's cavalry and when he discovered otherwise, it was too late to avoid a battle.[21]

When his corps was crushed, Ewell described how he and his staff had purposely ridden toward the VI Corps infantry, preferring to surrender to them than to the despised Sheridan. Ewell was telling this story when another Federal officer joined them and Wright introduced Ewell to Sheridan himself.

Ewell would have high praise for his division commanders:

> I deem it proper to remark that the discipline preserved in camp
> and on the march by General G. W. C. Lee, and the manner in
> which he handled his troops in action, fully justified the request I
> had made for his promotion. General Kershaw, who had only been
> a few days under my command, behaved with his usual coolness
> and judgment.[22]

At Ewell's request, the captive Major Stiles was brought to see him. Some of the Union officers earlier had complimented Ewell for his fight and had singled out Stiles' troops as especially courageous. Stiles would never forget the moment:

> Looking back upon the teeming recollections of this first and last
> retreat and this final battle of the Army of Northern Virginia, amid
> all the overpowering sadness and depression of defeat, I already

felt the sustaining consciousness of a real and a worthy success; but it is impossible to express how this consciousness was deepened and heightened when General Ewell sent for me on the field, after we were all captured, and in the presence of half a dozen generals, said that he had summoned me to say, in the hearing of these officers, that the conduct of my battalion had been reported to him, and that he desired to congratulate me and them upon the record they made.[23]

Ewell also lauded the heavy artillery brigade of Lee's Division. Despite the loss of their commander, Colonel Crutchfield, the gunners "displayed a coolness and gallantry that earned the praise of the veterans who fought alongside it, and even of the enemy."[24]

Kershaw realized that the hopelessness of his situation at Sailor's Creek did nothing to detract from the bravery and spirit of his division. "The conduct of the officers and men of the command under these trying circumstances is beyond all praise," he wrote in a postwar account written from his home in Camden, South Carolina. "On no battle-field of the war have I felt a juster pride in the conduct of my command." Kershaw also complimented Barham and his "little command" of dismounted cavalry for their combat actions.[25]

Ewell dined with Wright and after supper they joined other officers near Sheridan's bivouac. The group talked of West Point days and of what they expected on the morrow when the chase of Lee resumed. Ewell appeared quietly despondent for the most part, staring at the ground. Another Confederate recalled that "'Fighting Dick Ewell' looked like an old eagle with one of his wings clipped."[26] At one point he did open up and the Federals listened intently, one of them describing the diatribe. The Confederacy had been doomed on the day Grant besieged Petersburg, Ewell lamented. Peace negotiations initiated by the Southern government had been botched as well as being too late in coming. Because of these diplomatic foul-ups by Richmond, Ewell said that "For every man that was killed after this somebody would be responsible and it would be little better than murder," the Yankee officer recounted. "He could not tell what General Lee would do, but he hoped that he would at once surrender his army."[27]

Ewell closed by entreating Sheridan to demand Lee's surrender to prevent further bloodshed.

General Longstreet heaped laurels on the conduct of Anderson and Ewell at Sailor's Creek, writing that the generals "are barely known in the retreat, but their stand and fight on that trying march were among the most soldier-like of the many noble deeds of the war."[28] Fitz Lee, however, felt that Anderson erred in not attacking immediately when Custer's cavalry first broke his advance. "I am clearly of the opinion...that had the troops been rapidly massed when their march was first interrupted, they could have cleared the way," Lee wrote in his report.[29]

Longstreet's war memoir, in which he criticized Robert Lee, was acidic blasphemy to many aging Rebels. And "Old Pete" did not mince words in taking a shot at Fitz Lee's individual performance at Sailor's Creek: "The chief of cavalry was there, but his troopers were elsewhere, and he rode away, advising the force to follow him."[30] Longstreet added that Anderson and Ewell probably could have reached safety but that they "were true soldiers, and decided to fight, even to sacrifice their commands if necessary, to break or delay the pursuit..."[31]

In the April 15, 1865, edition of the New York *Herald*, was a report dated April 9 from correspondent S. T. Bulkley at Farmville. In this account, Bulkley gave his description of the Sailor's Creek battle scene:

> The slaughter of the enemy [Confederate] in the fight of the 6th inst. exceeded anything I ever saw. The ground over which they fought was literally strewn with their killed. The fighting was desperate, in many cases hand-to-hand. There were a number of bayonet wounds reported at the hospital.[32]

When Virginia Captain Thomas Blake read Bulkley's narrative years after the war, he reacted angrily:

> There was nothing said about the slaughter of his own men. We had an idea that we had done some "slaughtering" ourselves. At any rate, the letter shows that the fight at Sailor's Creek was no child's play...[33]

Another journalist's account better suited the Confederate veterans. William Swinton was a Scottish war correspondent for the Union whose *Campaigns of the Army of the Potomac* was published in 1866. Here he describes the Rebels' retreat and battles at Sailor's Creek:

> The misery of the famished troops passed all experience of military anguish...Thus pressed upon, with blazing wagons in front and rear, amid hunger, fatigue, and sleeplessness, they fared toward the setting sun...But even while thus environed these men showed they could exact a price before yielding. And when our advance was made by a part of the 6th Corps, they delivered so deadly a fire that a portion of that veteran line bent and broke under it. But the numbers were too unequal and overwhelming.[34]

CHAPTER 23
"AND YET MEN MUST DIE."

Much of the Union cavalry was widely scattered during the battle, victoriously romping through the woods and country roads to pistol, saber, or capture fleeing Rebels. The rattle of Spencers was incessant before the squadrons reassembled during the night and into the early hours of April 7. Other Federal horsemen kept up the chase. The troopers of Devin's Division hurtled through the dark Virginia forests, carbines spouting flame as they piled into elements of the Confederate rearguard.

The Rebels were driven back across Big Sailor's Creek where Devin's men were stopped cold. On the opposite bank was Mahone's Division, posted behind breastworks and bulwarked by artillery. Cannon and small arms fire stabbed the night, and Devin prudently withdrew his cavalry, encamping about a mile to the rear near midnight.

Some of Rosser's cavalry rejoined Lee's army after dark and went into battle line late Thursday night to protect what remained of the slow-moving wagon train. "Less than a mile away the camp-fires of Grant's army shone brightly through the gloom of that dismal night," remembered a Virginia captain.[1]

Sheridan, meanwhile, camped for the evening near Sailor's Creek. Colonel F. C. Newhall of his staff described "Little Phil":

> He is lying on the broad of his back on a blanket, with his feet to
> the fire, in a condition of sleepy wakefulness. Clustered about are
> blue uniforms and gray in equal numbers, and immediately around

his campfire are most of the Confederate generals. Ewell is sitting on the ground hugging his knees, his face bent down between his arms.[2]

Custer was a gracious host to the captured General Kershaw and Colonel Frank Huger, both of South Carolina. Huger and Custer reminisced about their West Point days, including a particularly golden incident. Huger had been among upperclassmen hazing plebe Custer when the two found some diversion in gambling. The Southerner had a set of ornately gold Spanish spurs supposedly worn by Mexican Presidente-General Antonio Lopez de Santa Anna when he was captured in 1836 during the war for Texas independence. A tumble of the dice sent the spurs home with Custer and Huger had ever since wailed that "Fanny" Custer had used loaded ivories.[3]

The ailing General Hunton also was brought to Custer to guard for the night and Hunton wrote that he was "treated very kindly." In a later letter to his wife, Hunton recalled: "General Custer, upon hearing that I was sick, sent his physician to me with a bottle of imported French brandy, and furnished me with a hair mattress to sleep on. He was as kind as a man could be, and I shall never forget his generous treatment."[4]

When Kershaw first entered Custer's camp, an aide introduced the Carolinian to his captor. Years after the war and Custer's legendary last stand at Little Big Horn, Kershaw wrote to Elizabeth Custer, describing this April 6–7 encounter and his stay at the wolverine's lair. Kershaw recounted that Custer greeted him with a handshake and smile:

> "I am glad to see you here. I feel as if I ought to know about you."
> "Yes," said I, "General, we have met very often but not under circumstances favorable to cultivating an acquaintance." This little passage of pleasantry made us quite at home immediately, and very soon the conversation became free, general and kindly around the camp fire. With a soldier's hospitality, we were made to feel welcome by our host, and notwithstanding our misfortunes, enjoyed not a little the camp luxuries of coffee, sugar, condensed milk, hard-tack, broiled ham, etc., spread before us upon the tent fly converted into a table cloth around which we all sat upon the ground. After supper we smoked and talked over many subjects of interest

to all of us dwelling, however, almost wholly upon the past. The future to us was not inviting, and our host with true delicacy of feeling avoided the subject. We slept beneath the stars, Custer sharing his blankets with me...[5]

"I hope peace is near at hand and that God in His goodness will again permit us to meet, never to be separated again," George Custer opened in a letter to his wife on April 7. He detailed brother Tom's adventures and the extent of his injuries. In closing, he penned, "Won't Father Custer and Father Bacon [the general's father-in-law] be delighted to hear of Tom's gallantry? Do you want to know what I think of him? Tom should have been the General and I the Lieutenant."[6] Not until Saturday, April 8, did Custer write to Elizabeth and describe the events of Sailor's Creek:

> Day before yesterday was another glorious day for our arms and particularly for the 3rd Cavalry Division. I again made a flank movement, got in rear of the Rebel army and routed their entire force, capturing six Generals, including one Lieutenant General, thirty battle flags, fifteen guns, ten thousand prisoners, three hundred wagons. All the above captures were made by the 3rd Division thanks to an all-wise Providence who guided us safely and triumphantly through the dangers of the battlefield and again crowned our efforts with victory.[7]

At Friday daybreak, many of the Federal horsemen were turned out to escort the thousands of Confederate prisoners to the rear. The Johnnies would be marched to Burke's Station and then east along the railroad toward Petersburg.

Some of these Rebs were guarded by the 1st Connecticut Cavalry on the first phase of their journey to prisoner of war camps. A Federal trooper recalled:

> They marched past [Third] Division headquarters in immense ranks. They had some spirit in them, notwithstanding all the hardships they had gone thro'. The Division Bands were playing as...they

marched; when they played "Yankee Doodle," "Hail Columbia," & kindred tunes, they would groan, but as…they struck up "Dixie," this called out rousing cheers from them…it was a noble sight [as] they moved off, with the manner & tread of trained soldiers, & it was impossible not to accord them respect as brave men. Often enough had we met them to prove this.[8]

Virginian David Johnston would recall that he and his comrades "had made a brave and gallant fight" but were "the victims of gross blunders on the part of someone in authority on the field, as well as [being] overwhelmed by superior numbers."[9]

At Custer's headquarters, prisoner General Kershaw awoke to blue cavalrymen scurrying about in brisk activity:

Our host [Custer] was already up and gave me a cheery greeting as I arose and joined him standing near the fire. He wore an air of thought upon his face, betokening the work of the day that lay before him and received and sent many rapid communications.[10]

As he breakfasted with Custer, Kershaw was distracted by the arrival of a Union rider bearing a Confederate flag. The Federal soon was joined by another cavalryman and then another, all carrying Rebel banners. Kershaw wrote:

One after another some 30 troopers rode up within a few rods, each dismounting and aligning himself, holding his horse by the bridle. Each also carried a Confederate battleflag, except my captor of the previous day whom I recognized in the ranks, and he bore two of our flags. He also, as he caught my eye and bowed, pointed to my own sabre worn with an air of pride and pleasure.

My curiosity was greatly excited by this group and I asked General Custer what it meant. "That," said he, "is my escort for the day. It is my custom after a battle to select for my escort a sort of *garde de honeur* those men of each regiment who most distinguished themselves in action, bearing for the time, the trophies which they have taken from the enemy. These men are selected as the captors of the flags which they bear."

I counted them. There were 31 captured banners representing 31 of our regiments killed, captured or dispersed the day before. It was not comforting to think of...

He [Custer] shook my hand, mounted a magnificent charger and rode proudly away followed at a gallop by his splendid escort bearing the fallen flags. As he neared his conquering legions cheer after cheer greeted his approach, bugles sounded and sabres flashed as they saluted. The proud cavalcade filed through the open ranks and moved to the front, leading that magnificent column in splendid array.[11]

Kershaw was among officers in a mass of Confederate prisoners getting ready to march to the Union rear when Custer again appeared with his entourage. Captain James H. Stevenson of the 1st New York Cavalry remembered the scene:

As Custer took the road he ordered his band to strike up "Bonnie Dundee." On approaching the prisoners he spied the group of officers and raised his hat, bowing politely as he galloped past. This action was repeated by his staff, and the rebels seemed electrified by the un-looked for civility. General Kershaw...turned to the others and, in the most enthusiastic manner, exclaimed: "By G-d that man is the embodiment of chivalry! And the next moment the well known 'rebel yell' was heard...Our boys returned the compliment with three rousing Yankee cheers, and the band struck up 'The Bonnie Blue Flag,' which almost made the prisoners wild with delight."[12]

Leaving his horse, Rifle, at Wright's headquarters, Ewell joined Kershaw and the other captured generals in gray. The eight settled into an ambulance for the journey to Burke's Station at the head of a five-thousand-man column of Southern prisoners. The Yanks actually had a ninth Confederate general in the ranks of the captives but did not realize it. Virginia Major James M. Goggin, 44, had temporarily commanded the South Carolina brigade of Brigadier General James Conner in Kershaw's Division at the battle of Cedar Creek after Conner had lost a leg in fighting a few days earlier. Goggin was promoted to brigadier general as of December 4, 1864, but his commission was subsequently cancelled for reasons that remain unclear.[13] Goggin was among the Sailor's Creek prisoners, apparently serving with Kershaw as a staff officer.

Before the gloomy procession set out, captured Georgia Major Basinger was requested to appear before Ewell. Basinger found Ewell sitting with an entourage of fellow prisoners around a campfire. The general thanked and commended him on the performance of his troops.

Included in the Union guard of the gray captives was the 49th Pennsylvania, which had broken in the face of the Confederate counterattack.[14]

Other elements of Sheridan's cavalry were in pursuit early on Friday, following Lee's main route toward Farmville.

Troopers in Crook's command rode past regiments of the VI Corps who, already on the march, were "singing, laughing, joking and apparently happy as they marched along, though a little inclined to growl at being obliged to let the cavalry have the road, while they took the rougher, harder-to-march-over ground at the side," a Maine trooper wrote. "Along the side were evidences around in loose profusion—a dead rebel soldier lying on the road where he halted for the last time, with every appearance of having died from hunger and exhaustion—dead horses, the infallible army guideboards, lying where they dropped, and others abandoned because unable longer to carry their riders—all informed the men that the men ahead of them were in a great hurry, and had an exhilarating effect upon their spirits."[15]

Multitudes of tired but cheering blue infantry clogged the roads, intent on finally finishing Bobby Lee. The mood had been much the same in July 1861, when Union columns, spurred by calls of "On to Richmond!" shined their muskets and swung out of camps around Washington, confidently intent on smashing the rebellion. That picnic lark had ended in ruinous rout along the banks of a tiny creek called Bull Run. But that was ancient history—long buried in the blood, pain, and dust of infinite skirmishes, campaigns, and grand battles.

The almost four years since then had been total and ceaseless war, no matter whether fought over a Missouri meadow, the New Mexico desert, or through a South Carolina backwater. Martial glory had long faded amid every loss of a comrade, friend, or relative to an Enfield bullet, the sudden burst of a Parrott shell or, most often, to pneumonia, fever, scurvy, or other ailment. Yet from the shameful waters of Bull Run, the Army of the Potomac emerged, an awesomely powerful weapon that had knifed Lee's jugular at another Virginia stream—Sailor's Creek.

Colonel Theodore Lyman of Meade's staff described how he rode along one of the roads taken by Lee's comatose regiments as the chase resumed that Friday:

> The way was completely strewed with tents, ammunition, officers' baggage, and above all, little Dutch ovens—such a riches of little Dutch ovens I have never seen! I suppose they bake hoecakes in them. You saw them lying about, with their little legs kicked up in the air, in a piteous manner.[16]

Foot-raw Maine Private John Haley found a pair of army brogans "that had been abandoned by some providential circumstance. I felt as if I had experienced a change of heart, so great and sudden was my relief. My heart was as light as my purse two days after payday."[17]

Like the previous days of the chase, the Yanks marched over and around the flotsam of a dying enemy army. Haley related:

> We moved on, going through the debris of yesterday's battles for three miles at least. One of our officers found a gold watch, another a gold chain, and still others scooped up abandoned treasure. The Rebs have made the mistake of loading their trains with foppery, but no food. Quite a lot of the aristocracy are fleeing in their own private carriages, but their goods are in the army wagons. Hence the frequent delays along the route. If it weren't for this, the Rebel army would doubtless leave us behind.[18]

"Yesterday, the old VI Corps had a grand fight and won a victory that must help to bring the war to a close," wrote Elisha Hunt Rhodes. "Thank God that I am alive. My heart is sad to think of the brave officers and men that died yesterday. So near the end and yet men must die."[19]

The dead and wounded of Sailor's Creek were left behind as both armies rapidly marched to their destinies. Union soldiers dug at least one mass grave near the stream to hold the Southern slain, but a multitude of Rebel corpses were left where they fell. Under the warm spring sun the bodies began decomposing rapidly and a number of area civilians, including former slaves, turned out to gather and inter them on the battlefield.

"One week after the battle I visited the field and could then have walked on Confederate dead...along the face of the heights held by the enemy when the battle opened," related General Keifer.[20] A number of men, foes united in death, were buried on the Hillsman farm. The Northerners later would be reinterred at Poplar Grove National Cemetery in Petersburg.

Making history was no comfort to the soldiers of both sides writhing in the agony of their wounds and awaiting medical attention. Burke's Station had been designated as the expected depot for the Army of the Potomac by the Federal high command on the night of April 6 and the Union medical corps set up camps there. They anticipated some two thousand five hundred wounded which was later proven to be a well-founded estimate.

A major problem immediately faced by the Union medics was the fact that a hotel and its outbuildings at the depot already were jammed with hurt Rebels as well as sick and wounded bluecoats. The Southerners had used the hotel as a hospital before the Yanks arrived. The Federals established divisional hospitals about the station and prepared a vacant warehouse and several nearby homes to hold the incoming injured.

Ambulances from the front trundled in during the night and early Friday with the rumble of cannon fire in the distance. About three hundred twenty soldiers of the VI Corps and one hundred sixty Rebels were among the first wounded brought to Burke's Station after initially being treated at field hospitals around Harper's farm. The bullet-riddled Lockett house served as a Union medical station for casualties suffered by both sides in the fighting at the Double Bridges. During the week after Sailor's Creek about two thousand five hundred Union and Confederate sick or wounded were sent by trains to the massive Union military hospital at City Point.

Surgeon John A. Lidell of the Union Medical and Hospital Department oversaw much of the clinical organization at Burke's Station, including treatment of the enemy's fallen. He reported:

> The Confederate surgeons told me that their wounded were well cared for, and all of whom I inquired (and the number was considerable) uniformly told me, even in the warehouses, that they had experienced good care and satisfactory attention to their wants.[21]

Lieutenant George Peck of the 2nd Rhode Island had been among bloodied Federals taken by litter bearers to the Hillsman house on Thursday. He recalled:

> I was then placed on the floor of a room in which there were two beds, each occupied by two severely wounded officers, while in the third corner, on the floor, were at least a half a dozen more. The only place found for me was in front of one of these beds; my head close beside the hall doorway, where stood the operating table, with surgeons working the entire night, my body forming the bound of a passage-way to the kitchen door in the fourth corner, whence people continually passed and repassed. Yet when my wet cloths had been removed…and myself wrapped in a couple of army blankets, I slept quietly, happily, until daylight.[22]

In another of the Union field hospitals near Sailor's Creek lay Captain Edwin F. Savacool of Company K, 1st New York [Lincoln] Cavalry. He had signed on as a private when the 1st was organized in 1861, and was one of a handful of enlisted men who had risen through the ranks. Savacool had captured three Confederate flags at Sailor's Creek before being severely wounded, he and his horse riddled by fire as the captain clutched a Rebel standard. He was awarded the Medal of Honor, but died of his injuries on June 2, 1865. Indeed, 57 Yanks earned the Medal for action at Sailor's Creek, either for gallantry or seizing enemy banners.

Confederate R. S. Rock had turned 16 a few days earlier. He was seriously wounded in the left side and collapsed 20 to 30 yards from the creek bank during the battle. In agony, he crawled forward to the water and drank from the muddy stream:

I must have fainted, for I knew nothing until I was arrested by a Federal soldier who was kneeling by me and bathing my face. I suppose his heart was touched by my extreme youth...He made me a cup of coffee…put his blanket over me, and remained with me all night...The name of the soldier who cared for me was George Hyatt from Indiana. In the morning he put me in an ambulance...[23]

A few days later, Rock was recuperating in a Federal hospital at Point Lookout, Maryland, when President Lincoln, who was visiting the wards, stopped to shake his hand. Based on Rock's account, a Northerner who observed the greeting said, "Mr. Lincoln, do you know that is a rebel?" Lincoln turned and replied, "Let me shake hands with him again." "I looked into his sad, good face, and when, a few days after, I heard of his assassination, not a soldier in the Federal army regretted it more than I," Rock recalled.[24]

CHAPTER 24

FLIGHT FROM FARMVILLE

A careworn Robert Lee rode across to the north bank of the Appomattox on the morning of April 7 to find out what, if anything, remained of the lost half of his army. Even as Traveller nosed down the country road, elements of the Union cavalry and infantry were preparing to march or already on the move, sniffing the kill. Lee had issued orders for surviving Confederate units and stragglers to converge on High Bridge and rejoin the army at Farmville, about four miles southwest of the gigantic span. As promised, Lee's commissary general had about eighty thousand rations waiting in seven trains of boxcars at the village.

Lee had few options as to his escape route. He would cross the Appomattox at Farmville and either strike south toward the Roanoke River to try to join Johnston's army or continue west and try to outrace his pursuers toward the mountains. Whatever the case, High Bridge and the nearby wagon bridge over the Appomattox were to be burned when the last elements of the army had reached the north bank. Mahone, now serving in rearguard capacity, was to ensure that the spans were destroyed and hold off any enemy attempt to cross the river.

Longstreet's Corps, accompanied by Rosser's cavalry, reached Farmville early on Friday and drew two days' rations, "the first regular issue since we left Richmond," Longstreet recalled.[1] They crossed to the north bank on the two bridges at the town and settled into fields to devour their riches. The spans at Farmville were yet another South Side Railroad bridge and a wagon route both crossing the snakelike

Appomattox. Longstreet's Divisions included those of Major General Charles W. Field, now the grenadier guard of the army with about five thousand infantry, and Mahone's approximately three thousand five hundred fighters. Both contained a cross-section of troops from the Confederate states.

Hour by hour other Rebels rejoined the army, coming in alone or in ragged formations of all sizes. Near Farmville, General Bushrod Johnson approached Lee, lamenting the destruction of his division. Shortly afterward, however, Lee met the largest of Johnson's Brigades, led by General Wise, marching toward him in precise order. With Wise was his son, John, the messenger from Jefferson Davis. The younger Wise had slept on a leaf bed and was awakened by the movement of Longstreet's men before daybreak. John Wise mounted his horse and had ridden only a short distance when he happened upon soldiers belonging to his father's brigade. The general and his 18-year-old son had a warm but brief reunion before marching toward Farmville. "Demoralization, panic, abandonment of all hope, appeared on every hand," John Wise remembered of the soldiers they passed on the ride.[2]

Behind Wise's troops of about two thousand, seven hundred came the South Carolinians of Wallace's Brigade, who had largely escaped being engaged, about two hundred fifty Alabamans of General Young Moody's command, and 80 North Carolina troops from Ransom's Brigade. Trailing these survivors from Anderson's Corps were the bedraggled and bloodied five thousand veterans of Gordon's Corps.[3] Most of these fragmented corps, divisions, brigades, and regiments had marched through the cold night, which included some snow flurries, to rejoin Lee. Gordon's men and Wise's Brigade also were issued two days' rations, including bacon and meal to make cornbread, which they set about cooking over campfires.[4]

Pickets from the 35th Virginia Cavalry Battalion were briefly halted near Farmville when the full might of the enemy appeared before them. "Now the country being open the thousands of men in blue could be seen, drawing close along the flank and rear...," wrote Rebel Captain Frank Myers.[5] As the gray cavalrymen watched, a lone Union horseman galloped toward them carrying a white flag. The Federal said he had a letter from General Grant to General Lee, but Myers, the squadron leader, said he would not accept the dispatch until a line of enemy infantry marching forward in the distance had been stopped. Undismayed, the Yank rode back and the Union line was soon halted. Myers sent a courier to Lee with the letter, which contained good news: Custis Lee had been captured and was unharmed.[6]

The Confederates spent considerable time on Friday waiting for other stragglers who trickled back to the army, among them about two hundred of Joseph Kershaw's men. The wait afforded time for many exhausted soldiers already with Lee to finally fall into sleep bordering on comas. "The troops were lying there more like dead men than live ones," a Southerner wrote. "They did not move, and they had no sentries out. The sun was shining upon them as they slept."[7]

General Wise added some comic relief to the melancholy. Other than what he wore, he had lost all of his clothing and other personal articles in the flight and was marching afoot. Around his shoulders he wore a coarse gray blanket held together by a pin. With no other option, he had washed himself in a puddle, leaving his face streaked with red clay that Lee compared to an Indian wearing war paint.[8]

Lee had little time to do anything except try to reorganize his decimated army and march. He issued orders to slim his command to two corps—Longstreet's and Gordon's, the latter assimilating what was left of any survivors from Anderson, Pickett, and Bushrod Johnson, plus Wise's Brigade.[9]

The aroma of sizzling bacon soon garnished the air in the fields around Farmville and hundreds of other Rebels lined up at the trains to receive their precious rations. A Confederate wrote of the scene at Farmville:

> The roads and fields were filled with stragglers. They moved looking behind them, as if they expected to be attacked...Demoralization, panic, abandonment of all hope, appeared on every hand. Wagons were rolling along without any clear order or system. Caissons and limber-chests, without commanding officers, seemed to be floating aimlessly upon a tide of disorganization.[10]

Suddenly, cries of alarm spread among the clots of soldiers in the streets. The enemy was advancing! Something had been botched in burning the bridges and the Yankees were crossing! An enraged General Lee wondered what had gone wrong as the boxcars of food were closed up and the trains chugged west to escape this threat.

Something indeed had gone wrong at High Bridge. Mahone was to have coordinated the spans' destruction with Confederate engineers, but the bridges had not been torched when Union infantry from Barlow's Division appeared. The Rebels frantically fired High Bridge and the wagon bridge, but the Federals were able to douse the flames before the spans were destroyed. Screaming rounds from Federal artillery soon made it even hotter for the Confederates at the bridges and they hustled back toward Farmville with Union troops not far behind them. General Humphreys of the II Corps was on the scene by now and led the divisions of de Trobriand and Miles to the northwest to cut off any Confederate escape toward Lynchburg.

Barlow, meanwhile, caught up with Gordon's baggage train near Farmville and destroyed a number of wagons. He then smacked into elements of Gordon's Corps, which remained full of fight. The Union advance was temporarily blunted with about 130 of Barlow's men taken prisoner and Brigadier General Thomas A. Smyth of the Third Brigade being mortally wounded by an enemy sharpshooter's ball in the face.[11]

Crook's cavalry rode into Farmville from the south and found that the Rebels had destroyed the two bridges there after they crossed to the north side of the Appomattox. With Colonel Gregg's Brigade in the lead, the blue troopers forded the river about 4 p.m.—and promptly rode into a Confederate trap.[12] Gregg saw enemy wagons ahead and galloped forward to take them. But the wagons were the bait for an ambush and Gregg's force quickly found itself attacked in front and flank by Rebel cavalry. Gregg and several of his staff were captured while his command sustained "severe" losses.[13]

Sharp fighting occurred between Mahone's command and Miles' Division at a crossroads near Cumberland Church, about three miles north of Farmville. Longstreet sent in more troops after Mahone's flank was dangerously threatened and the Federals withdrew. Despite these minor victories, Lee was again on the run, having lost more invaluable time to feed and rest his dwindling army. Once again, he had eluded total defeat, but this combat cost the Confederates a half-day's march they could ill afford in evading the enemy.

With the Union VI Corps and Crook's horsemen gnashing at his rear, and Ord, Humphreys, and Griffin shadowing his flanks, Lee and his troops plodded west again, drawing ever closer to Appomattox Court House and a date on the army's doomsday.

CHAPTER 25

"THEIR FIELD OF GLORY"

Ulysses Grant rode into Farmville late Friday afternoon and was told by Sheridan that Union troops were being arrayed to capture four trainloads of enemy supplies waiting at Appomattox Station, 25 miles to the west. Sheridan guessed that Lee was now marching west toward Lynchburg rather than trying to make a break to the southwest in the direction of Danville. He decided that the best tactic would be to race forward with his cavalry and delay the enemy until the infantry could come up and seal the issue.[1]

To block Lee's drive on Lynchburg, Sheridan would concentrate his cavalry at Appomattox Station where, according to his scouts, the ration trains were waiting for the arrival of Lee's army. Indeed, one of Sheridan's scouts, wearing a Confederate uniform and flashing a copy of the Rebel commissary general's orders intercepted earlier, had talked to the train crews, persuading them to wait for Lee at Appomattox Station.

Grant secured a room at Farmville's Prince Edward Hotel on Friday. In the streets, bonfires and torches blazed, cheers echoed and bands played as the Federal troops celebrated the expected end of the war. "Soldiers waved their muskets in the air as whole regiments sang 'John Brown's Body,' which had risen to the dignity of a national anthem," a Union officer recalled.[2]

Grant sat on the hotel porch and watched the proud soldiers of the VI Corps march into the village. Wright's Veterans "came swinging through the main street of the village with a step that seemed as elastic as on the first day of their toilsome tramp," Colonel Porter wrote. "It was now dark, but they spied the commander-in-chief watching them with evident pride from the piazza of the hotel as they marched past...The night march had become a grand review, with Grant as the reviewing officer."[3]

Knowing the damage his troops had inflicted on the Confederate army since the Petersburg evacuation, the Union commander hoped to quickly put an end to the bloody chase where men were killed or maimed at virtually every crossroads and creek ford. Grant decided to send a surrender entreaty to Lee and a courier soon was heading toward the Rebel army with a 5 p.m. Friday dispatch from the Union army commander in chief:

APRIL 7, 1865.

General R. E. LEE:

GENERAL: The result of the last week must convince you of the hopelessness of further resistance on the part of the Army of Northern Virginia in this struggle. I feel that it is so, and regard it as my duty to shift from myself the responsibility of any further effusion of blood, by asking of you the surrender of that portion of the C. S. Army known as the Army of Northern Virginia.

U. S. GRANT,
Lieutenant-General.[4]

Grant received a reply from Lee, dated April 7, early on Saturday, April 8, before the Union chieftain left Farmville:

Lieutenant General U. S. GRANT:

GENERAL: I have received your note of this date. Though not entertaining the opinion you express on the haplessness of further resistance on the part of the Army of Northern Virginia, I reciprocate your desire to avoid useless effusion of blood, and therefore, before considering your proposition, ask the terms you will offer on condition of its surrender.

R. E. LEE,
General[5]

Grant's answer was immediate:

APRIL 8, 1865.

General R. E. LEE:

GENERAL: Your note of last evening, in reply to mine of same date, asking the condition on which I will accept the surrender of the Army of Northern Virginia, is just received. In reply I would say that, peace being my great desire, there is but one condition I would insist upon, namely, that the men and officers surrendered shall be disqualified for taking up arms again against the Government of the United States until properly exchanged. I will meet you, or will designate officers to meet any officers you may name for the same purpose, at any point agreeable to you, for the purpose of arranging definitely the terms upon which the surrender of the Army of Northern Virginia will be received.

U. S. GRANT,
Lieutenant-General[6]

Even while he replied to Grant, Lee knew that his options were running out. Federal columns of infantry and cavalry even then were sweeping around his flanks like the tendrils of a deadly vine. Grant was with Meade about midnight when a messenger arrived with Lee's latest response:

APRIL 8, 1865.

Lieutenant General U. S. GRANT:

GENERAL: I received at a late hour your note of to-day. In mine of yesterday I did not intend to propose the surrender of the Army of Northern Virginia, but to ask the terms of your proposition. To be frank, I do not think the emergency has arisen to call for the surrender of this army, but as the restoration of peace should be the sole object of all, I desired to know whether your proposals would lead to that end. I cannot, therefore, meet you with a view to surrender the Army of Northern Virginia, but as far as your proposal may affect the C. S. forces under my command, and tend to the restoration of peace, I should be pleased to meet you at 10 a. m., to-morrow, on the old stage roads to Richmond, between the picket-lines of the two armies.

Very respy your Obt Sevt

R. E. LEE,
General[7]

Lee kept his divisions on the move west as he traded correspondence with Grant. During a stop at the hamlet of New Store on Saturday, he made some major changes among his generals based on his losses at Sailor's Creek.

Anderson, Pickett, and Bushrod Johnson were relieved of their commands, supposedly because their ranks had been so decimated due to battle casualties and other attrition that they no longer were worthy of operating as independent units. Certainly Lee greatly considered their less-than-stellar combat performances on the retreat in making his decision. The generals' remaining troops were shifted to other divisions.[8]

After Sailor's Creek, William Mahone described Anderson as "the sad picture of a man who was whipped."[9] The Carolinian indeed was emotionally spent, believing that his corps had been destroyed when, in fact, much of it survived to march to Appomattox Court House. The despondent Anderson rode off toward his home in South Carolina, but Pickett and Johnson remained with the troops, either ignoring or never receiving word of their dismissals. Seeing Pickett amid his men hours before the final surrender, Robert Lee derisively asked, "Is that man still with this army?"[10]

At one point, General Pendleton of the artillery asked to see Lee. Pendleton said that he represented a group of senior officers who had met the night before and decided that the time had come to discuss negotiations with the Yankees. Lee would have none of it, telling Pendleton that the army still had "too many brave men to think of laying down our arms." He added that all of the soldiers should be resolved to "die at our posts" rather than face the humiliation of surrender.[11] Yet even though he spoke with the determination and courage of old, Lee realized that he likely would have to make that choice within the next few days.

As Grant and Lee focused on the bigger picture, their lieutenants concentrated on making war as if the battles would never end. The cavalry of Custer, Devin, and Crook regrouped at Prospect Station on Saturday and all three commands moved on the 20-mile road to Appomattox Station to block Lee's line of march as Sheridan intended. "And now began a rollicking stern chase," wrote Major Albert Barnitz of the 2nd Ohio Cavalry, "capturing stragglers, artillery, baggage wagons and other debris of war."[12]

Custer led the cavalry drive and was within two miles of the depot near sundown. Receiving word about the four Confederate supply trains at the station, he decided to attack immediately. Despite the dimming day, Custer's First Brigade horsemen under Colonel Pennington charged pell-mell down to the station. Yanks of the 1st Connecticut and 2nd Ohio captured the trains other than one engine which some of the fleeing Southerners uncoupled and used to escape. The cars of the latter train were burned, but it is unclear if they were torched by Union, Confederate, or were accidentally destroyed.[13]

Custer had some former railroaders in his ranks and these men climbed into the captured locomotives and proceeded to pull them out of the depot, away from the grasp of Lee's dying army. The Federals at the throttles gleefully tooted the train whistles to rival the cheers of other arriving bluecoats. The celebration abruptly ended with a boom when Custer's men unexpectedly came under fire from enemy artillery. Incoming shells exploded around the station or hurtled over the trains, which were hastily run back toward Farmville.

The Confederate artillery column of Brigadier General R. Lindsay Walker of Longstreet's Corps was nearing the station when the Rebels saw that blue cavalry had taken the trains.[14] Walker unlimbered about 30 guns and began shelling the depot, sending the Federals scurrying for cover. These were the surplus cannon Lee had sent ahead of the army from Amelia Court House.[15] In the evening's murkiness, Custer located the guns by their flashes and went on the attack. Walker's resistance, however, was stout and Custer had to call for support from Devin to gain an upper hand.

Much of the fighting was done in total darkness, the foes clashing by the flames of musket and cannon fire. When the engagement sputtered out about 9 p.m., the bluecoats had captured about 30 Rebel guns, a number of baggage wagons, including those of General W. H. F. Lee, and a sizeable haul of prisoners and battle flags.[16]

Among the captives was the sickly Confederate General Young Moody, 42, who had been riding in the wagons. He had not been healthy since a serious wound at Drewry's Bluff the previous May and had been unable to lead his brigade of Alabamans in Anderson's Corps at Sailor's Creek.[17] Union losses were slight, according to Custer.

Custer was not done for the evening. His advance resumed towards Appomattox Court House, less than three miles away to the northeast where Lee's army was massing. Some of these blue horsemen "charged fairly into the rebel camp...riding over & between the tired and sleeping rebels & out again before they were sufficiently awake to stop them," Custer related.[18] The cavalryman Merritt wrote that night:

> It is impossible to overestimate the value of this day's work. The enemy's supplies were taken, as it were, out of their mouths. A strong force, they knew not how strong, was posted along their line of retreat at a point where they did not expect opposition. Night was upon them; tired, dispirited, and starving they lay at our feet. Their bravest soldiers, their hardiest men, gave way when they heard the noise of battle far in the rear, and the night of despair fell with the night of the 8th of April darkly and terribly on the Army of Northern Virginia.[19]

At Danville, Jefferson Davis did not learn of the debacles at Sailor's Creek and High Bridge until April 8. He had spent Thursday and Friday still waiting for any word from Lee, but incoming telegrams bore no solid information.

Finally, Secretary of War Breckinridge had left the army near Farmville and found a telegraph station on the Richmond & Danville from which he could send a message to the president. In his dispatch, Breckinridge briefly detailed the two battles and his plans for dealing with a force of Union cavalry raiders further to the west. He described the Sailor's Creek disaster as "a serious reverse" and told Davis that

Lee still was trying to reach North Carolina, but starkly added, "The straggling has been great, and the situation is not favorable..."[20]

Davis was discussing Breckinridge's report with the other cabinet members after dinner that night at the Sutherlin house when a courier arrived to see him. The messenger was Lieutenant John Wise who had ridden back from Lee's army. Wise's depiction of the situation was grim to say the least and left Davis almost no hope that the Confederacy could be saved. Within hours the Rebel president and his cabinet were on the move south out of Virginia. They would never return to the state in their official capacities, and Davis was captured by Federal cavalry near Irwinville, Georgia, on May 10.

Grant dispatched a reply to Lee's last letter of April 8 early on the morning of Palm Sunday, April 9, before heading off to join Sheridan:

Headquarters Armies of the United States

APRIL 9, 1865.

General R. E. LEE,
Commanding C.S. Armies

GENERAL: Your note of yesterday is received. As I have no authority to treat on the subject of peace; the meeting proposed for 10 a.m. to-day could lead to no good. I will state, however, General, that I am equally anxious for peace with yourself, and the whole North entertains the same feeling. The terms upon which peace can be had are well understood. By the South laying down their arms they will hasten the most desirable event, save thousands of human lives, and hundreds of millions of property not yet destroyed. Seriously hoping that all our difficulties may be settled without the loss of another life, I subscribe myself, &c.,

U. S. GRANT,
Lieutenant-General
U. S. Army[21]

In his campaign report, Grant briefly described the events that followed: "General Ord's command and the V Corps reached Appomattox

Station [actually Appomattox Court House] just as the enemy was making a desperate effort to break through our cavalry. The infantry was at once thrown in. Soon after a white flag was received, requesting a suspension of hostilities pending agitations for a surrender."[22]

Grant had not yet caught up with Sheridan when he received the following from Lee:

APRIL 9, 1865.

Lieutenant General U. S. GRANT,
Commanding U. S. Armies.

GENERAL:

I received your note of this morning on the picket-line, whither I had come to meet you and ascertain definitely what terms were embraced in your proposal of yesterday with reference to the surrender of this army. I now ask an interview in accordance with the offer contained in your letter of yesterday for that purpose.

Very respectfully, your obedient servant,

R. E. LEE,
General[23]

Grant sent Lee a letter of agreement and the hilly, gravelly Virginia roads led both commanders to the tiny village of Appomattox Court House where they met in the home of Wilmer McLean. "Glory to God in the highest. Peace on earth, good will to men!" wrote Elisha Hunt Rhodes. "Thank God Lee has surrendered, and the war will soon end."[24]

Lee's grace as the unbowed warrior and Grant's magnanimity, despite his fire and sword might to demolish his foe with lethal precision, mark one of the greatest chapters in the American saga. Yet there likely would have been no storied surrender at Appomattox if the Confederates had not blundered so often and tragically at Sailor's Creek. Obviously, Lee might have held on at least a few days longer, but the outcome is unquestioned.

The Federals eventually issued paroles to 28,231 soldiers of Lee's army at Appomattox.[25] Scores of these men, however, were wounded, ill, unarmed, stragglers, or disabled by battle fatigue and lack of provisions. Also included in this total were the piecemeal units of Fitz Lee's

cavalry, some of which drifted back to the army after Lee's formal surrender. Robert Lee likely provides the most accurate picture of the troops
he had on hand facing the enemy on Sunday, April 9:

> On the morning of the 9th...there were 7892 organized infantry
> with arms, with an average of seventy-five rounds of ammunition
> per man. The artillery, though reduced to sixty-three pieces, with
> ninety-three rounds of ammunition, was sufficient... I have no ac-
> curate report of the cavalry, but believe it did not exceed 2100
> effective men.[26]

In essence, Lee's loss of infantry when the Army of Northern
Virginia was surrendered was approximately the same as his overall
casualties at Sailor's Creek. General Meade offered this contrast of
Union forces concentrated around Appomattox:

> We had at least 50,000 around [Lee], so that nothing but madness
> would have justified further resistance.[27]

Other Federals within quick striking distance of Lee's army were
just as numerous.

For New York drummer Delavan Miller, the war ended with a
pitiful and sorrowful encounter with a dying youngster from South Carolina who had been grievously wounded either at Sailor's Creek or in the
Farmville fighting. The Rebel, not old enough to carry a musket, was
found in a wagon taken by Union troops at the Appomattox surrender.
Miller told the story:

> He, too, was a drummer boy and had been wounded two or three
> days before. We got our surgeon and had his wound dressed and
> gave him stimulants and a little food, but he was very weak, "all
> marched out," he said, and was afraid that he would not see his old
> Carolina home again. We bathed his face and hands with cold wa-
> ter and his lips quivered and tears coursed down his cheeks as he
> faintly whispered of his widowed mother. We, too, were "marched
> out," and had to lie down and rest, but before leaving "Little
> Gray,"as we called him, two boys knelt by his side and repeated

the Lord's prayer that had been learned at a mother's knees. In the morning the little Confederate from the Palmetto state was dead, and we buried him on the field with his comrades.[28]

After reaching Burke's Station on Friday, April 7, the Confederate prisoners from Sailor's Creek, including Ewell and the other generals, were marched east along the South Side Railroad toward Petersburg. The generals continued to travel by ambulance and Ewell also moved about on his crutches when the column stopped.

At least one of his colleagues did not approve of the way Ewell fraternized with the Yanks. Eppa Hunton recalled that Ewell "seemed bent on making himself popular," adding that Ewell told Federals that the South was as guilty as the North in devastating enemy property. Based on Hunton's account, Ewell also told his captors that the Richmond government had been cruel in their treatment of Yankee prisoners. "I was very indignant with General Ewell," Hunton recalled later. "He was thoroughly whipped and seemed to be dreadfully demoralized."[29]

On April 10, the Rebels were separated at Wilson's Station. Sick and weakly soldiers were put aboard trains headed for City Point. The healthier enlisted men were halted at the depot to await rations.

The generals and the other eight hundred or so Confederate officers continued along the railroad toward Ford's Station. En route, a rider brought word of Lee's surrender. To the Southerners the news elicited a mixed reaction of deathly despair, disbelief, and grief compounded with hope and happiness that the war was all but over. Certainly Joe Johnston was fighting on—they had heard nothing to the contrary—and there were other scattered Confederate commands still active. But Robert E. Lee had been the fountainhead for the cause. Ewell's response to the news was to throw his arms in the air and exclaim, "The jig is up!"[30]

Lee's soldiers who capitulated at Appomattox were paroled and allowed to return to their homes. Learning this, Ewell tried to obtain the same terms for the Sailor's Creek prisoners, but Union officials denied the request. Thus, the Rebels captured on April 6 were headed to Union military prisons while the rest of their comrades who laid down their arms with Lee were free.[31]

The captives' march on April 11 was within 10 miles of Petersburg when it was interrupted with a report for Custis Lee that his mother was deathly ill in Richmond. The Federals released Lee to go to her bedside. Lee hurried to the capital where he learned that the story was untrue. Some of his friends in the Union army had perpetrated the hoax so that Custis would escape any prison time. Bewildered, Lee immediately turned himself in to the provost marshal's office in Richmond, but was allowed to go home. He was the only Confederate general taken at Sailor's Creek who was not incarcerated.[32]

After reaching City Point on April 12, Ewell and the other generals were among Rebel officers taken by ship to Washington, arriving on the afternoon of Friday, April 14. The Southerners came ashore to catcalls and jeers from an unruly crowd of several hundred, but escaped harm. Ewell was soon greeted by his oldest sister, Rebecca, and others, including former United States Postmaster General Montgomery Blair, a friend of the family. Blair gave Ewell money that had been forwarded to him from Ewell's wife, Lizinka.[33]

Georgia Major Basinger was among prisoners from Sailor's Creek herded through the streets of Petersburg that April 14. Also in the column was Captain Thomas Blake of Virginia. Many of the Rebels were held temporarily in a large tobacco warehouse before resuming their march to City Point. Blake recounted:

> The citizens of Petersburg, especially the ladies, visited us in numbers and brought us delicacies to eat. Friends also brought me clothing, of which I was sorely in need, and gave me money in small silver coins, which proved to be a godsend.[34]

While in Petersburg, Basinger wrote to his mother, Mrs. J. S. Basinger, in Savannah:

> My dear Mother,
>
> On our way, a sad train of captives from the unfortunate field of Sailor's Creek of Apl. 6th, to I know not whither, I seize an opportunity to let you know what has befallen me. I lost everything, the most common necessities. As soon as I am sure of a

permanent place of confinement, I will draw on you for a little money. I know how embarrassed you all are in that way. But I will make the draft as small as possible.

I cannot think of the splendid conduct and of the losses of my noble little command without mingled emotions of admiration and grief. Of 85 engaged, I lost 24 killed, 28 wounded and the rest prisoners. Rice, Turner and King were killed. Tupper mortally wounded. Starr painfully, but doing well...For the conduct of the command, let it suffice to say, that everyone I meet, from Ewell down to the privates, congratulates me upon it. Major Robt. Stiles, was under my immediate command, behaved himself more like a hero than any man I ever saw, and is with me, a prisoner.

I have prepared a list of casualties for the *N.Y. Herold* [*sic*], and will write fully as soon as I get a chance.

Thank God for his wonderful preservation of my life, and believe me ever your affte son, and my sister's affte brother.[35]

As Basinger wrote, Union authorities in Washington were preparing to send the Sailor's Creek generals and Commodore Tucker to imprisonment at Fort Warren in Boston Harbor. The lower-ranking Rebel officers, other than Campbell Brown, Ewell's stepson and aide, who was allowed to accompany Ewell, were ordered to Johnson's Island on Lake Erie.

A train carrying the generals left Washington about 7:30 p.m., Friday, less than three hours before the shooting of President Lincoln shocked the country. Lincoln was watching a play at Ford's Theater in Washington that night when an assassin shot him in the head while the president was seated in his private balcony box. Lincoln died early the next day, even as an intensive manhunt and investigation to identify and arrest his killer and any conspirators were spreading like a web in every direction from the capital. Union Secretary of State William H. Seward had been critically wounded by an assailant in his home the same evening of Lincoln's shooting.

With the emergence of actor and Southern sympathizer John Wilkes Booth as a prime suspect in the president's slaying, there was rapidly mounting Northern opinion that the night's horrors were the result of a Confederate conspiracy. Blind rage and howls for revenge mingled with tears of shock and anguish as telegraph lines, newspapers, and word of mouth carried the terrible news to the far corners of the fragile Union. Some hard-shell Rebels were elated by Lincoln's death but most, like the captive generals, were deeply saddened by the tragedy. Ewell is said to have wept.

Throughout April 15, the train carrying the Confederate senior officers was beset by threatening crowds at virtually every depot from New York City through Connecticut and into Massachusetts. Rocks were hurled at the cars and the Union escort was hard-pressed to hold back bloodthirsty gangs shouting for Ewell and the others to be hung. When the train chugged into Boston about 5 p.m., it was met by a force of Federal soldiers who ensured that the generals got safely aboard a boat to carry them across the harbor to Fort Warren. Here they settled into cold and damp casemates converted to cells, unsure of their fate.

Within hours of their arrival, however, the Confederates had voiced their feelings about Lincoln's murder. "The general officers confined at this post as prisoners of war have, from the moment of the reception of the news, expressed their regret for the loss of President Lincoln, and their utmost horror of the act and detestation of his murderers," Union Major John Appleton, the post commander, wrote in a report forwarded to General Grant.[36] Appleton's message accompanied an April 16 letter written to Grant by General Ewell, who stated that he represented the feelings of the imprisoned officers:

> Of all the misfortunes which could befall the Southern people, or any Southern man, by far the greatest, in my judgment, would be the prevalence of the idea that they could entertain any other than feelings of unqualified abhorrence and indignation for the assassination of the President of the United States and the attempt to assassinate the Secretary of State. No language can adequately express the shock produced upon myself, in common with all the other officers confined here with me, by the occurrence of this appalling crime, and the seeming tendency in the public mind to connect the South and Southern men with it.

Need we say that we are not assassins, nor the allies of assassins, be they from the North or from the South, and that coming as we do from most of the States of the South we would be ashamed of our own people, were we not assured that they will reprobate this crime. Under the circumstances I could not refrain from some expression of my feelings. I thus utter them to a soldier who will comprehend them.[37]

Among the officers who "heartily concur with me in what I have said," Ewell listed Kershaw, Barton, Corse, Hunton, DuBose, and Simms as well as Commodore Tucker.[38] Hunton later wrote that he bitterly disagreed with what Ewell had done and in no way endorsed it. In fact, Hunton claimed that the other officers also voted against sending the message but that Ewell did it anyway.

"I asked them if they thought it becoming for thirteen gentlemen who were thought worthy to wear the stars of general officers of the Confederate Army to declare to the world that they were not assassins," Hunton recalled. "By great exertions, and the efforts of several who came to my aid, the resolution was defeated."[39] This controversy further deepened Hunton's loathing of Ewell. "I asked General Ewell where the leg he lost at [S]econd Manassas was buried; that I wished to pay honor to that leg, for I had none to pay to the rest of his body. He replied that he did not know where it was."[40]

The Rebel officers remained incarcerated at Fort Warren for some three months before they were allowed to take an oath of allegiance and were freed in late July 1865. Major Basinger was among Southern prisoners aboard a steamer bound from City Point to Washington when he wrote another letter to his mother on April 16:

My grief for my men and for the misfortunes of our country have made the last 10 days the most wretched of my life...Be of good courage, and don't give up. God will not abandon us. It is only on Him now that we can rely.[41]

The battle stench of Sailor's Creek reigned for months after Lee's surrender. On May 31, Grant sent this message to General Henry W. Halleck, the army's chief of staff:

> I am informed that a great many bodies have been left unburied at Appomattox Court-House. It is possible that some may have been left in the same way at Sailor's Creek. I think a small cavalry force had better be sent to each place to bury any that may still be left above ground.[42]

The macabre dispatch met with this response about two weeks later:

HEADQUARTERS PROVOST-MARSHAL,
Amelia Court-House, June 15, 1865.

> I have the honor to report that according to instructions I sent a portion of this command to examine into the condition of the dead on the different battle-fields mentioned. The officer in command reports having buried five Federal soldiers on Foster's plantation, two of which had lain on the field since the battle. Found seventeen bodies at Sailor's Creek (ten of which were Confederate) that the recent heavy rains had washed the covering from. These were reburied; also one found near Amelia Springs. Diligent search was made at Appomattox Court-House but found no bodies uncovered.

> I have the honor to be, very respectfully your obedient servant,

S. R. CLARK,
Brevet Colonel and Provost-Marshal, Amelia Co., Va.[43]

The 18th Georgia Battalion had been one of the few, if the only Confederate unit in the retreat, to have musicians with them. Their fife and drum corps, composed of a handful of black freedmen, apparently remained devoted to the cause until the end. These men provided lively music at intervals along the doleful march and "greatly picked up the spirits of all within hearing distance," Major Basinger recounted.[44] Under enemy fire, the band was ordered to the rear before the battle. After being paroled at Appomattox, one of the players, who is unidentified, went back to Sailor's Creek to learn the fate of his friend, Georgia Captain John R. Dillon, who belonged to Basinger's unit.

The musician found Dillon's bloody coat and sword at the battleground, but no other trace of the officer. Walking back to Savannah and believing Dillon dead, the bandsman delivered the jacket and sword to Dillon's sister. Dillon, however, was alive. Badly wounded in the combat, he had spent some time in a Federal hospital, but recovered.

He was the leader of a group of Savannah Volunteer Guards members who went to New York in 1870 and successfully negotiated for the return of the Guards' "Victory or Death" flag captured by the 121st New York at Sailor's Creek.[45]

On New Year's Eve, 1865, military burials were held for 18 Confederate soldiers at Laurel Grove Cemetery in Savannah, Georgia. Their remains, and those of other men of the Savannah Volunteer Guards slain at Sailor's Creek as members of the 18th Georgia Battalion, had been disinterred from the battlefield and brought home.

Major Basinger had been imprisoned at Johnson's Island for several months after his command had been destroyed at Sailor's Creek. Upon his release Basinger, still wearing his Confederate uniform, headed for New York where he set about collecting debts owed to him since his days working there as an attorney before the war. With some of this money in his pockets, Basinger returned to Sailor's Creek where he located the burial sites of some of the Georgians who had fallen in the battle.

The major brought these men back to Savannah to rest in their native soil. Seven of these dead were claimed by relatives and taken to family plots or cemeteries. But the other eleven, although recognized as Guards, could not be fully identified and were buried in the Savannah Volunteer Guards section of the cemetery.

"Notwithstanding the inclemency of the day...a very large number of our most respectable citizens, ladies and gentlemen and youth, including the relatives and friends of the gallant dead, had assembled," stated the *Savannah Daily Morning News* on January 1, 1866. The caskets were placed side by side and "covered with laurel wreathes and bouqets [*sic*] of choice flowers." Among the entourage was the

Metropolitan Fire Company that included some Confederate veterans, "companions in arms of those whose names they had come to honor." After a "solemnly impressive" burial service, the unknown soldiers were lowered into their graves "together, as they had mingled their blood on 'their field of glory.'"[46]

NOTES

Chapter 1

1. Burke Davis, *The Long Surrender*, pp. 19–21.
2. Harwell, *Lee*, p. 466.
3. Ibid.
4. Ibid., p. 467.
5. Elisha Hunt Rhodes in Rhodes, *All For The Union*, p. 227.
6. Buel and Johnson, *Battles and Leaders of the Civil War* (hereafter referred to as *Battles and Leaders*), vol. 4, p. 718.

Chapter 2

1. Benson, *Berry Benson's Civil War Book*, p. 195.
2. Ibid.
3. Blake, "The Artillery Brigade at Sailor's Creek," *Confederate Veteran*, vol. 28, no. 6, p. 213.

Chapter 3

1. Anderson, *The Generals*, p. 433.
2. Burke Davis, *To Appomattox*, p. 190.
3. Harwell, p. 471.
4. Davis, *To Appomattox*, pp. 190–91.
5. Calkins, *The Appomattox Campaign*, p. 76.
6. Davis, *To Appomattox*, pp. 191–92.
7. Ibid.
8. Ibid.
9. Starr, *The Union Cavalry*, vol. 2, p. 462.
10. Calkins, pp. 86–87.
11. Ibid.
12. Rhodes, p. 227.
13. *The War of the Rebellion: A Compilation of the Official Records of the Union and Confederate Armies*, pt. 1, chap. 46, pp. 1106–7 (hereafter referred to as the *OR*).
14. Ibid.
15. Charles S. Wainwright in Nevins, *A Diary of Battle*, p. 518.
16. Freeman, *Lee's Lieutenants*, vol. 1, p. 690.

17. Trudeau, *Out of the Storm—The End of the Civil War—April–June 1865*, p. 192.

18. Blake, p. 213.

19. Donnelly, *The Confederate States Marine Corps*, p. 58.

20. Ibid., p. 62.

21. Blackford, *War Years With Jeb Stuart*, p. 283.

22. Ibid.

23. Pfanz, *Richard S. Ewell*, p. 435.

24. Blackford, p. 283.

25. Pfanz, p. 435.

26. Myers, *The Comanches*, pp. 371–72.

27. Methvin, *Confederate Reminiscences and Letters*, vol. 8, p. 66.

28. Stern, *Soldier Life in the Union and Confederate Armies*, p. 354.

29. Ibid.

30. Douglas, *I Rode With Stonewall*, p. 316.

31. Methvin, p. 67.

Chapter 4

1. Hutton, "Paladin of the Republic," *Military History Quarterly* (hereafter referred to as *MHQ*), vol. 4, no. 3, p. 88.

2. Ibid., p. 88.

3. Ibid.

4. Ibid., p. 83.

5. Warner, *Generals in Blue*, p. 438.

6. Hutton, pp. 84–85.

7. Ibid., p. 87.

8. Nevins, p. 518.

9. Pfanz, pp. 423–24.

10. Ibid.

11. Trudeau, p. 100.

12. Calkins, p. 183.

13. Trudeau, p. 100.

14. Davis, *To Appomattox*, pp. 224–25.

15. Myers, pp. 372–73.

16. Starr, vol. 2, p. 95.

Chapter 5

1. Patterson, *Rebels From West Point*, p. 162.

2. Warner, *Generals in Gray*, p. 179.

3. Stern, p. 355.

4. Calkins, p. 94.

5. Buel and Johnson, *Battles and Leaders*, vol. 4, p. 724.

6. Anderson, p. 434.

7. Davis, *To Appomattox*, p. 196.

8. Blake, p. 213.

9. Starr, vol. 2, p. 466.

10. Davis, *To Appomattox*, p. 233.

11. Buel and Johnson, *Battles and Leaders*, vol. 4, p. 719.

12. *OR*, pt. 1, chap. 46, pp. 630–31.
13. Haley, *The Rebel Yell & the Yankee Hurrah*, p. 260.
14. Rhodes, p. 227.
15. *OR*, pt. 1, chap. 46, p. 1107.
16. Nevins, p. 518.
17. Haley, p. 260.
18. Trudeau, p. 193.
19. *OR*, pt. 1, chap. 46, p. 55.
20. Anderson, p. 435.
21. Davis, *To Appomattox*, p. 235.
22. Ibid.
23. Ibid.

Chapter 6

1. Anderson, pp. 434–35.
2. Freeman, p. 696.
3. Grimes, *Extracts of Letters of Major-Gen'l Bryan Grimes To His Wife*, p. 113.
4. Buel and Johnson, *Battles and Leaders*, vol. 4, p. 724.
5. Benson, p. 196.
6. Davis, *To Appomattox*, p. 228.
7. Stern, p. 355.
8. *Recollections and Reminiscences*, vol. 1, p. 45.
9. Davis, *To Appomattox*, pp. 228–29.
10. Ibid.
11. *Recollections and Reminiscences*, vol. 1, p. 45.
12. Freeman, p. 696.
13. Anderson, p. 435.
14. Davis, *To Appomattox*, p. 243.
15. *OR*, pt. 1, chap. 46, p. 1387.

Chapter 7

1. Longstreet, *From Manassas To Appomattox*, p. 611.
2. Davis, *To Appomattox*, p. 229.
3. Rodick, p. 57.
4. *OR*, pt. 1, chap. 46, p. 631.
5. Warner, *Generals in Blue*, pp. 575–76.
6. Davis, *To Appomattox*, p. 266.
7. Sheridan, *Civil War Memoirs,* p. 337.
8. Starr, vol. 2, p. 468.
9. Ibid., p. 467.
10. *OR*, pt. 1, chap. 46, p. 1150.

Chapter 8

1. Warner, *Generals in Gray*, p. 184.
2. Myers, p. 373.
3. *OR*, pt. 1, chap. 46, pp. 1301–2.
4. Rodick, p. 57.

5. Stern, p. 355.
6. Jones, *Lee's Tigers*, p. 225.
7. Davis, *To Appomattox*, p. 246.
8. *Recollections and Reminiscences*, vol. 1, p. 45.
9. Harwell, p. 474.
10. Blake, p. 213.
11. Freeman, p. 699.
12. Gordon, *Reminiscences*, p. 38.
13. Pfanz, p. 268.
14. Ibid., p. 273.
15. Steiner, *Medical-Military Portraits*, p. 290.
16. Pfanz, p. 398.
17. Ibid., pp. 402–3.

Chapter 9

1. *OR*, pt. 1, chap. 46, p. 597.
2. Buel and Johnson, *Battles and Leaders*, vol. 4, p. 748.
3. Warner, *Generals in Blue*, pp. 240–41.
4. *OR*, pt. 1, chap. 46, p. 602.
5. Ibid., p. 778.
6. Warner, *Generals in Blue*, pp. 121–22.
7. *OR*, pt. 1, chap. 46, p. 778.
8. Ibid., p. 674.
9. Ibid., p. 682.
10. Korn, *The Civil War—Pursuit To Appomattox*, p. 117.
11. Rodick, p. 64.
12. Korn, p. 116.
13. Benson, p. 196.
14. Davis, *To Appomattox*, p. 229.
15. Rodick, pp. 56–57.
16. Pickett, *The Heart of a Soldier*, p. 177.
17. Stern, p. 355.
18. Haley, p. 260.
19. Stern, p. 355.
20. *OR*, pt. 1, chap. 46, p. 779.
21. Ibid.
22. Ibid.
23. Dowdey, *Lee's Last Campaign*, p. 194.
24. Douglas, p. 226.
25. Warner, *Generals in Gray*, p. 111. Some accounts state that Gordon's commission was not confirmed and that he was reappointed brigadier in May 1863.
26. Trudeau, p. 107.
27. Haley, p. 260.
28. Ibid., p. 261.
29. *OR*, pt. 1, chap. 46, p. 713.
30. *OR*, pt. 1, chap. 58, p. 599.
31. Ibid., p. 609.

32. Ibid., pp. 784–86.
33. Ibid.
34. Gordon, pp. 422–24.
35. *OR*, pt. 1, chap. 46, p. 600.
36. Haley, p. 261.
37. *OR*, pt. 1, chap. 46, p. 1125.
38. Pickett, p. 177.
39. Buel and Johnson, *Battles and Leaders*, vol. 4, p. 724.
40. Warner, *Generals in Blue*, pp. 102–3 and 260–61.
41. *OR*, pt. 1, chap. 46, p. 1142.
42. Freeman, p. 701.

Chapter 10

1. Starr, vol. 2, p. 468.
2. Basinger, "Crutchfield's Artillery Brigade," *Southern Historical Society Papers* (hereafter referred to as *SHSP*), vol. 25, pp. 38–44.
3. *OR*, pt. 1, chap. 46, p. 1107.
4. Ibid., p. 1126.
5. Ibid., p. 1108.
6. Starr, vol. 2, p. 469.
7. Boatner, *The Civil War Dictionary*, p. 216.
8. Wert, *From Winchester To Cedar Creek*, p. 73.
9. Warner, *Generals in Blue*, pp. 108–9.
10. Urwin, *Custer Victorious*, p. 245.
11. Johnston, *The Story of a Confederate Boy in the Civil War*, p. 328.

Chapter 11

1. Freeman, p. 708.
2. Calkins, p. 101.
3. *OR*, pt. 1, chap. 46, p. 1161.
4. Buel and Johnson, *Battles and Leaders*, vol. 4, p. 750.
5. *OR*, pt. 1, chap. 46, p. 1161.
6. Longstreet, p. 612.
7. *OR*, pt. 1, chap. 46, p. 1161.
8. Ibid.
9. Ibid., p. 1169.
10. Ibid., p. 1162.
11. Ibid., p. 1169.
12. Korn, p. 120.
13. Calkins, p. 143.
14. *OR*, pt. 1, chap. 46, p. 1169.
15. Ibid., p. 1162.
16. Myers, p. 379.
17. Davis, *To Appomattox*, p. 264.
18. Korn, p. 130.
19. *OR*, pt. 1, chap. 46, p. 1167.
20. Myers, p. 380.

21. Calkins, p. 143.
22. Freeman, pp. 708–9.
23. Korn, p. 120.
24. *OR*, pt. 1, chap. 46, p. 1214.
25. Ibid., p. 1218.
26. Ibid., p. 1167.
27. Longstreet, pp. 615–16.
28. *OR*, pt. 1, chap. 58, p. 611.
29. Freeman, p. 709.

Chapter 12

1. Starr, vol. 2, p. 469.
2. *OR*, pt. 1, chap. 46, p. 1136.
3. Ibid., p. 1120.
4. Ibid., p. 1132.
5. *OR*, pt. 1, chap. 58, p. 611.
6. James, "Battle of Sailor's Creek," *SHSP*, vol. 24, p. 84.
7. Ibid.
8. *OR*, pt. 1, chap. 58, p. 599.
9. Ibid., p. 609.
10. Ibid.
11. Ibid.

Chapter 13

1. *OR*, pt. 1, chap. 46, p. 1132.
2. Ibid., p. 1125.
3. Warner, *Generals in Blue*, pp. 123–24.
4. Ibid.
5. Ibid.
6. *OR*, pt. 1, chap. 46, p. 1125.
7. Ibid., p. 1120.
8. Ibid., p. 1302.
9. Basinger, "Battle of Sailor's Creek—The Savannah Guard," *SHSP*, vol. 24, pp. 251–52.
10. *OR*, pt. 1, chap. 46, p. 1289.
11. Gordon, pp. 111–12.
12. Buel and Johnson, *Battles and Leaders*, vol. 4, p. 724.
13. *OR*, pt. 1, chap. 58, p. 1294.
14. Ibid., p. 1293.
15. Ibid., pp. 1283–84.
16. Ibid., p. 1295.
17. Gordon, p. 430.
18. Harwell, pp. 474–75.
19. Warner, *Generals in Gray*, p. 157.
20. *OR*, pt. 1, chap. 46, p. 1290.
21. Ibid.
22. Selcer, "George Pickett: Another Look," *Civil War Times Illustrated* (hereafter referred to as *CWTI*), vol. 33, no. 3, pp. 64–67.

23. Ibid.
24. Ibid., p. 69.
25. Pfanz, p. 438.
26. Letter from R. T. W. Duke in the *Richmond Dispatch*, April 25, 1897.
27. Freeman, p. 706.
28. *OR*, pt. 1, chap. 58, p. 1295.
29. Pfanz, p. 438.

Chapter 14

1. *OR*, pt. 1, chap. 46, pp. 561–62.
2. Ibid., p. 1108.
3. Ibid.
4. Ibid., p. 1003.
5. Buel and Johnson, *Battles and Leaders*, vol. 4, p. 749.
6. Warner, *Generals in Gray*, p. 277.
7. Scharf, *History of the Confederate States Navy*, p. 196.
8. Robert Stiles, *Four Years Under Marse Robert*, p. 329.
9. Blake, p. 213.
10. *OR*, pt. 1, chap. 46, pp. 561–62.
11. Calkins, p. 105.
12. Korn, p. 122.
13. *OR*, pt. 1, chap. 46, pp. 561–62.
14. Davis, *To Appomattox*, p. 268.
15. Basinger, "Crutchfield's Artillery Brigade," *SHSP*, vol. 25, p. 39.
16. Ibid.
17. *Recollections and Reminiscences*, vol. 1, p. 45.
18. Robert Stiles, p. 330.
19. Ibid.
20. *OR*, pt. 1, chap. 46, pp. 561–62.
21. Blake, p. 213.
22. *OR*, pt. 1, chap. 46, p. 914.
23. Warner, *Generals in Blue*, p. 553.
24. Korn, p. 123.
25. Robert Stiles, p. 330.
26. Korn, p. 122.
27. Blake, p. 213.
28. *OR*, pt. 1, chap. 46, p. 1284.

Chapter 15

1. Johnston, p. 327.
2. Warner, *Generals in Blue*, pp. 321–22.
3. Starr, vol. 2, p. 319.
4. Patterson, p. 161.
5. Warner, *Generals in Gray*, pp. 8–9.
6. Patterson, p. 22.
7. Sorrel, *Recollections*, pp. 213–14.
8. Ibid., p. 107.

9. Katcher, *The Army of Robert E. Lee*, p. 299.

10. Calkins, p. 224.

11. *OR*, pt. 1, chap. 58, p. 1142.

12. James, *SHSP*, vol. 24, p. 85.

13. Pickett, pp. 178–79.

14. Johnston, p. 327.

15. *OR*, pt. 1, chap. 58, p. 1151.

16. Ibid., p. 1145.

17. Ibid., p. 1142.

18. Ibid., p. 1151.

19. Johnston, pp. 328–29.

20. *OR*, pt. 1, chap. 58, p. 1145.

21. Ibid., p. 1142.

22. Trudeau, p. 110.

23. James, *SHSP*, vol. 24, p. 85. C. F. James erroneously describes Terry on the field in this phase of the fighting. He had to be referring to Colonel Williams or other officers of Terry's Brigade.

24. Johnston, p. 329.

25. James, p. 85.

26. Ibid.

27. Mitchell, *The Badge of Gallantry*, p. 56.

28. Starr, vol. 2, p. 471.

29. Trudeau, p. 111.

30. Kinsley, *Favor the Bold*, p. 277.

31. Urwin, p. 247.

32. Ibid., p. 248.

33. The U.S. War Department apparently misidentified the flag after the conflict as belonging to the 18th Florida Infantry, a nonexistent unit since Florida only fielded 11 infantry regiments in the war. Now in the collection of the Museum of Florida History, the banner is believed to be that of the 5th Florida Infantry which fought at Sailor's Creek.

34. Mitchell, p. 57.

35. Ibid.

36. Trudeau, p. 111.

37. Johnston, p. 329.

38. *OR*, pt. 1, chap. 46, p. 1132.

39. Blake, p. 214.

40. *OR*, pt. 1, chap. 46, p. 1145.

41. James, *SHSP*, vol. 24, p. 86.

42. Ibid.

43. Ibid.

44. Ibid.

45. *OR*, pt. 1, chap. 46, p. 864.

46. Ibid.

Chapter 16

1. *OR*, pt. 1, chap. 46, p. 998.

2. McNeily, "Incidents of Sailor's Creek," *Confederate Veteran*, vol. 28, no. 9, p. 329.

3. *OR*, pt. 1, chap. 46, p. 942.

4. Ibid., p. 1001.
5. *OR*, pt. 1, chap. 58, p. 988.
6. *OR*, pt. 1, chap. 46, p. 914.
7. Trudeau, p. 109.
8. *OR*, pt. 1, chap. 58, p. 949.
9. Calkins, p. 119.
10. Rhodes, p. 227.
11. Ibid., pp. 227–28.
12. *OR*, pt. 1, chap. 46, p. 953.
13. Blake, p. 213.
14. *OR*, pt. 1, chap. 46, pp. 938–39.
15. Ibid., p. 914.
16. Ibid., pp. 951–52.
17. Calkins, p. 119.
18. Ibid.
19. *OR*, pt. 1, chap. 46, p. 914.
20. Ibid., p. 938.
21. Rodick, p. 60.
22. Calkins, pp. 120–21.
23. Ibid.
24. *OR*, pt. 1, chap. 58, p. 946.
25. Davis, *To Appomattox*, pp. 251–54.
26. Robert Stiles, p. 331.
27. Calkins, p. 121.
28. Robert Stiles, pp. 331–32.
29. *Recollections and Reminiscences*, vol. 1, p. 45.
30. Basinger, *SHSP*, vol. 25, p. 39.
31. *OR*, pt. 1, chap. 58, p. 1001.
32. *OR*, pt. 1, chap. 46, p. 1108.
33. Rhodes, pp. 228–29.
34. Ibid.
35. *OR*, pt. 1, chap. 46, p. 949.
36. Ibid., p. 942.
37. Davis, *To Appomattox*, p. 251.
38. Robert Stiles, p. 332.
39. Blake, pp. 213–14.
40. Basinger, *SHSP*, vol. 25, p. 39.
41. Blake, pp. 213–14.
42. Robert Stiles, p. 332.
43. Blake, p. 214.
44. Sheridan, *Civil War Memoirs*, p. 340.
45. Calkins, p. 121.
46. Trudeau, pp. 111–12.
47. *OR*, pt. 1, chap. 46, p. 984.
48. Ibid., p. 980.
49. Ibid., p. 984.

50. Ibid., pp. 946–47.

51. Ibid.

52. Ibid., p. 1297.

53. Davis, *To Appomattox*, p. 251. V.M.I. archive alumni files indicate that Crutchfield was never married.

54. *Recollections and Reminiscences*, vol. 1, p. 45.

55. Blake, p. 214.

56. Calkins, p. 122.

57. Blake, p. 214.

58. Trudeau, p. 112.

59. Sheridan, *Civil War Memoirs*, p. 340.

60. *OR*, pt. 1, chap. 46, pp. 950–51.

61. Ibid., p. 949.

62. Ibid.

63. Basinger, *SHSP*, vol. 25, p. 40.

64. Henry Kennedy, *History of the Savannah Volunteer Guards*, p. 101.

65. Ibid.

66. Basinger, *SHSP*, vol. 25, p. 41.

67. Ibid.

Chapter 17

1. *OR*, pt. 1, chap. 46, p. 1284.

2. *OR*, pt. 1, chap. 58, p. 939.

3. *OR*, pt. 1, chap. 46, p. 1295.

4. Ibid., p. 1001.

5. McNeily, p. 329.

6. Ibid.

7. *OR*, pt. 1, chap. 46, p. 1284.

8. McNeily, p. 329.

9. Ibid.

10. *OR*, pt. 1, chap. 46, p. 1302.

11. Ibid.

12. Blackford, pp. 216–17.

13. Basinger, *SHSP*, vol. 25, p. 41.

14. Ibid.

15. Basinger letter to his mother, April 16, 1865.

16. Ibid.

17. Henry Kennedy, p. 104.

18. Ibid., p. 102.

19. Blake, p. 214.

20. *OR*, pt. 1, chap. 46, p. 1297.

21. Warner, *Generals in Gray*, pp. 18–19.

22. *OR*, pt. 1, chap. 46, p. 998.

Chapter 18

1. Scharf, p. 749.

2. Davis, *To Appomattox*, p. 255.

3. *OR*, pt. 1, chap. 46, p. 998.
4. Robert Stiles, pp. 333–34.
5. Ibid.
6. Korn, p. 121.
7. Watson, "The Fighting at Sailor's Creek," *Confederate Veteran*, vol. 25, no. 10, p. 451.
8. *OR*, pt. 1, chap. 46, p. 947.
9. Ibid.
10. Rodick, pp. 61–62.
11. Robert Stiles, p. 334.
12. Scharf, p. 749.
13. Ibid.
14. Trudeau, p. 112.
15. Rodick, p. 62.
16. *OR*, pt. 1, chap. 46, p. 906.
17. Ibid., p. 998.
18. Scharf, p. 749.
19. Donnelly, p. 62.
20. *OR*, pt. 1, chap. 46, p. 914.
21. Donnelly, p. 61.
22. Scharf, p. 196.
23. James, *SHSP*, vol. 24, p. 87.
24. Davis, *To Appomattox*, p. 258.
25. *OR*, pt. 1, chap. 58, p. 604.

Chapter 19

1. Warner, *Generals in Gray*, p. 319.
2. Ibid., pp. 120–21.
3. Ibid., p. 83.
4. Gordon, pp. 429–30.
5. Rodick, p. 61.
6. *OR*, pt. 1, chap. 46, p. 600.
7. Methvin, pp. 67–68.
8. *OR*, pt. 1, chap. 46, p. 786.
9. Ibid., p. 779.
10. Ibid., p. 657.
11. Ibid.
12. *OR*, pt. 1, chap. 58, p. 793.
13. Trudeau, p. 110.
14. Methvin, p. 67.
15. Grimes, p. 114.
16. Gordon, pp. 429–30.
17. Stern, p. 358.
18. Ibid.
19. *OR*, pt. 1, chap. 46, p. 713.
20. Warner, *Generals in Blue*, pp. 322–23.
21. Ibid.

22. Buel and Johnson, *Battles and Leaders*, vol. 4, p. 748.
23. Stern, p. 358.
24. Ibid.
25. Ibid., p. 359.
26. Douglas, p. 316.
27. Stern, p. 359.
28. Davis, *To Appomattox*, p. 262.
29. Trudeau, p. 110.
30. Ibid.
31. Korn, p. 127.
32. Grimes, p. 114.
33. *OR*, pt. 1, chap. 46, p. 713.
34. Stern, p. 359.
35. Ibid.
36. Stern, pp. 359–60.
37. Ibid.
38. Ibid.
39. Trudeau, p. 110.
40. Gordon, p. 424.
41. Buel and Johnson, *Battles and Leaders*, vol. 4, p. 724.
42. Rodick, p. 64.
43. *OR*, pt. 1, chap. 46, p. 779.
44. Stern, p. 360.
45. Grimes, pp. 114–15.
46. Stern, p. 208.
47. Ibid., p. 361.
48. Methvin, p. 67.
49. *OR*, pt. 1, chap. 46, p. 595.

Chapter 20

1. Harwell, pp. 474–75.
2. Longstreet, pp. 614–15.
3. Harwell, p. 475.
4. Rodick, pp. 63–64.
5. Ibid.
6. James, *SHSP*, vol. 24, p. 88.
7. Davis, *To Appomattox*, p. 261.
8. Rodick, p. 64.
9. Harwell, p. 476.
10. Rodick, pp. 62–63.
11. Ibid.
12. Ibid.
13. *Recollections and Reminiscences*, vol. 5, p. 200.
14. Rodick, p. 67.
15. Basinger in Henry Kennedy, p. 101.
16. Blake, p. 214.

17. Buell, *The Warrior Generals*, p. 417.
18. Ibid.
19. Rodick, p. 67.
20. Botkin, *A Civil War Treasury*, p. 482.
21. Ibid.
22. Rhodes, p. 229.
23. Haley, p. 261.
24. McNeily, p. 329.
25. Ibid.

Chapter 21

1. *OR*, pt. 1, chap. 46, p. 1295.
2. Ibid., p. 1132.
3. Ibid., pp. 985–86.
4. Ibid.
5. Ibid., p. 984.
6. Ibid.
7. Ibid., p. 953.
8. Ibid.
9. Gordon, p. 429.

Chapter 22

1. *OR*, pt. 1, chap. 58, p. 610.
2. Ibid., pp. 594–95.
3. Ibid., p. 596.
4. Ibid., p. 620.
5. Sandburg, *Abraham Lincoln—The War Years*, vol. 4, p. 185.
6. Rodick, p. 63.
7. Blake, p. 214.
8. Freeman, p. 712.
9. Longstreet, p. 616.
10. Ibid., p. 614.
11. Strode, pp. 175–76.
12. Ibid.
13. Trudeau, p. 115.
14. *OR*, pt. 1, chap. 46, p. 915.
15. Ibid., p. 907.
16. Ibid., p. 947.
17. Ibid., p. 1011.
18. Ibid., p. 562.
19. Ibid., p. 841.
20. Pfanz, p. 440.
21. Ibid., p. 441.
22. *OR*, pt. 1, chap. 46, p. 1295.
23. Robert Stiles, p. 335.
24. *OR*, pt. 1, chap. 46, p. 1295.
25. Ibid., p. 1294.

26. Pfanz, p. 442.
27. Ibid.
28. Longstreet, p. 614.
29. *OR*, pt. 1, chap. 46, p. 1302.
30. Longstreet, p. 613.
31. Ibid.
32. New York *Herald*, April 15, 1865.
33. Blake, p. 214.
34. McNeily quote of Swinton, p. 330.

Chapter 23

1. Myers, p. 382.
2. Davis, *To Appomattox*, pp. 270–71.
3. Kinsley, p. 280.
4. Rodick, p. 66.
5. Urwin, p. 248.
6. Reynolds, *The Civil War Memories of Elizabeth Bacon Custer*, p. 138.
7. Ibid., p. 139.
8. Starr, vol. 2, p. 474.
9. Johnston, p. 329.
10. Urwin, pp. 248–49.
11. Ibid., pp. 249–50.
12. Rodick, p. 66.
13. Warner, *Generals in Gray*, p. 109.
14. *OR*, pt. 1, chap. 46, p. 949.
15. Starr, vol. 2, p. 475.
16. Buell, p. 418.
17. Haley, p. 261.
18. Ibid.
19. Rhodes, p. 227.
20. Watson, p. 451.
21. *OR*, pt. 1, ch. 46, p. 633.
22. Calkins, p. 122.
23. Rodick, p. 67.
24. Ibid., pp. 67–68.

Chapter 24

1. Longstreet, p. 616.
2. Trudeau, p. 117.
3. Freeman, p. 768.
4. Ibid., p. 715.
5. Myers, p. 386.
6. Ibid., p. 387.
7. Davis, *To Appomattox*, p. 282.
8. Freeman, p. 715.
9. Ibid., p. 712.

10. Davis, *To Appomattox*, p. 283.
11. Warner, *Generals in Blue*, p. 466. Smyth lingered until the morning of April 9, unaware that Lee would surrender a few hours later. The last Union general to die in the war, he was posthumously promoted to major general.
12. Starr, vol. 2, p. 476.
13. Ibid.

Chapter 25

1. Starr, vol. 2, p. 477.
2. Korn, p. 133.
3. Ibid.
4. *OR*, pt. 1, chap. 58, p. 56.
5. Ibid.
6. Ibid.
7. Ibid.
8. Trudeau, p. 127.
9. Patterson, p. 140.
10. Ibid.
11. Trudeau, p. 129.
12. Urwin, p. 250.
13. Starr, vol. 2, p. 480.
14. *OR*, pt. 1, chap. 46, p. 1132.
15. Starr, vol. 2, p. 480.
16. Ibid.
17. Calkins, p. 155.
18. Starr, vol. 2, p. 481.
19. *OR*, pt. 1, chap. 46, p. 1121.
20. Ibid., p. 1389.
21. *OR*, pt. 1, chap. 58, p. 57.
22. Ibid.
23. Ibid.
24. Rhodes, p. 229.
25. Freeman, pp. 767–68.
26. Ibid.
27. Ibid.
28. Rodick, p. 69.
29. Pfanz, p. 443.
30. Ibid., p. 444.
31. Ibid.
32. Ibid., pp. 444–45.
33. Ibid., p. 446.
34. Blake, p. 214.
35. Basinger letter to his mother, April 14, 1865.
36. *OR*, pt. 1, chap. 46, p. 787.
37. Ibid.
38. Ibid.

39. Pfanz, pp. 450–51.
40. Ibid.
41. Basinger letter to his mother, April 16, 1865.
42. *OR*, pt. 1, chap. 46, p. 1280.
43. Ibid.
44. Basinger in Henry Kennedy, p. 555.
45. Ibid., p. 104.
46. *Savannah Daily Morning News*, January 1, 1866.

BIBLIOGRAPHY

Allardice, Bruce S. *More Generals in Gray*. Baton Rouge and London: Louisiana State University Press, 1995.

Anderson, Nancy Scott and Dwight. *The Generals—Ulysses S. Grant And Robert E. Lee*. New York, N.Y.: Wings Books, 1987.

Basinger, William S. "Battle of Sailor's Creek—Part Taken in It by the Savannah Volunteer Guard," *Southern Historical Society Papers*, vol. 24, Richmond, Va., 1897.

———. "Crutchfield's Artillery Brigade—Report of its Operations, April 3–6, 1865, when it was captured with Lee's Division at Sailor's Creek," *Southern Historical Society Papers*, vol. 25, Richmond, Va., 1897.

Benson, Berry (Susan Williams Benson, ed.). *Berry Benson's Civil War Book—Memoirs of a Confederate Scout and Sharpshooter*. Athens, Ga.: University of Georgia Press, 1962.

Billings, John D. *Hardtack and Coffee, or, The Unwritten Story of Army Life*. Boston, Mass.: George M. Smith & Company, 1887.

Blackford, Lieutenant Colonel W.W. *War Years With Jeb Stuart*. New York, N.Y.: Charles Scribner's Sons, 1945.

Blake, Captain Thomas B. "The Artillery Brigade at Sailor's Creek," *Confederate Veteran*, vol. 28, no. 6, June 1920, Nashville, Tenn.

Boatner, Mark M., III. *The Civil War Dictionary*. Rev. ed., New York, N.Y.: David McKay Company, Inc., 1987.

Botkin, B.A., ed. *A Civil War Treasury of Tales, Legends And Folklore*. New York, N.Y.: Random House, Inc., 1960.

Buel, Clarence C., and Robert V. Johnson. *Battles and Leaders of the Civil War: Being for the Most Part Contributions by Union and Confederate Authors*. 4 vols. New York: Century Co., 1887.

Buell, Thomas B. *The Warrior Generals—Combat Leadership in the Civil War*. New York, N.Y.: Crown Publishers, Inc., 1997.

Calkins, Chris M. *The Appomattox Campaign*. Conshohocken, Pa.: Combined Books, Inc., 1997.

Catton, Bruce. *This Hallowed Ground*. Garden City, N.Y.: Doubleday & Company, Inc., 1956.

Commager, Henry Steele, ed. *The Blue and the Gray—The Story of the Civil War As Told By Participants*. 2 vols. New York, N.Y.: The Bobbs-Merrill Company, Inc., 1950.

Couper, Colonel William. *One Hundred Years at V.M.I.* Vol. 2. Richmond, Va.: Garrett and Massie, Inc., 1939.

Davis, Burke. *The Long Surrender*. New York, N.Y.: Random House, Inc., 1985.

———. *To Appomattox—Nine April Days, 1865*. New York, N.Y.: Holt, Rinehart and Winston, 1959.

Davis, Kenneth C. *Don't Know Much About The Civil War*. New York, N.Y.: William Morrow and Company, Inc., 1996.

Donnelly, Ralph W. *The Confederate States Marine Corps: The Rebel Leathernecks*. Shippensburg, Pa.: White Mane Publishing Company, Inc., 1989.

Douglas, Henry Kyd. *I Rode With Stonewall*. Chapel Hill, N.C.: The University of North Carolina Press, 1940.

Dowdey, Clifford. *Lee's Last Campaign*. New York, N.Y.: Bonanza Books, Crown Publishers, Inc., 1960.

Eggleston, George Cary. *A Rebel's Recollections*. New York, N.Y.: Hurd and Houghton, 1875.

Evans, Clement Anselm. *Confederate Military History, Volume VI—Georgia*. Atlanta, Ga.: Confederate Publishing Company, 1899.

Fehrenbacher, Don E. *Abraham Lincoln, Speeches and Writings, 1859–1865*. New York, N.Y.: The Literary Classics of the United States, Inc., 1989.

Freeman, Douglas Southall. *Lee's Lieutenants: A Study in Command.* Vol. 1. New York, N.Y.: Charles Scribner's Sons, 1942.

Gallagher, Gary W., ed. *Lee—The Soldier.* Lincoln and London: University of Nebraska Press, 1996.

Gordon, General John B. *Reminiscences of the Civil War.* New York, N.Y.: Charles Scribner's Sons, 1903.

Gragg, Rod. *Confederate Goliath—The Battle of Fort Fisher.* New York, N.Y.: HarperCollins Publishers, 1991.

Grimes, Bryan. *Extracts of Letters of Major-Gen'l Bryan Grimes To His Wife, Written While In Active Service In The Army Of Northern Virginia—Together With Some Personal Recollections Of The War, Written By Him After Its Close, Etc.* Raleigh, N.C.: Edwards, Broughton & Co., Steam Printers and Binders, 1883.

Haley, John W. Ruth L. Silliken, ed. *The Rebel Yell & the Yankee Hurrah—The Civil War Journal of a Maine Volunteer.* Camden, Me.: Down East Books, 1985.

Harwell, Richard. *Lee.* Abridgment of Douglas Southall Freeman, *R.E. Lee.* 4 vols. New York, N.Y.: Charles Scribner's Sons, 1961.

Hoehling, A. A. and Mary. *The Day Richmond Died.* San Diego and New York: A. S. Barnes & Company, Inc., 1981.

Hotchkiss, Major Jedediah. *Confederate Military History, Volume III—Virginia.* Atlanta, Ga.: Confederate Publishing Company, 1899.

Hutton, Paul Andrew. "Paladin of the Republic," *Military History Quarterly*, vol. 4, no. 3, spring 1992, New York, N.Y.: MHQ, Inc.

James, C. F. "Battle of Sailor's Creek—Recollections of the Battle at Marshall's Crossroads by Hunton's Brigade," vol. 24, *Southern Historical Society Papers*, Richmond, Va., 1896.

Johnston, David E. *The Story of a Confederate Boy in the Civil War.* Portland, Ore.: Glass & Prudhomme Company, 1914.

Jones, Terry L. *Lee's Tigers—The Louisiana Infantry in the Army of Northern Virginia*. London and Baton Rouge: Louisiana State University Press, 1987.

Jordan, William B., Jr. *Red Diamond Regiment—The 17th Maine Infantry, 1862–1865*. Shippensburg, Pa.: White Mane Publishing Company, Inc., 1996.

Katcher, Philip. *The Army of Robert E. Lee*. New York, N.Y.: Arms and Armour Press, Sterling Publishing Company, Inc., 1994.

Kennedy, Francis H., ed. *The Civil War Battlefield Guide*. Boston: Houghton-Mifflin Co., 1990.

Kennedy, Henry J., compiler and ed. *History of the Savannah Volunteer Guards, Inc.—1802–1992*. Greenville, S.C.: Southern Historical Press, Inc., 1998.

Kinsley, D. A. *Favor the Bold: Custer—The Civil War Years*. New York, N.Y.: Henry Holt & Company, 1967.

Korn, Jerry, and the Editors of Time-Life Books. *The Civil War—Pursuit To Appomattox*. Alexandria, Va.: Time-Life Books, Inc., 1987.

Laboda, Lawrence R. *From Selma To Appomattox—The History of the Jeff Davis Artillery*. Shippensburg, Pa.: White Mane Publishing Company, Inc., 1994.

Longstreet, James. *From Manassas To Appomattox—Memoirs of the Civil War in America*. Philadelphia, Pa.: J. B. Lippincott Company, 1896.

McCarthy, Carlton. *Detailed Minutiae of Soldier Life in the Army of Northern Virginia, 1861–1865*. Richmond, Va.: B. F. Johnson Publishing Company, 1899.

McNeily, J. S. "Incidents of Sailor's Creek," *Confederate Veteran*, vol. 28, no. 9, September 1920, Nashville, Tenn.

Methvin, John Francis. *Confederate Reminiscences and Letters, 1861–1865*. Vol. 8. Atlanta, Ga.: Georgia Division of the United Daughters of the Confederacy, 1998.

Mitchell, Joseph B. *The Badge of Gallantry—Recollections of Civil War Congressional Medal of Honor Winners*. New York, N.Y.: The Macmillan Company, 1968.

Myers, Frank M. *The Comanches: A History of White's Battalion, Virginia Cavalry, Laurel Brigade, Hampton Division, Army of Northern Virginia*. Baltimore, Md.: Kelly, Piet & Company, 1871.

Nevins, Allan, ed. *A Diary of Battle—The Personal Journals of Colonel Charles S. Wainwright 1861–1865*. New York, N.Y.: Da Capo Press, Inc., 1962.

Patterson, Gerard A. *Rebels from West Point*. New York, N.Y.: Doubleday, Inc., 1987.

Pfanz, Donald C. *Richard S. Ewell—A Soldier's Life*. Chapel Hill and London: The University of North Carolina Press, 1998.

Pickett, George E. *The Heart of a Soldier, As revealed in the Intimate Letters of Genl. George E. Pickett C.S.A.* New York, N.Y.: Seth Moyle, Inc., 1913.

Recollections and Reminiscences, 1861–1865, Through World War I. 6 vols. South Carolina Division, United Daughters of the Confederacy, 1992.

Reynolds, Arlene, ed. *The Civil War Memories of Elizabeth Bacon Custer*. Austin, Tex.: University of Texas Press, 1994.

Rhodes, Robert Hunt, ed. *All For the Union—The Civil War Diary and Letters of Elisha Hunt Rhodes*. New York, N.Y.: Orion Books, 1985.

Rodick, Burleigh Cushing. *Appomattox: The Last Campaign*. New York, N.Y.: Philosophical Library, Inc., 1965.

Sandburg, Carl. *Abraham Lincoln—The War Years*. 4 vols. New York, N.Y.: Harcourt, Brace and Company, Inc., 1939.

Scharf, J. Thomas. *History of the Confederate States Navy*. Avenel, N.J.: Random House Value Publishing, Inc., 1996.

Selcer, Richard F. "George Pickett: Another Look," *Civil War Times Illustrated*, vol. 33, no. 3, July/August 1994, Harrisburg, Pa.

Sheridan, General Philip H. (Paul Andrew Hutton, ed.). *Civil War Memoirs*. New York, N.Y.: Bantam Domain Books, 1991.

Sheridan, Philip H. *Personal Memoirs of P. H. Sheridan, General, United States Army*. 2 vols. New York, N.Y.: Charles L. Webster & Company, 1888.

Smith, Derek. *Civil War Savannah*. Savannah, Ga.: Frederic C. Beil, Publisher, Inc., 1997.

Sorrel, G. Moxley. *Recollections of a Confederate Staff Officer*. New York, N.Y.: Neale Publishing Company, 1905.

Starr, Stephen Z. *The Union Cavalry in the Civil War*. 3 vols. Baton Rouge and London: Louisiana State University Press, 1985.

Steiner, Paul E., M.D., Ph.D. *Medical-Military Portraits of Union and Confederate Generals*. Philadelphia, Pa.: Whitmore Publishing Company, 1968.

Stern, Philip Van Doren. *Soldier Life in the Union and Confederate Armies*. New York, N.Y.: Bonanza Books, 1961.

Stiles, John C. "Confederate States Navy at Sailor's Creek, Va.," *Confederate Veteran*, vol. 28, no. 7, July 1920, Nashville, Tenn.

Stiles, Robert. *Four Years Under Marse Robert*. New York, N.Y.: The Neale Publishing Company, 1904.

Strode, Hudson. *Jefferson Davis—Tragic Hero, 1864–1889—The Last Twenty-five Years*. First Edition, New York, N.Y.: Harcourt, Brace & World, Inc., 1964.

Thomas, Wilbur. *General James "Pete" Longstreet—"Lee's Old War Horse"—Scapegoat For Gettysburg*. Parsons, W.Va.: McClain Printing Company, 1979.

Trudeau, Noah Andre. *Out of the Storm—The End of the Civil War—April–June 1865*. Baton Rouge, La.: Louisiana State University Press, 1994.

Urwin, Gregory J. W. *Custer Victorious—The Civil War Battles of General George Armstrong Custer*. East Brunswick, N.J.: Associated University Presses, Inc., 1983.

Walker, Charles D. *Institute Memorial—Collection of Biographical Sketches on VMI Graduates Who Died in the Civil War*. Philadelphia, Pa.: J. B. Lippincott & Co., 1875.

Warner, Ezra J. *Generals in Blue: Lives of the Union Commanders*. Baton Rouge, La.: Louisiana State University Press, 1964.

———. *Generals in Gray: Lives of the Confederate Commanders*. Baton Rouge, La.: Louisiana State University Press, 1959.

The War of the Rebellion: A Compilation of the Official Records of the Union and Confederate Armies. 128 vols. Washington, D.C.: U.S. Government Printing Office, 1880–1901.

Watson, W. A. "The Fighting at Sailor's Creek," *Confederate Veteran*, vol. 25, no. 10, October 1917, Nashville, Tenn.

Wert, Jeffry D. *From Winchester to Cedar Creek—The Shenandoah Campaign of 1864.* Carlisle, Pa.: South Mountain Press, 1987.

Wise, John S. "The End of an Era," *Atlantic Monthly*, vol. 83, Issue 498, April 1899, Boston, Mass.

Newspapers

New York *Herald*

Richmond Dispatch

Savannah Daily Morning News

INDEX

254

L

Lafayette Guard, 62

Lake Erie, 225

Lamkin, James N., 31

Lathrop, Joseph H., 82, 83

Laurel Grove Cemetery, 229

Lee, Fitzhugh, 9, 21, 33, 53, 54, 86, 93, 94, 101, 151, 163, 169, 197, 221

Lee, George W. C., 10, 12, 21, 22, 29, 33, 35, 43, 45, 56, 75, 91, 93–97, 106, 107, 109, 114, 133, 135, 137, 140–44, 149, 150, 152, 185, 188, 196, 211, 224

background, 34

capture of, 154

praise from Ewell, 195

Lee, Robert E., 17–21, 23, 29, 30, 33–38, 40–42, 44, 46–50, 53, 54, 56–57, 66, 70, 72, 79–81, 84, 87, 88, 94, 95, 97, 98, 104, 110, 117, 118, 133, 160, 164, 171, 177, 183, 184, 188–93, 196, 197, 199, 204, 205, 210–14, 218, 222–23, 228

correspondence with Grant, 215–17, 220–21

in first phase of Richmond-Petersburg evacuation, 1–15

opinion of Ewell, 58–59

at Sailor's Creek, 178–80

Lee, Stephen Dill, 34

Lee, William H. F. "Rooney," 33, 53, 151, 169, 174, 219

Leonard, Charles H., 185–87

Libby Prison, 11

Lidell, John A., 207

Lincoln, Abraham, 7, 8, 28, 190, 208, 225, 226

Lincoln Cavalry. *See* New York Units, 1st Cavalry

Livermore, Thomas L., 181

Lockett, James S., 95

Lockett Farm, 95, 164–69, 172, 206

Lockwood, Abram L., 175

Longstreet, James, 3, 9, 11, 13, 15, 33, 34, 36, 43, 48, 53, 56–58, 72, 79–81, 85, 87–89, 94, 115–18, 163, 177, 178, 180, 182, 191, 192, 209–12, 218

criticism of Fitzhugh Lee, 197

Louisiana Units

15th (CSA), 55

Washington Artillery of New Orleans, 15

Lyman, Theodore, 77, 205

Lynchburg, Va., 19, 36, 56, 80, 85, 193, 212, 214

M

McAllister, Robert, 170, 175

McCarthy, Carlton, 24, 35, 169–71, 173–76

McCausland, John, 83

McClellan, George B., 28, 60, 78

McDonald, Andrew N., 132, 141

McGlashan, Peter A. S., 108

McNeill, Jesse, 73

McNeily, J. S., 131, 149–51, 184

McNeily, W. P., 150

MacDougall, Clinton D., 169, 175

Mahone, William, 20, 23, 33, 72–74, 87, 178–80, 182, 191, 192, 209, 210, 212, 217

Mahone's Division (CSA), 20, 177, 199

Maine Units

1st Cavalry, 181

1st Heavy Artillery, 62

17th, 39, 69, 174, 182

Malvern Hill, Battle of, 103

Marion, Francis, 126

Marshall, Charles, 192

Marshall's Crossroads, 87, 88

Maryland Units

6th (U.S.), 105, 131, 149

Mason, James M., 112

Mason-Slidell Affair, 112

Massachusetts Units

4th Cavalry, 81, 83, 84

10th Artillery, 70

22nd, 169

37th, 133, 135, 142, 154, 158, 162, 193

54th U.S. Colored Troops, 103

Mattocks, Charles P., 182

Meade, George G., 6, 7, 17–19, 41, 42, 49–51, 60, 61, 70, 89, 90, 163, 166, 176, 188, 189, 205, 222

clashes with Sheridan, 27, 32, 37

Mechanicsville, Battle of, 165

Merrill, Samuel H., 181

Merritt, Wesley, 18, 75, 76, 88, 93, 115, 116, 122, 129, 150, 185, 219

Methvin, John Francis, 23, 24, 166, 167, 176

Metler, James S., 120

Mexican War, 26, 33, 57, 98, 103, 106, 117, 118

Michigan Units

2nd Cavalry, 26

Miles, Nelson, 2, 50, 61, 62, 65, 70, 71, 169, 170, 173, 175, 176, 182, 183, 212

Millen, Richard, 152

Miller, Delvan S., 182, 222

Miller, Marcus P., 75, 76, 92

Mine Run Campaign, 49

Missionary Ridge, 27

Monroe, Mich., 78

Moody, Young M., 118, 119, 127, 210, 219

Monitor, USS, 107

Morrill, W. C., 154